STUDIES IN CHURCH HISTORY

Volume VIII

Edited by

James H. Nichols   Wilhelm Pauck

Prize Essay
of the
Frank S. Brewer Fund

In original form this study was submitted to the Faculty of the Graduate School of Yale University in Candidacy for the Degree of Doctor of Philosophy. Portions have been published in *The Union Seminary Quarterly Review*, *The Mennonite Quarterly Review* and *The Journal of Religious Thought*.

To

William Walker Rockwell

Teacher and Friend

THE ANABAPTIST VIEW
OF THE CHURCH

An Introduction to Sectarian Protestantism

By

Franklin Hamlin Littell

AMERICAN SOCIETY OF CHURCH HISTORY
1952

TABLE OF CONTENTS

ABBREVIATIONS USED IN THE FOOTNOTES

ADB............ *Allgemeine Deutsche Biographie*
CH................ *Church History*
CR................ *Corpus Reformatorum*
CSchw.......... *Corpus Schwenckfeldianorum*
DB................ *Doopsgezinden Bijdragen*
HZ................ *Historische Zeitschrift*
ML................ *Mennonitisches Lexikon*
MQR............ *The Mennonite Quarterly Review*
SVRG.......... *Schriften des Vereins für Reformationsgeschichte*
TSK.............. *Theologische Studien und Kritiken*
ZKG.............. *Zeitschrift für Kirchengeschichte*
ZTK.............. *Zeitschrift für Theologie und Kirche*

Beck.............. Beck, Josef, ed., *Die Geschichts-Bücher der Wiedertäufer in Österreich-Ungarn* (Wien, Carl Gerold's Sohn,
1883); XLIII *Fontes Rerum Austriacarum* (Hist. Comm.
Kaiserl. Akad. der Wiss. in Wien), 2te Abth.

Egli.............. Egli, Emil, ed., *Actensammlung zur Geschichte der
Zürcher Reformation in den Jahren 1519-1533* (Zürich, J.
Schabelitz, 1879), 2 volumes.

KSch............ Schottenloher, Karl, *Bibliographie zur Deutschen Geschichte im Zeitalter der Glaubensspaltung, 1517-1585*
(Leipzig, Karl W. Hiersemann, 1933-39), 5 volumes.

WTQ1930.... Bossert, Gustav, ed., *Quellen zur Geschichte der Wieder-
täufer: Herzogtum Württemberg* (Leipzig, M. Heinsius
Nachf., 1930); XIII:1 *Quellen und Forschungen zur
Reformationsgeschichte.*

WTQ1934.... Schornbaum, Karl, ed., *Quellen zur Geschichte der Wiedertäufer: Markgraftum Brandenburg* (Leipzig, M. Heinsius Nachf., 1934), XVI:2 *Quellen und Forschungen
zur Reformationsgeschichte.*

WTQ1938.... Müller, Lydia, ed., *Glaubenszeugnisse oberdeutscher
Taufgesinnten* (Leipzig, M. Heinsius Nachf., 1938); XX:
Quellen und Forschungen zur Reformationsgeschichte.

Z.................. Zieglschmid, A. J. F., *Die älteste Chronik der Hutterischen Brüder* (Philadelphia, Carl Schurz Memorial
Foundation, 1943).

PREFACE

Several serious impediments have customarily beset those who turned their minds to a discussion of "Anabaptist" church life and thought. These impediments have proved fatal to most previous studies, and are of consuming concern to the present writer.

The first difficulty is that it is impossible to assume that the average reader has any adequate concept of the "Anabaptists." Information on the groups so termed has been notoriously scarce, and has rested in the main upon hostile polemics. In the first chapter we will discuss the way in which present evidence calls into question four centuries of partial interpretation by defenders of state-church Protestantism. In addition to Martin Luther and Ulrich Zwingli the traditional authorities have been Justus Menius and Heinrich Bullinger, who were also very partisan opponents of the radical groups. We shall see that the typical history of the Reformation in English still rests upon the attacks which these stalwarts made upon the "Anabaptists," although documentary material and German monographs have now made imperative a re-assessment of the entire movement. The primary sources now available require a thorough revision of prevailing judgments regarding those called "Anabaptist." Contemporary students who approach the radicals not infrequently comment quite vigorously upon the paucity of reliable interpretative writing, a paucity the more remarkable because the newer resources obviously make timely a thorough re-working of the field.[1]

Not only were the "Anabaptist" students of many decades plagued by descriptions of the movement of doubtful value; further difficulty was given by the complexity of the movement itself. We shall see that the groups that broke away from state-church Protestantism on the Continent were marred initially by many confusions and incoherences; it is not easy to extract a central concept or classifying principle. Various attempts at such classification will be discussed in this study, and the author will make a recommendation of his own.

The term itself gives no assistance in our problem. Very evidently a study of "The Anabaptist View of the Church" will come to grief at an early paragraph unless some more precise

use of the word is adopted than has been usual. The word
wants a definition, as will be plain from its history. The problem
of defining and classifying is related in Chapter II. But at this
point the use of the word must be checked; it has been one of
the stumblingblocks for every generation of historians.

What Does "Anabaptist" Mean?

The word "Anabaptist," is a Latin derivative meaning
"one who re-baptizes" (German: *Wiedertäufer*). Lutherans
and Zwinglians applied it in the beginning to those who separated themselves off from the main body of the state-church. As for
the radicals, themselves:

"They repudiated the name, insisting that infant baptism did not constitute
true baptism and that they were not in reality re-baptizers. Their argument was of no avail. The name was so conveniently elastic that it came
to be applied to all those who stood out against authoritative state religion."[2]

We shall see later that even Baptism itself was not the primary
matter in the testimony of the radical movement.[3] The radicals
wanted to be known only as *"Brüder"* (brethren) or by some
other non-sectarian name, and were far indeed from the later
insistence on formal precision in ritual. Baptism only became
important because it was the most obvious dividing line between two patterns of church organization, and especially because it afforded the authorities a means for suppressing the
radicals. The insistent use of the term *"Wiedertäufer"* or *"Anabaptistici"* by enemies of the movement was because the groups
fell thereby subject to the death penalty under the ancient Roman
law against the re-baptizers (Donatists).[4] The propaganda
campaign succeeded; at Speyer, 1529, the Emperor ruled against
the "Anabaptists" in final fashion, and persecution by imprison-
ment and exile and death spread throughout the length and
breadth of the Empire.[5] But the movement itself cannot properly be classified in terms of the baptismal rite.

Historically, the term "Anabapist" became a slippery
word, a term flung contemptuously, in much the way the word
"Bolshevik" was hurled at those of unpopular views a few years
ago.[6] In fact, the term has very limited value, and is used in this
study only because it has found an accepted place in historical
studies. The terms "Swiss Brethren," "Hutterian Brethren,"
"Mennonites," are more precise. "South German Brethren"
also carries some meaning, although our material on the lead-

ers and groups of Nürnberg, Augsburg and Strassburg leaves something to be desired. The Swiss and South Germans were one party, however, and they are not always distinguished even by specialists in "Anabaptist" affairs.

A WORKING HYPOTHESIS

When we review the various sixteenth century groups on the basis of the newer materials we are struck with the central significance of the church view among those usually termed "Anabaptists." The function of Chapter II is to show how this happened, and the argument is historical; the view of the church came to dominate the movement, although initially there were several grounds for disagreement with the state-churches. The concern for "The True Church" was a center about which various groups coalesced, and from which other groups broke away from "Anabaptism" proper. As the principle of voluntary religious association has come to be of striking importance to contemporary Christianity, the incidents surrounding its origin and validation become vital to both theology and sociology. In this perspective a study of the "Anabaptist" church view is a study in the origins of sectarian Protestantism.

There has been a marked change in writing about the "Anabaptists" in recent decades. Scholars are no longer content with sweeping generalizations about the movement, based on polemical Lutheran and Reformed writings. Various schemes of classification have been attempted, to separate off different groupings among the radicals.[7] After studied review of the materials at hand, assayed with attention to evidence yet largely unavailable to the American scholar, the writer has come to the point where an arbitrary definition seems both logical and inevitable. Such a definition can reflect, however, the verdict of history in favor of those radical groups, among others, which were able to resolve certain incoherences and approximate their ideal. For working purposes, *the Anabaptists proper were those in the radical Reformation who gathered and disciplined a "True" Church (rechte kirche) upon the apostolic pattern.* The doctrine of the church affords a classifying principle of first importance.

Fritz Heyer, in his detailed coverage of the field, came to a similar but less precise proposition about the church view in an effort to tie the several wings of the movement together:

"The ultimate significance of the Anabaptism (*Schwaermertum*) of the sixteenth century is grounded in the concept of the church."[8]

His treatment is a rather traditional state church apologetic however, whereas we shall concern ourselves primarily with concrete group experience. In a broadly theological context, we might use "Anabaptism" (in quotation marks) as Heyer uses it; but the term is applied most appropriately to those groups who effected a vigorous church life upon what they thought to be the pattern of the primitive church. Chapters III, IV and V will show what they thought that pattern was; Chapters I and II will discuss the Anabaptist congregations ("churches") and the way they are to be viewed.

FORMER TREATMENTS OF ANABAPTISM

INTRODUCTION TO THE CRITICAL PROBLEMS

The average seminarian in America knows little about the Anabaptist movement. He is able to find only a few summary statements in the surveys of the Reformation with which he is familiar, and these brief paragraphs do little to fill in the outlines of a blurred impression. He would be surprised indeed to learn that the leaders and groups of the radical Reformation were early champions and martyrs for a view of the church which he now takes for granted. When we review the reference works best known to him, the reason for his lack of knowledge becomes plain.

Most historians who have written about the Reformation in the intervening four centuries have treated those they called "Anabaptists" in one of two ways: they have dismissed them as peripheral with swift and easy strokes, or they have based their elaboration of the subject upon extremely hostile polemics. The Anabaptists are the abandoned people, who pass in dim review behind the glittering personalities of the chief Reformers and their protecting princes. In the usual fashion, a *History of the Reformation* recently re-published by the Cambridge University press dismisses them in three rapid pages out of six hundred.[1] We are left to assume that the radical groups were totally peripheral to the main concerns of Protestantism, and are barely worthy of passing reference. Certainly there is no suggestion that a reader might be led to a fuller understanding of contemporary religious life by familiarity with the primary sources of Anabaptism. There is no footnote to indicate that such sources exist.

A treatment typical of the second type of writing, and perhaps more common among surveys, is that found in Preserved Smith's *The Age of the Reformation*. Without apology he relied upon secondary sources of doubtful value:

"Mary of Hungary was not far wrong when she wrote that they planned to plunder all churches, nobles, and wealthy merchants, in short, all who had property, and from the spoil to distribute to every individual according to his need."[2]

Even in 1907, and certainly by 1920, there was enough source

1

material accessible to call into question a simple reliance upon
the polemical writings of those who drove those they termed
"heretics" to exile or death. The Anabaptists could no longer be
properly dismissed in a casual fashion; neither could a fair and
thorough work rely uncritically upon hostile testimony *about*
the radicals, without regarding the growing body of *direct* evidence. Both Whitney and Smith, however, reveal the traditional
tendential dependence upon the colored reports of Luther, Menius, Zwingli, Bullinger and the like. The sources edited by Cornelius, Keller, Beck and Egli, although available, were not given
a hearing in their pages, and the in-group writings of the Swiss
and South German Brethren, Hutterians and Dutch were apparently unknown to the authors.

The currently used volume by Thomas M. Lindsay, in the
International Theological Library,[3] presents a more comprehensive handling of sources. His list of references includes the
best materials available before 1903; the author was evidently
anxious to present a fair picture.[4] In spite of limited sources he
went far to give a generous estimate of some aspects of the
movement. He appreciated their passionate ethical concern and
hit upon a clue of key significance in discussing their uniform
aversion to a State Church.[5] In final analysis, however, he depended upon other writers who classified the Anabaptists as the
remnants of medieval brotherhoods.[6] Although his work is to
be praised beyond the volumes by Whitney or Smith, still it
must be emphasized that the most significant primary sources
now available have been exhumed from the archives since his
survey was written. The large mass of newly published court
testimony, sermons, confessions of faith and other records—
although only the beginning of a full representation—go far
to refute his fundamental conceptions. Yet Lindsay's writing,
along with the two previously mentioned, is that commonly allowed to stand in our seminaries and universities. The three
standard surveys of the Reformation in English are thus ruled
inadequate simply from the point of view of sources utilized.
If the Anabaptists have any significance for an informed discussion of contemporary church life, the priority of these surveys becomes even more intolerable.[7]

We find a similar inadequate use of source-material in more
limited studies, such as Vedder's *The Reformation in Germany*
(1914) and Allen's *A History of Political Thought in the Sixteenth Century* (1928). Henry C. Vedder was far more gener-

ous in his estimate than the authors mentioned. As his eyes swept over the scattered fragments of Anabaptism which were then exposed to view, he concluded:

"They were the only party among those protesting against the errors of Rome who were logical and thoroughgoing. They alone accepted in absolute faith and followed to its necessary consequences the principle avowed by the leading reformers, that the Scriptures were the sole source of religious authority. . . . The Anabaptists alone had penetrated beneath the surface of traditional Christianity and comprehended the real Gospel of Jesus. They were centuries in advance of their time in perceiving that the Good News of Salvation, as taught by Jesus, was a social gospel, and that the acceptance of it implied and necessitated a reconstruction of society until all institutions could endure the measurements of the Golden Rule. In a word, the Anabaptists were the real reformers, and the only real reformers, of the Sixteenth century."[8]

Spoken like a good American Baptist! But where is the documentation for such a sweeping opinion? And where may we find the Anabaptist writings on church reform which make clear what they were driving at? The references will not be found in Vedder's footnotes. In turning to Allen, we deal with an author who cites primary sources at length; but his basic interpretations are frequently far afield, and his chapter on those he thought "Anabaptists" is the poorest in the book. The evidence contradicts several of his basic assertions:

"Belief in the 'inner light' seems to have been the most fundamental of the beliefs that characterized the Anabaptists." (p. 39)[9]

"The Magistrate, so far from being a lieutenant of God, is simply the most persistent offender against God's law. They do not merely deny his right to coerce them into religious conformity—they deny his right to exist at all." (p. 41)[10]

"There appears (sic) to have been in Moravia communities of Anabaptists who actually had a common store of goods from which distribution was made by an elected official. But there is little evidence of any organized or systematic communism among the Anabaptists." (p. 42)[11]

"I do not think it can be said, even, that the Anabaptists proclaimed any principle of religious toleration, otherwise than indirectly. They denied of course the right of the Magistrate to punish heretics, but they denied his right to punish anyone." (p. 47)[12]

He missed the most significant single contribution of the radicals to political thought! His whole writing, although detailed, shows dependence upon the usual polemics—interspersed with citations from "Anabaptists" whose connection with the main line of the movement was very attenuated.

The outstanding limitation of the dominant interpretation of Anabaptism is this: when the authors give any detail at all they usually rely upon the traditional Lutheran and Reformed polemics against the radical groups. This procedure is in part a sign of unwise dependence upon partial evidence, but in good part it reflects the serious problem of getting at the sources in the field. The major primary materials have only lately become generally accessible, and scholars in the English-speaking world are not yet habituated to their use. As a result, there has been little "concrete'" study of the movement. Opinions expressed can generally be said to reflect the theology of the Reformers more than the economy of the Anabaptists.

The important point to register at this level of our discussion is simply this: *the treatment generally afforded those called "Anabaptists" in surveys and general studies is extremely faulty, and primarily because it is not informed by an adequate use of the primary sources now available.* There were, even by 1907 and 1920, documents which critical scholars should have used; today there is no excuse whatever for permitting to pass unchallenged that slighting notation which dismisses the radicals as peripheral and unworthy of intensive study at first-hand, or the morbid dependence upon questionable sources which seems to satisfy many of those historians who do pause to assess the movement.

The realization comes hard that the most significant materials upon which informed judgments might be based have lain relatively untouched for four hundred years in the archives of Swiss, Austrian and Czechoslovakian, German, and Dutch cities. For more than three centuries, most historians depended entirely upon the colored and partial reports of the enemies of the Anabaptists. Only within fifteen years have materials of greatest value become generally available, making possible a thorough re-writing and re-assessment of the movement. Only a beginning was made before World War II; used along with the work of other editors, however, the initial volumes of the "Wiedertäuferakten" of the *Archiv für Reformationsgeschichte*[13] provide enough data to launch a re-interpretation. Any discussion of the Anabaptists must cling closely to the primary sources; a structural analysis of Anabaptism, in fact, must begin with the romance of source-exhumation and re-discovery.

Traditional Interpretations of Anabaptism

The inadequacy of the currently used surveys of the Reformation will be further evident, as we review the progress of Anabaptist historiography. And it will be clear that there is a major problem prior to all contemporary discussions about the Anabaptists and their point of view: *to establish the comparative reliability and value of the authorities usually cited in Anabaptist studies.* Within recent decades there has been, as we shall see, a notable shift of attention from polemics about those called "Anabaptists" to primary sources of the movement itself.

Some former treatments can be grouped according to schools of thought, and we may well begin with those writings of the dominant groups which for long determined all semi-official interpretations and are still definitive for many.

The views of Martin Luther will be considered in their proper setting at Wittenberg.[14] In the meantime, there were several of his disciples who were distinguished for their polemics against those they called "Anabaptists," men whose historical writings helped to shape a school of thought about them. Of these, the most noted were Justus Menius, Urbanus Rhegius, Philipp Melanchthon and Andreas Althamer. J u s t u s M e n i - u s (1499-1558) whote two very widely circulated works, which Luther prefaced: *Der Widdertauffer lere vñ Geheimnis/ aus heiliger schrift Widderlegt* (with Myconius, 1530),[15] and *Von dem Geist der Wiederteuffer* (1544).[16] Menius tried to move Philipp of Hesse to more strenuous measures against the radicals, and as Superintendent in Ansbach "put out many much needed writings against the *Stenkfeldischen* and Anabaptists."[17] Menius is still one of the most commonly cited writers in any discussion of "Anabaptists." U r b a n u s R h e g i u s (1489-1541) wrote more polemics against them than Menius, but his writings have been less highly regarded.[18] Nevertheless, Luther looked favorably upon them and several have seen large use: *Wider den newen Taufforden Notwendige Warnung an alle Christglaeubigen . . .* (against Hans Hut, 1527);[19] *Widerlegung der Münsterischen newen Valentinianer vnd Donatisten* (1535);[20] *De Restitutione regni Israelitici . . .* (1536).[21] P h i l i p p M e l a n c h t h o n (1497-1560) was a prolific writer against "Anabaptists," and his authority was for long second only to Luther's, although his treatment is not especially keen or useful. He thought of them in terms of Müntzer and Münster.[22] A n d r e a s   A l t h a m e r   (1500-1539) was active against the Anabaptists at the time of the Bern Disputation, and against Denck's *Wer die Wahrheit wirklich lieb hat* he wrote *Dial/lage, hoc est,/conciliatio loco/rum scripturae qui prima facie inter se pugnare wi/dentur.* (1527), which saw many editions, including a German translation by Sebastian Franck (1528).[23] As a regional leader of the Reformation, Althamer found other occasions to strike against the ideology and practice of the radicals.

Menius' views may be considered typical of the Lutheran theological interpretation of radical dissent. Like the breaking forth of the Turk, the false prophets were also signs of the end:

"Nothing makes it plainer than the false teachings whereby he causes many factions and sects to appear within Christendom."[24]

"But when the Devil is a God he also has a Gospel, and in the nature of his gospel he also sends apostles out for it, and in the nature of his apostles they also build a church. Now our dear Lord Christ said the devil was an arch-liar and murderer; therefore his gospel is also not a gospel of grace and peace but rather directed toward murder and revolution with a lie as foundation. Therefore he sends his apostles not as Christ did—as sheep among wolves—but as raging and roaring wolves to rob and murder among the sheep. . . ."[25]

"For although Müntzer is thrown down, yet his spirit is not; it lives even yet, indeed rules in many corners—especially in the Anabaptist sect which was planted by Müntzer in this part of the land—and it has been impossible up to now to root it out."

Anabaptists are thereby classified as social incendiaries, and to their writings the traditionalists add lurid descriptions of the Münster episode of revolution, communism and polygamy. This has remained a standard assessment.

In later Lutheran writing, the learned monographs prepared by Heinrich Böhmer's Seminar are useful; yet they are colored by the intention to show that Luther's view of the origin and consequences of Anabaptism was sound. We do not find even in modern Lutheran historians any great willingness to modify the old views.[26] Karl Holl, it, is true, was prepared to admit the special significance of Anabaptism for the free churches; but this but proved the case for his theological criticism of "the sects."[27] Fritz Heyer's *Der Kirchenbegriff der Schwärmer* (1939) is a penetrating and exhaustive study, which is, nevertheless, committed to the traditional intention to prove Luther right in grouping revolutionaries and pacifists, mystics and Biblicists together in a common condemnation.[28] The entire body of Lutheran interpretation is generally marked by an unfamiliarity with the primary sources of Anabaptism, and by a studied determination to uphold that understanding of the radical groups which came from the Reformer himself. In the twentieth century, some Lutheran sociologists have allowed new schemes of classification,[29] but the apologetic intent remains the same for the "official" writings. They entertain with difficulty the thought that the church view of the radicals may have had integrity and vitality of its own, distinct from the opinions of Martin Luther.

In the Reformed churches the polemics of Zwingli, Bullinger and Calvin were circulated on a wide front against "Anabaptists." Bullinger is still the most frequently used writer among the traditionalist historians of both Lutheran and Reformed camps, Menius excepted. Ulrich Zwingli was the fountain source of the Swiss Brethren and through them of the South Germans and Hutterians.[30]. Yet when the radicals broke with a landchurch in 1524, public disputations were held in several cities and Zwingli wrote bitterly against his opponents on the left.[31] December 7, 1524, he countered their attack on the tithes with *Wer ursach gebe zu Aufruhr, wer die wahren Aufrührer seien, und wie man zu Christlicher Einigkeit und Frieden gelangen möge.*[32] In 1525 he published the well-known *Vom touf, widertouf und kindertouf,*[33] which precipitated an exchange; *Von Predigtamt und Wahrhafte und gegründete Antwort auf Dr. Balthasars Taufbüchlein* followed.[34] In July, 1527, appeared *In Catabaptistorum elenchus.*[35] Zwingli was sorely troubled by his former associates, who derived their radical Biblicism and doctrine of the Lord's Supper from his own teachings. His disciple and successor in the battle of ideas was H e i n r i c h B u l l i n g e r (1504-75), who began writing against the radicals after the Disputation of January 17, 1527. His polemics were widely read and are still cited with definitive accent: *Von dem vnuerschamptē fräfel, ergerlichem verwyrren, vnnd vnwarhafften leeren, der selbsgesandten Widertöuffern, vier gespräch Bücher* (1531), and *Der widertöufferen ursprung fürgang/ Secten- /wäsen/ etc.* (1560).[36] J o h n C a l v i n (1509-61) was also among those whose writings lent misunderstanding to the historiography of the Anabaptists.[37] Among widely read authors probably none understood them less. His *Briève Instruction pour armer tous bons fidèles contre les Erreurs de la Secte Commune des Anabaptistes* was written against the Seven Arti-

cles of Schlatten am Randen (1527),[38] and when he attacked the
free-thinking spirituals at Geneva he believed he was dealing
with the same movement.[39] Calvin thought "Anabaptists" were
individualists, descendants of the medieval mystics, and he made
no distinction between the spiritualist and the Biblicist wings of
the movement—if, indeed, he knew there was such a distinction.

The writings of Bullinger may be taken as authoritative
for the Reformed churches. Again and again he returns to attack those who spread dissension and factionalism in the Church:

"Their first article is that they hold up and remonstrate and teach themselves to be the one true God-blessed Church and the community of Christ/
and they are raised up in this community through re-baptism (and) of
course shall have nothing in common either with the Evangelicals or
any other church. This article has two parts/which they universally
maintain. The first is that the Baptist Churches are alone the right God-
blessed churches. The other is that the Anabaptists hold to their own
church alone/and have no community at all with any (other) churches
and also not with the Evangelicals."[40]

Bullinger felt that true and humble Christians should not be so
hasty to display their pride, neither should they sever themselves
too eagerly from their fellows. Let each remain in the calling
wherein he is called in the social order, and let none hasten to
rend the community of Holy Church because of some matter of
secondary importance. Bullinger believed "Anabaptism" began
with Thomas Müntzer, but divided them into eleven types—a
wide variance due to the religious subjectivism which he condemned. He especially opposed Adult Baptism (*Erwachsenen-
taufe*), which meant a sundered community. His writings were
definitive in Reformed circles until Emil Egli went back to the
primary sources.[41]

Along with those of Lutheran and Reformed writers, the
Roman Catholic polemics deserve mention. Among the early
authors of this tradition none gained a wider hearing than
C h r i s t o p h   E r h a r d and C. A.   F i s c h e r. Both
functioned in opposition to the Hutterian Brethren. Erhard was
associated with the Counter-Reformation under Adam von
Dietrichstein at Nikolsburg (c. 1583)[42]; Fischer appears to have
been a Jesuit opponent of Claus Braidl (c. 1600).[43] Both were
very prolific writers and enjoyed the approval and encourage-
ment of Roman Catholic rulers.

In general, Lutheran and Reformed and Roman Catholic
writers have inclined to look upon Müntzer and Münster as rep-

resentative evidence regarding the movement. The latter have also informed the reader that the revolutionaries represent Protestantism carried to its logical extreme of religious anarchy. The logic of "Anabaptism" is discovered in connection with the Peasant Revolt and the "New Jerusalem" at Münster. The Swiss phase of the movement is credited to short visits by Müntzer and Karlstadt, and Menno Simons' strict pacifism is considered a kind of "tired radicalism" following the collapse of revolutionary hopes.

The secondary sources which we have considered above have generally prevailed in the various writings about the Anabaptists, and we may no longer be surprised at the lack of insight which characterized those who depended upon them. Nor is it surprising that the orthodox opinion still prevails in many quarters when the name "Anabaptist" is mentioned. Generation after generation they have been called up for trial by the historians, the words of their accusers have been heard, and the Anabaptists have been sentenced to oblivion without having an opportunity to speak in their own behalf.

IN-GROUP RECORDS AND WRITINGS

To a certain extent the continued misunderstanding of Anabaptism can be explained in a single very brief statement: *the writings and records of the movement were quite successfully suppressed, whereas the polemics of their enemies circulated widely and were early translated into various languages* (including English). From the beginning this fact has played a large part in the dominance of hostile views. Even the churches descended from the radical groups have frequently lacked vital validating records, and discriminating historians who might have judged impartially have lacked the primary sources on which to build a case.

The Anabaptist writings, as orginally printed, found only limited circulation. Many never existed in other than manuscript form. The very important history attributed to Carl of Ghent, *Het beginsel en voortganck der geschillen, scheuringen en verdeeltheden onder degene die Doopsgezinden genoemt worden, in dese laetste eeuwe van hondert jaren herwaerts, tot op den jare 1615, getrouwelick beschreven door J. H. V. P. N.,* circulated in handwritten form for 43 years before finding a printer.[44] Because of dangers to life and limb the persecuted "heretics"frequently sought protection in anonymous publication;

the printer also might well hesitate to let his responsibility be known.[45] Writer and printer knew that the authorities of church and state were efficient and thorough, collecting both men and books for the flame. The religious and political powers endeavored to suppress both opinions and radical leadership; court actions and attendant judgment by the clergy frequently list the titles of writings to be confiscated. The authorities were determined to destroy the ideas which the Anabaptists represented; and they were, to a marked extent, successful in preventing informed discussion both in their own time and subsequently.

A bibliography of Anabaptist works will contain a large majority of rare items. Many of the most significant books within the group, originally published secretly and in limited numbers, exist today only in single copies or are lost altogether. The story of the Greater Chronicle of the Hutterian Brethren is not a-typical. Although this comprised the core of tradition, records and rules by which a major Anabaptist party lived, Josef Beck was unable to find a copy by 1883 and assumed it to be lost.[46] Re-discovered in the American settlements in this century, it was edited by Rudolph Wolkan in 1923 and A. J. F. Zieglschmid in 1943. Among the most significant long-lost writings was Pilgram Marpeck's *Vermahnung* (1542), written during the dispute with Schwenckfeld; it is the basic source for the South German concept of "the True Church." In recent years a copy was found by John Horsch in the British Museum, and another by Ernst Crous in the Württembergische Bibliothek.[47] Among the lost items, none is more to be mourned than Johannes Campanus' *Contra totum post-apostolos mundum,* listed by Melanchthon as *Wider die Lutherischen und alle Welt nach den Aposteln und derselben wunderbarlicke und seltzame Irrthumb* (1531). This is the fountain source among various radical groups for the idea of the Fall of the Church.[48]

The Bible was the only book which could not be taken from them, and which could not be kept from circulation. And they relied upon it implicitly. For an understanding of their ethical teachings, however, it would be very useful to have more of the "commentaries." These have been kept from other generations by the conspiring forces described above. The *Ausbund*[49] and *Märtyrer-spiegel*[50] were the only in-group records widely circulated, and to those out-group scholars who had them in hand these must have seemed only the mournful and credulous apologetic of a harried people.

Just as their enemies wrote broadly in their attacks, so the Anabaptists made sweeping claims for themselves in their apologetic. Their writings must be viewed with the same critical eye that we turn to the polemics of their enemies. They picture themselves as "the True Church," a Christian gathering of eternal significance.[51] From the beginning of history only a small band went the right way, and the Anabaptists stood in that line of the faithful. Their hymns and records of martyrdom are the self-conscious account of a people of integrity, whom God has chosen to carry the meaning of history.[52] With the fresh life of those given a primary religious experience, the community kept records like those of the early church: uncritical and inspired sermons, confessions of faith, epistles to the saints. This naive picture persisted in the more isolated American communities almost to the present day; even such an informed historian as the late John Horsch was resistant to the comparative method and critical research by students outside the group.

In Europe, however, the Mennonite historians imbibed earlier the spirit of German historical criticism, and were able to regard their own movement with a certain measure of detachment. This second level of in-group writing was heralded by Samuel Müller's *Jaarboekje voor de Doopsgezinden Gemeenten* (1837-50). In the next few years appeared Steven Blaupot ten Cate's regional histories of the Dutch Mennonites,[53] and separate studies by A. M. Cramer and S. Hoegstra. These histories will compare favorably with other studies written in the period, both for use of sources and devotion to the historical method.

FRIENDLY OUT-GROUP WRITING

For a long time the only historians to treat the radicals with any degree of sympathetic understanding and constructive analysis were independent thinkers like Sebastian Franck, and Pietists like Gottfried Arnold, von Mosheim, and Füsslin. Sebastian Franck (1499-1542/43)[54] was a great independent writer and contemporary who reported the "sect" critically but in great detail. He condemned all "sectarianism" —Catholic, Lutheran, Reformed, Anabaptist,—in the name of the God of true inward religion, and was most critical of all those who would not tolerate dissent in the things of the inner man. He was therefore a champion of the persecuted, and published extensive excerpts from the early documents of the Anabaptist movement. Gottfried Arnold (1666-1714)[55] was more widely read by eighteenth century Mennonites than any other out-group author. Products of Pietism, his writings were sympathetic treatments of the "heretics" and brotherhood movements across the centuries. J o h a n n   L o r e n t z   v o n   M o s h e i m[56] and J o h a n n   K o n r a d   F ü s s l i n[57] represent in the eighteenth century a highly developed historiography of similar ring: the "heretics" carry the True Church, which has existed only in dispersion since the time of Constantine the Great. From this theoretical base they give sympathetic hearing to the persecuted groups of the Reformation epoch.

Two writers, not alien to this way of looking at the radical groups, have more recently introduced novel propositions to classify the Anabaptists: Ludwig Keller and Albrecht Ritschl. L u d w i g   K e l l e r, whose significance in the excavation of sources will be considered later,[58] endeavored to trace back a continuous succession of radicalism from the insurgents of the Reformation to the pre-Reformation brotherhood movements. He interpreted the Anabaptists in terms of medieval mysticism and ethical concern.[59] They looked for true inwardness, and were not content with faith alone; they thought ethical concern would flow from a true repentance. A l b r e c h t   R i t s c h l proposed a similar scheme, relating the Anabaptists to the Franciscan tertiaries. Anabaptism stands clearly on the side of the middle ages and Catholicism in two important respects: claiming a visible church, perfecting the religious life. Poverty, pacifism, and the return to Jesus in the whole of life were common concerns of both the Franciscan circles and the Anabaptists.[60] Although the evidence is too slight to sustain the weight of speculation, Keller and Ritschl represent friendly attempts to classify and define the Anabaptists in terms of earlier radical movements.

Another frame of mind which leads to sympathetic interpretation of the Left Wing of the Reformation is that revealed by the modern "social" writers. The German Social Democrat, Karl Kautsky, and the English Guild Socialist, Belfort Bax, make a like case for Anabaptism.[61] They are unfamiliar with the best sources, and for them "Anabaptism" is the religious overtone of the revolutions of peasant and guild-worker. They place marginal events in the Peasant War and at Münster at the center of the stage. In effect, this is to accept the traditional misunderstanding, giving praise rather than blame.

CURRENT DEVELOPMENTS IN INTERPRETATION

The traditional interpretation of Anabaptism has been doctrinaire, and the apologetic of the group or friendly out-group comments have usually been founded in a doctrine opposed to institutional church life. More recently there has come a review of the movement which seeks to remain critically aware and at the same time understand Anabaptism as a church-type in itself. This approach owes most to two forces: the impact of the religious sociologists, and the re-discovery of primary materials.

A marked change in interpretation came in the twentieth century, when certain trained sociologists analyzed the Anabaptist church life and significance "concretely." The traditional historiography dealt with the leaders and groups in terms of certain fixed ideas and categories apart from historical evidence, but the sociologists departed from this well-worn path.

Before wide use could be made of the edited sources now available, a great sociologist—Ernst Troeltsch— displayed his acute judgment in comprehending the movement as a body of phenomena of unique character, with a pattern different from that of the dominant state-churches.[62] He recognized that the nature of the Anabaptist congregation and the structure of Anabaptist thought grew out of a Christian discipleship far distant in viewpoint from the teaching and practice of the Reformers. Troeltsch also distinguished between individual radicals (*Spiritualisten*) and the radical congregations (*Täufer*).[63] Finally, he concluded that the evidence pointed to an origin of the movement in Zürich rather than Wittenberg, a finding which threw him into strong controversy with Karl Holl and the other champions of orthodox historiography.[64] The watershed between the traditional and newer writings has come to be at this point: *whether the movement took its start with Müntzer and Karlstadt at Wittenberg, or with Grebel and Manz and Reublin at Zürich.*

Among those who have added to the evidence at this level we may note especially Ernst Correll. In Germany and America his research has carried on the great tradition of Troeltsch and Weber, with *Das Schweizerische Täufermennonitentum,*[65] and articles in *Mennonitisches Lexikon* (1913, 1937, ...) and *The Mennonite Quarterly Review.*

This "concrete" approach to the Anabaptist groups has had a profound effect upon the writing of both hostile and in-group writers. The Lutheran and Reformed scholars have come to give more time and attention to the radicals, realizing that the careers of Luther and Zwingli cannot be interpreted intelligently without portraying the insurgency on the left with which they were in conflict. On the other hand, the modern Mennonite scholar takes seriously the findings of the critics outside the group. He is resolved to relate the Anabaptist teaching to the concrete historical situation in which the doctrine took shape, and to relate the ideological conflicts to the real issues in the life of the congregations. Cornelius Krahn's *Der Gemeindebegriff des Menno Simons im Rahmen seines Lebens und seiner Theologie* may serve as an example of this type.[66]

Strange to say, Continental historians have to date been more moved by the recent analyses, and have shown more concern for proper revision of the traditional opinions than have the scholars of the English-speaking countries. And yet the Anabaptist view of the church is most significantly related to the Protestant sectarianism important in England and dominant in the United States.

Along with the contributions in the field of the sociology of religion we must mention the changes effected by the excavation of new source materials. Although a great deal of data is yet unworked, and the project begun by the *Verein für Reformationsgeschichte* is only in progress, significant gains have been made in recent years both in the discovery and publishing of primary materials.

The first outstanding contributions in the way of using and making difficult sources more generally available were made by two independent scholars of leftist tendencies: C. A. Cornelius and Ludwig Keller. C. A. C o r n e l i u s (1819-1903) was in a position of political responsibility in 1848, and was moved by the revolution of that year to study the Münster episode and related concerns. He energetically sought new sources and distinguished himself from the polemical writers by the breadth of his treatment; he wrote frequently and well, and documented his reports with copious footnotes and appendices.[67] A man of large churchmanship, he was among those Catholic leaders who broke with Rome at the time of the affirmation of papal infallibility (July 18, 1870). Ludwig Keller (1849-1915) represented a new and significant turning point in modern treatment of Anabaptism. His *Ein Apostel der Wiedertäufer* (1882) instituted a new and stimulating interpretation, which he continued in a number of brilliant and provocative volumes.[68] In October, 1890, he established the *Comeniusgesellschaft* for furthering sympathetic research in the brotherhoods, and its publications contain some valuable items too little used by historians of the Reformation. In 1897 Keller joined the Freemasons, hoping to find there fellow-champions of the free and ethical religion which attracted him in his studies to the radicals of the Reformation time.

Although some interpreters, of whom Cornelius and Keller are most worthy of note, made their fellow historians aware of hitherto unknown evidence, the most conclusive work was done by editors: Beck, Egli, Cramer, and Wolkan. Through their hard work a new assessment of the radical movements became possible to those who share their diligent concern for the early records. First we consider E m i l   E g l i (1848-1908), like Cornelius an Old Catholic, and editor of sources which have become invaluable to students of the Swiss Reformation dealing with the origins of the Anabaptist movement in Zürich. Especially noteworthy are the two volumes, *Actensammlung zur Geschichte der Zürcher Reformation in den Jahren 1519-1533.*[69] In 1897 he founded *Zwingliana,* an organ whose pages have continued to provide first class historical scholarship to the present day. Next in line is J o s e f   B e c k (1815-87), Knight of Mannagetta, who found time in a busy career to prospect many lost sources. He edited *Die Geschichts-Bücher der Wiedertäufer in Osterreich-Ungarn,*[70] and exhumed other materials which have seen light of day in the articles of Johann Loserth. He first opened the teachings of the Hutterian Brethren to the careful scholar. Priceless materials of the Dutch wing of the movment, including fragments sometimes extant only in one or two copies, were made available through the devoted erudition and sacrifices of S a m u e l   C r a m e r (1842-1913). Cramer participated from the beginning in the *Doopsgezinde Bijdragen* (N.F. 1867f), and wrote a large number of critical essays on Dutch Mennonite history. His monumental work was the ten volume *Bibliotheca Reformatoria Neerlandica,* completed after his death by F. Pijper. [71]

More recently, the available source materials of the Hutterian Brethren have been greatly enlarged; the Greater Chronicle, which Josef Beck had thought to be lost, was edited by Rudolph Wolkan (1923) and A. J. F. Zieglschmid (1943).[72] Some other valuable single items have recently been published in usable form. Foremost among them is Peter Ridemann's *Rechenschaft* of first importance to the movement in Moravia; this has been issued in beautiful edition by the new communities of the Hutterian Brethren in England and Paraguay (1938).[73] The last sixty years of Anabaptist study have been high-lighted, then, by the digging up and editing of long-lost and previously circumscribed records of the movement in Switzerland, Moravia and the Netherlands. The work of these editors is directly responsible for rescuing the Anabaptists from the limbo to which they have been consigned by their enemies, and from those historians who have for three and four centuries depended upon the polemics of their enemies in analyzing Anabaptist thought and practice.

Any discussion of the Continental sources would be incomplete without a mention of the information contributed by *The Mennonite Quarterly Review*, beginning January, 1927. The *MQR* continued the *Review Supplement* to the *Goshen College* (Indiana) *Record,* which appeared three times, in January, May-June and September of 1926. The magazine has frequently made known some of the rare materials collected at Goshen College (Harold S. Bender, Librarian), and through the industry of the late John Horsch and Edward Yoder at, Scottdale, Pennsylvania. The American "Mennonites" stem mainly from Swiss and South German fore-runners, and their later historians have pursued the Continental as well as American records. The Mennonite Historical Society is today one of the most active and significant groups among American historians, with a sharp concern for bringing forth the early sources. The Society has also encouraged the preparation of critical monographs by out-group as well as Mennonite writers.

We are now familiar with the way in which the Hutterian, Swiss and Dutch wings of the movement have come up for review in the light of recently published sources. Within recent years the German phase has also been presented more adequately. Certain monographs (largely in German) had previously been written which suggested re-orientation, but of greatest moment are the volumes made available through the *Verein für Reformationsgeschichte*. In 1930 was published the first, of thirteen planned volumes, sources on Anabaptism in Württemberg edited by Gustav Bossert; in 1934 appeared the Markgraftum Brandenburg sources, edited by Karl Schornbaum, and in 1938 the South German sources, edited by Lydia Müller.[74] Sermons, Confessions of Faith, Court testimony, Pastoral letters and other priceless materials have for the first time become generally accessible, and their significance for a proper assessment of the Anabaptist movement can hardly be exaggerated. Although only 5 of the 13 proposed volumes have been published, these volumes are more important, perhaps, than those dealing with other wings of the movement: we recall that both Lutheran and Reformed writers (since Menius and Bullinger) have traditionally found the point of origin of Anabaptism in the union of economic rebellion and religious enthusiasm in Thomas Müntzer, and given a German point of origin to the whole movement. The continuation of this series of source-books is a matter of first importance to historians; fortunately, American Mennonites have contributed a fund and worked out a plan with leading German scholars to carry the *Akten* toward completion.

We may do well in passing to note the existence of another largely unexplored mine of information about the movement: the Disputations. A favorite device of the Reformers was to hold public debate with the radicals, seeking thereby to discredit "subversive" opinions. Not infrequently, however, the keen wit and Biblical information of the illegal preachers turned public opinion their way. More often, the hearings were before selected circles from university and clergy. Sometimes the dissenters were guaranteed safe conduct to come to the Disputation; frequently they were brought from prison cell to be faced with the mortal charges levelled against them by the authorities of state and church. The records of such Disputations were sometimes published and distributed by one or more parties to the controversy, and afford an interesting but little used body of evidence on the opinions of the Anabaptists. Among the most famous of these meetings which dealt with Anabaptism were those at Zürich (1525), Basel (1525), Bern (1528), St. Gall (1530), Zofingen (1532), Pfeddersheim (1557), Frankenthal (1571), Emden (1578). The reports from these and other such hearings need to be re-worked so that historians can make ready use of the materials contained in them.[75] As it is, they are little used; they are not part of the rediscovery discussed above, and do not yet figure to a major extent in the re-assessment which is occurring.

In Conclusion

The comparatively recent discovery of most vital primary sources, unknown and unused by most historians for four centuries, calls for a thorough re-working of our understanding of the Left Wing of the Reformation. In this re-working, as it relates to Anabaptism, the modern historian will concern himself with information drawn directly from the movement, seeking to understand and define what the leaders and congregations hoped to accomplish. And their vision will be judged not by what their enemies feared and wrote about them but by what they were in fact able to accomplish. For the first time the sources and analytical equipment are available for such an assessment. It may be well to remark in passing that the data in hand suggest not only a new interpretation of the radical leaders and groups, but a re-writing of current representation of the major Reformers. If the Reformers were incorrect in appraisal of such opponents, they are themselves set in a new light. This will be noted in the course of the study, although our first concern is to understand the Anabaptists. The Anabaptist life is especially relevant to present problems in Sectarian Protestantism, and coming to grips with their church-view will have both historical and contemporary significance.

The Anabaptists have commonly been judged on the basis of insufficient evidence. It is time for a re-trial.

THE QUEST FOR THE ESSENCE OF ANABAPTISM

The first step toward an understanding of Anabaptism is a descriptive treatment in the light of the newer sources, a treatment which will review much of Left Wing Protestantism. The radical tendencies first appeared in the very centers of the Reformation.

RADICALISM IN THE CENTERS OF REFORM

Among the students who flocked to Wittenberg and Zürich and Strassburg were numbers who lamented the fallen estate of the Church, and judged her great sins and weaknesses in the light of the Church before Constantine. As time was to prove, the great Reformers were cautious and responsible men; they hesitated to abandon the parish pattern of the medieval church. At this point the radicals passed beyond, demanding a purging of errors accumulated during the period of wandering in the wilderness; small groups embraced the New Testament pattern with eagerness, pressing forward to restore the undefiled spirit and customs of the first centuries. Such men were impatient with compromise. As Walter Rauschenbusch said, the Anabaptists were "the root and branch party" of the Reformation.[1] They said of Luther that he

". . . tore down the old House, but built no new one in its place"[2],
and of Zwingli that he
". . . threw down all infirmities as with thunder strokes, but erected nothing better in place."[3]

Discontent with the slowly-moving brethren grew steadily, and rifts appeared between the party of the Reformation and the party of the Restitution. With bitter disappointment the radical party turned against the "half-way men,"[4] their former leaders, and against their former brethren who rested in large part in the unseparated condition of the medieval church.

". . . there is no people under the sun who disgrace God's name, suffering, martyrdom and death (more) than the so-called Christians."[5]

In the beginning period this discontent was not clearly defined. The attitude of the Reformers to the church underwent some significant changes, and the Anabaptists also separated

19

slowly and painfully from the dominant party. As we review the experiences at the three great centers of early Protestantism, we shall see that it took time to clarify the issues and define the distinctions between the Reformers and the Anabaptists. But it will be plainly seen also that the lines became clear in time to both parties, and that what was truly at stake was the concept of the Church, and the pattern of Church life involved in a genuine re-formation.

Anabaptism did not have in the beginning a clearly conceived doctrine of the Church. As a radical protest, it early enrolled in its ranks prophets and Biblicists, anti-Trinitarians and orthodox, revolutionaries and non-resistants, independents and covenanters. With the passing of months and years of persecution the movement acquired discipline and integrity. For convenience we speak today of "an Anabaptist movement," but we must avoid reading back into the Reformers and radicals a logical coherence which neither party possessed until after a series of hard-fought controversies. The Anabaptists had both to distinguish themselves from the dominant party and also to achieve unity within their own ranks.

In North Germany the first radical upsurge of importance came at Wittenberg in late 1521, while Luther was in refuge at the Wartburg. Martin Luther (1483-1546) was adored as a champion by many different classes and for as many reasons. He seemed to voice German national needs against those who bled the Germans for a trans-alpine master. The lesser knights hoped to find in him an advocate against the Imperial pressures. He called for religious reform against a system of outward display and inward sterility. Among those who rallied to his banner were many to whom he appeared as a social reformer as well as religious. Such groups looked with excited eye upon the heightened economic and religious tensions, and awaited with eager hearts the revolutionary Day which should usher in a New Age of history.

The point of separation was Luther's policy of Reformation. However much the Anabaptists may resemble medieval sects in certain respects, they did not spring from pre-Reformation movements directly. In their records they refer to Luther half in praise and half in sorrow, as a leader whom they first followed but who did not carry them through to as thorough a reformation as they had hoped. In the first explosion of radical

discontent, certain men from Zwickau, experienced in meetings
where anyone possessed of the Holy Spirit could proclaim with
authority the truths of the inner life, advocated thorough-going
change with such insistence that some at Wittenberg were won
to their cause and even Melanchthon was temporarily carried
away. The prophets strongly demanded a return to the usage of
the Apostles, as they understood it, and condemned the temporiz-
ing attitude in which the Reformer still allowed some practices
introduced by the Pope.[6] Marcus Thome (Stübner) claimed a
special revelation from the Angel Gabriel (*sonderliche offenbarung und erleuchtung.*)

"Finally it was declared that the Holy Scripture was undependable for
the instruction of men. For men must be taught only by the Spirit. If God
had wanted to teach men with scripture, he would have sent forth a Bible
from heaven."[7]

There was a great impatience in their words as well as harshness
toward the slow leaders, for soon the Turk would break forth
into the land; and the end of the world in a mighty battle, the
elevation of the righteous and the slaying of the godless were
close at hand.[8] Such enthusiastic spirit revealed dependence upon
Hussite teaching (both Stübner and his colleague, Thomas
Müntzer, had peregrinated to Prague). They preferred the Living Word to the written, used Tauler's Sermons frequently.
They also cited the Commentary on Jeremiah attributed to Joachim of Fiore.[9] From chiliastic, mystical and prophetic sources
they drew proof that true religion is inwardly authoritative and
free from external compulsion or evaluation. But they went further, to conform the social order to their spirit.

"This knotty spirit further taught that the secular magistrate and rule
must be reformed."[10]

With insistent demand for a thorough-going reform and ethical
renewal they pressed through the *Rat* certain measures of "Puri-
tanical" reform in town and church. In six blunt articles they
terminated the Roman rites, eliminated bawdy houses and tav-
erns, proposed to supervise the religious and moral life of the
people.[11] Popular feeling was aroused in support: images were
smashed, Infant Baptism suspended, the Mass celebrated in
both kinds. Among prominent Wittenbergers won to the new
cause was Andreas Karlstadt, who married in open break with
the old church order.

When Luther heard what was occurring, he returned in

haste from his "Patmos"; his eight vigorous sermons against the radicals stopped the new departures in mid-flight. With strong plea for moderation he condemned those who brought innovations by unbrotherly violence.

"As a mother gives milk to the child we should also serve our brother, carry with him for a time and bear and help carry his weakness, even nurse him along—as it happened to us, until he becomes strong; and not go heavenward alone, but bring along our brother who is not now our companion. . . ."[12]

To Luther, the issues are less important than unity, and laws and general rules which give offense to some should not be made about non-essentials. For example, take images. An Emperor and Pope once warred about this matter, and both were wrong; the issue is not important.[13] So also with fasting; we should carry our Christian freedom so as not to give offense to bound brethren.[14] Luther later accused Karlstadt of violating Christian freedom as much as the Catholics by enforcing legalisms of minor significance.[15] Above all, force should be avoided.

". . . for the word shaped heaven and earth and all things; it (the Word) must bring things to pass and not we poor sinners. In sum, I will preach, I will speak, I will write. But I will drive and compel no one with power, for faith is to be voluntary, proclaimed without compulsion."[16]

Yet the approval and even assistance of the temporal power was invited in the interests of order.

With like energy Luther wrestled against the spirit of "inspirationism" and "enthusiasm" (*Schwarmgeisterei*) among the radicals. He feared the consequences of their subjectivism; when they asserted an infallible inner authority he declared that the hidden God is revealed only in the objective word and not by vision.[17] The prophets were more probably inspired by the devil than by the Angel Gabriel. Under such hammer blows, the radicals were discredited and soon left the city. Luther was confirmed in his blunt opposition to all confusion of religious and social concerns, whether Roman Catholic or what he termed "Anabaptist."

At this distance no clear view of the Church can be seen to emerge from the words of the radicals who grouped so briefly at Wittenberg, and their later individual contributions are just as problematical. In spite of traditional Lutheran and Reformed interpretations, which have been discussed above,[18] we may question whether Stübner, Cellarius and Zwilling, Müntzer and Karlstadt, are properly termed "Anabaptists" at all. We review them in part for traditional reasons, and especially because of their influence upon the great Reformer himself. Furthermore, the Wittenberg radicals introduce some of the ideas which in time became common to various left wing groups of the time: repudiation of Infant Baptism, "Puritan" reform of morals, world-view.

After the Eight Sermons, Luther wrote frequently against those he grouped as *"Schwärmer."* Among the better known of his polemics are *Wider die himmlischen Propheten* (1525),[19] *Von den Schleichern und Winkelpredigern* (1532),[20] and the prefaces to Menius' tracts and Rhegius' polemics of 1535.[21] He thought that he was dealing with the fruit of "Anabaptist" enthusiasm when he wrote *Ermahnung zum Frieden auf die zwölf Artikel der Bauernschaft in Schwaben* (1525)[22] and *Wider die räuberischen und mörderischen Rotten der Bauern* (1525).[23] In the process of resisting those who urged "that corner masses or separate masses must be performed,"[24] and in putting down the civil revolt led by religious revolutionaries, Luther's own view of the Church underwent a marked transformation. At first he had embraced a fairly free view: In the Lectures on Romans he had spoken of the Church as a persecuted remnant, always small, hiding in the world. The view points toward Sebastian Frank's dissolution of any visible Church. On the other hand, in the Address to the German Nobility he spoke in terms of *Corpus Christianum* or *Volkskirche,* even a *Landeskirche.* However, in the Right of a Congregation he held that believers, if in some new or heathen land, had a perfect right to set up their own organization. Here was the congregational ideal.[25] In dealing with the Peasant Revolt and the spread of corner-meetings and irregular assemblies his view changed.[26] Dissent became a very serious matter, a breach of brotherly relations.

"Even if it were true that the Mass implies a good work, and Dr. Karlstadt were in good blood, he would have addressed us first and warned, before he made such a great shame of us publically before all the world."[27]

With embittered eyes he watched Müntzer and Karlstadt proclaim the prophetic messages which confused social and religious issues, played havoc with the political standing of the cause of the Reformers. Upon a basis of inner inspiration they spiritualized the Sacraments,[28] preached upheaval and poured contempt upon himself and his colleagues. The Lutheran leaders appealed more and more to the magistrate, and in their lands the *"Sakramentierer"* (Zwinglians, Schwenckfeldians, those called "Anabaptists") were proscribed in a common condemnation; the ethical concern of the radicals seemed to throw them into focus as revolutionaries and supporters of peasant and guild revolt. Upon Luther their effect was like that of the Donatists upon Augustine, turning him against all dissenting movements in the years to come.[29] He would not later tolerate even quiet separation.

The Peasant Revolt was the major turning point in the attitude of the dominant groups to the radicals. The spread of the Bible among the common people produced many literal-minded efforts to re-establish God's law among men. The confused and discrepant programs of the peasants acquired a Biblical coloring. While some appealed to the Law of Nature many invoked the Word of God and expected support from Luther.[30] Late in 1524 Swabia was in ferment, and throughout the early months of 1525 the revolt spread throughout South Germany. Among the Swabian peasants appeared the famous Twelve Articles, asserting historic rights and among other things calling for a located clergy, gospel from the Bible, and congregational control. The peasants offered, in conclusion, to surrender any point which could not be sustained by the Bible. For long the anonymous writing was attributed to Hübmaier or another "Anabaptist,"[31] and the Reformers denounced the episode as a mistakenly extreme reading of Biblical truth. They had some cause for this interpretation. As the movement spread northward to Thüringia T h o m a s M ü n t z e r came to the fore, again claiming the day of upheaval was at hand. In God's law, *omnia sunt communia*; all oppression in the world, both secular and religious, was to be violently overthrown.[32] His teaching was in good part responsible for peasant action, and Luther thought that the revolt was the logical outcome of the confused and excited prophetism with which he had three years earlier contended.[33] At first he condemned the princes and lords whose injustices had precipitated the revolt:

"Our sins are before God; therefore we have to fear His wrath when even a leaf rustles, let alone when such a multitude sets itself in motion."[34]

But the violence of the mob alienated him.

"For Christians fight for themselves not with sword and gun, but with the Cross and with sufferings. . . ."[35]

Events moved apace, and anarchy seemed to be at the door; the peasants had to be treated as robbers, suppressed for perjury (having sworn to be good subjects), rebellion and blasphemy (calling themselves "Christians").[36] The revolt was crushed with bloody excess, and Müntzer died by the sword he had drawn, at Mühlhausen. When, in later years, the quiet Brethren came before Luther's eyes, his imagination called up in their shadow the figure of Thomas Müntzer with the sword of Gideon. But the radicals with whom Luther dealt were hardly more than peripheral to the Anabaptist movement, for only in their initial opposition to the Mass and to Infant Baptism did they have common ground with those who came to be the main line of Anabaptism. As we shall see, the Anabaptists proper repudiated subjectivism and condemned revolution.

Although the fascinating figure of Thomas Müntzer has usually claimed the center of the stage in orthodox discussions of "Anabaptism," the community at Orlamünde was probably of more relevance to the movement than the coterie of prophets which rotated about Mühlhausen. Karlstadt, having lost his influence at Wittenberg after the return to the established order in the spring of 1522, took up residence outside the city as a layman and peasant. Then he assumed the leadership of the church at Orlamünde, and for two years strove to accomplish there the ethical reforms which had met short shrift at Wittenberg. If we value the vigorous, congregation-centered ethic, then the radical efforts at Wittenberg and Orlamünde must be sympathetically viewed;[37] in our case, the line of attack is of some significance for the permanent character of Anabaptism. It is clear, however, that the radicals did not make the break from the old parish system and develop a strictly congregational (internal) ethic. Karlstadt's concern was very little with baptism and the attendant voluntarism on the part of adults; he read *Acts* to the people and spoke warmly of the priesthood of all believers, but went no further. In his system the whole question of leadership (*Amt*) in the Church was interwoven with religious subjectivism and radical interpretation of the Mass in a way to defeat the clear lines of free association which marked the Swiss Brethren and other mainline Anabaptists. In September, 1524, this experiment ended; Karlstadt was expelled with his family from the land, along with his associates.[38] After travelling for a time with Melchior Hofmann, he turned to a vigorous literary work in South Germany and Switzerland.

Luther moved through successive disillusionment to a more conservative Church policy. In his early days he thought in terms of voluntary cells (*ecclesiolae*) within the territorial church. He was unable to recruit the committed members. The choice then lay between the *Landeskirche* or separatist congregations. Luther made his choice for the parish and denounced the "false prophets" who "have gone out from us, but . . . are not of us" (I *John* 4:1). There were many students and associates besides the better known—Müntzer, Karlstadt, Hofmann, Franck, Schwenckfeld—who broke away when the great Reformer's economic and ecclesiastical conservatism became evident. Some were lost in the swamps of speculation and chiliasm, "standing still" in frustration or dying as revolutionaries; a few contributed an idea or practice to that movement which can rightly be termed "Anabaptism." Most unfortunate is the fact that Luther's experience with the "Anabaptists" (if the *Schwärmer* may be so termed) was so limited, for early in his ministry he favored that inner concern and discipline which marked the main line of Anabaptism. His attitude to Anabaptism was moulded by a succession of unfortunate events, and he turned from toleration through banishment to the death penalty for sedition and for "blasphemy" (a term which in practice was largely equated with what hitherto had been called heresy).[39] Luther gave a new turn to religious persecution by directing it not against error as such so much as against the sociological and ecclesiastical effects. Yet we may doubt whether he and his colleagues would have reacted differently to more responsible congregational leaders. The corner-preachers and alley-congregations of the *Stille* also seemed revolutionary to those who attached salvation to the preaching of the Word and the administration of the Sacraments, for which the pulpit, the altar and the font must be undisturbed.

A number of those who broke away from Wittenberg found their way southward to Switzerland at one time or another; Müntzer, Karlstadt, and Cellarius were among them. In the period before the modern documentary studies and sourcebooks were available it was customary to attribute the origin of Anabaptism in Switzerland to their influence; the point of departure in discussing Anabaptism was, therefore, Wittenberg.[40] Gottfried Arnold, with habitual liberality, stated that Anabaptism had its origins in two different groups: first, Storch, Stuebner, Cellarius, Müntzer; further, "*Hubmeyer*", "*Mant-*

zer", "Graebel", Blaurock.[41] In fact, from the earliest times the Swiss Brethren and Hutterians condemned the revolutionaries and dissociated themselves from their violence;[42] and, with the Dutch, they traced their origin to Zürich. The point of view of the historian has obviously for long determined the selection of a geographical point of origin, and the matter of point of view involved has been previously discussed.[43] For the time being, let us refer to the record.

In Switzerland.

From 1514, Erasmus was at the University of Basel. There he became the center of a vigorous humanistic circle, pressing study of the Bible in the original languages and stressing the development of inward religion.[44]

"You may mark your houses, your vestments, and your churches, with the cross, as much as you please; but Christ will recognize no other badge than that which he himself prescribed, love of one another."[45]

His concern for the simplification of dogma and institution led his students toward Anabaptism and Anti-Trinitarianism. Although overshadowed and embittered by the Reformers, he remained for many the champion of a purified visible Church. As such, his teaching affords a significant link between the Great Church and the radicals.[46] He was a hero to many "Protestants" whose ethical insistence made them discontented with both Rome and Wittenberg.[47]

Zwingli was indebted in some respects more to Erasmus than to Luther, for the effect on Zwingli of Luther's attack on indulgences was to resolve to adopt the principle of rejecting in doctrine and practice whatever did not conform to the Biblical pattern. Zwingli was deeply concerned for the ancient and inner things of the faith, and by a radical Biblicism moved beyond Luther, who was bound far more solidly to the traditions of the church.

In 1522 and 1523 a wave of lay reading groups spread throughout the Allied District.[48] Andreas Castelberger was leading an adult reading group in Zürich in 1522, and Johannes Kessler was prominent as a reader in St. Gall—having been invited to function because of his training at Wittenberg. The reading groups trained leaders and were fruitful in encouraging Biblical radicalism among the common people. In October, 1524, Kessler stopped holding private Bible meetings at the request of the St. Gall City Council, but many of the lay readers throughout the Swiss cities went on to become potent figures in the emerging Anabaptist movement.

An impatience with the reforming leadership was first strongly expressed in the circle which associated with Zwingli at Zürich. At first Zwingli had opposed Infant Baptism, as had also Vadian; because there is nothing about it in the New Testament, they were resolved to hold to the Biblical pattern.[49] But when it became evident that the gathering of a church by faith baptism and the maintenance of a state-church were not compatible, Zwingli held to the latter line. Nevertheless, in his theory of spiritual communion only in the sacraments he remained in accord with the sectarian position and thereby permanently offended the German Reformers.[50] In the First Disputation (January 29, 1523) there was unity of Reformers and radicals against the Romanists. During the following summer Stumpf approached Zwingli on gathering a church of believers only; but Zwingli would have nothing of a "Donatist" church and answered with "he who is not against us is for us" and the Parable of the Tares.[51] By the time of the Second Disputation (October 26-28, 1523), the radicals were already committed to a program of the complete restitution of apostolic Christianity, and demanded less compromise with the Council's slow motion.

The chief leader of the Anabaptists during this hectic period was C o n r a d G r e b e l,[52] and with him were Felix Manz, Wilhelm Reublin, Georg Blaurock; Balthasar Hübmaier also took a prominent part in the Second Zürich Disputation. Grebel and Stumpf urged complete abolition of the Mass without further hesitation; when the Council left it to the discretion of each priest, Stumpf resigned from the priesthood and continued as minister to several lay meetings. On November 3, 1523, the Council ordered him into exile. Thereupon Zwingli launched his attack in writing and speaking; the radicals replied by making faith baptism authoritative. On January 21, 1525, four days after a Third Disputation in which Zwingli had taken the position that the initiation of children into Christianity by baptism was comparable to the initiation of infants into Judaism by circumcision, occurred the famous ceremony in which Grebel baptized Blaurock. Opposition to the baptism of children had moved over to Believers' Baptism; Scriptural radicalism had moved from opposition to what was outside the Bible over to a positive position. On March 16, 1525, the Council decreed that all who would henceforth be re-baptized should be exiled. The Anabaptists, in return, nourished the most bitter resentment toward those who had refused to go the whole way on the New Testament pattern. They called Zwingli "more false than the Old Pope,"[53] and "the Zürich popular preachers the true anti-Christs."[54] The breach between the party of the Reformers and the radical New Testament party was thus complete.

The important point to emphasize is that the real issue here was not the act of Baptism,[55] but rather a bitter and irreducible battle between two mutually exclusive concepts of the Church. Zwingli was finally committed to the state-church, and the continuance of the parish system on the level of the cantons; the Anabaptists were out to restore Apostolic Christianity. Baptism became important because it was the most obvious dividing line between the two systems,[56] and because it afforded the authorities an issue for suppressing the radicals by force.

S t. G a l l was next to Zürich as an important center of Anabaptist missionary work. Lay reading groups had flourished there in the pre-Reformation period. Leaders were Lorenz Hochrütiner (who had been in Castelberger's groups at Zürich) and Wolfgang Schorant called "Uolimann" (who replaced Kessler as leader when the latter submitted to Council's ruling against the groups); Dr. Christoph Schappeler (probably the author of the *Twelve Articles*)[57] and Dr. Balthasar Hübmaier of Waldshut were later most active. Grebel was in St. Gall from March 25th to April 10th, 1525, preaching and baptizing. On April 25th Uolimann and his associates were called before the Council and asked to desist, but they said that only by Bible proof could they "stand still." On May 12th a Disputation was held with Grebel's brother-in-law, Vadian, in the leadership of the Evangelicals. Zwingli's book on baptism had appeared, dedicated to the Burgomeister, people and Councillors of St. Gall; the St. Gall Council concluded by forbidding re-baptism and the separate "breaking of bread." June 5th, Vadian read his "Book" and the persecution began. At about the same time that Roman practices were finally ended, in 1528, a Synod of the state-church attempted to pull together some of the lessons learned in dealing with the Anabaptists. Meeting at Rheineck and led by Dominic Zili, the Synod decided to adopt church discipline as in *Matth.* 18 and I *Cor.* 5. This obvious attempt to meet the Anabaptist organizational intensity failed, as did also Oecolampadius' similar effort at Basel.[58] Thus, while the Anabaptist meetings were suppressed and two hundred men were sworn in as special police to

suppress the movement, the first of a series of notable attempts
was made to adapt to the state-church some of the lessons of
Anabaptism. Meanwhile, the leaders of the Anabaptist movement were exiled and their followers terrorized.[59] The restoring
of primitive Christianity was bringing persecution such as the
Early Church had borne.

B e r n is especially interesting, because the large majority
of Swiss Brethren who later came to America were descended
from families there. The Council had early ordered Scriptural
preaching, but did not abolish the Roman rites for several years;
various Disputations were held between the Brethren and the
representatives of the state-church (notably Berthold Haller
and Sebastian Hofmeister). A famous meeting was held at
Zofingen, July 1-9, 1532, in which the radicals held to Scriptural radicalism—including ordination by the local congregation, purified and disciplined; they also disapproved of serfdom.
In general, the Bern Council tried at first to follow the more
moderate policy of Strassburg: tolerating those outside of con-
venticles and exiling those organized. But they finally demanded
oaths of all to obey the Council, and used the special police to
hound into exile or death those who would not conform.[60]

B a s e l, through the influence of Erasmus and Amerbach,
was for many a city of refuge. In due time we find there Curione,[61] Castellio (unwelcome in Geneva), Martin Borrhaus (Cellarius), Hans Denck (who died there), Karlstadt, and finally
the "Anabaptist flammingo" David Joris.[62] Oecolampadius arrived there in November, 1522, and in the same year Erich Hugwald, a professor at the University, wrote a book against infant
baptism. The first Anabaptist "church" was gathered by visiting
missioners, in August 1525, who began "eine 'wincklechtige Ver-
sammlung'" which included Jakob Hochrütiner and Hugwald
(a friend of Müntzer).[63] The First Basel Disputation was held
in August, 1525, with Oecolampadius leading the Reformers'
party; the results were inconclusive.[64] On July 6, 1526, the
Council forbade rebaptism and ordered infant baptism. On June
10, 1527, a Second Disputation was held, but no record survives.
On March 14, 1528, a law was made that all Täufer not forsak-
ing their errors were to be fined five pounds, as were also those
giving them hospitality. In February, 1529, the party of the Reformers seized control of the city by force of arms and abolished
the Roman rites; from then on controls grew more hostile to the

Anabaptists and finally all property in their name was subject to confiscation.

With persecution increasing in the various Swiss cities, the Brethren began to spill over into the Tyrol to the southeast and north into South Germany. Missioners had travelled widely from the first,[65] and now family migrations became frequent. A center had already developed just across the border in W a l d s h u t, where delegates had gathered in 1524 in Hübmaier's home and agreed upon a statement of faith and polity.[66] At Easter time, 1525, Wilhelm Reublin was there preaching and baptizing; Hübmaier and sixty parishioners were re-baptized, and about three hundred eventually followed suit. B a l t h a- s a r H ü b m a i e r had taken over from the early Zwingli the belief in an *allgemeine Kirche* and *Einzelkirche*, both visible and resting upon Confession—"visible community and not (only) imagined."[67] This belief was translated into concrete form at Waldshut, although Hübmaier's predilection to mysticism forbade his conceding more than earthly authority to the congregation.[68] Upon accepting Faith Baptism as a visible sign of the restored Christian Community, Hübmaier resigned as priest and was immediately re-elected as minister by the congregation.[69] This is a most significant point in Anabaptist history, for it introduced the congregational principle of government. In the Swiss cities small congregations were gathered; at Waldshut an Evangelical congregation was won over bodily to Anabaptism. The break came so clearly in Waldshut because the town was in Roman Catholic territory, and there were not the delaying factors which in Zürich and other Evangelical territories prevented an early and complete break with a "Protestant" state-church pattern. Hübmaier's career in Waldshut and the life of the Anabaptist congregation were cut short by the coming of Austrian forces. The leader escaped December 5, 1525, spent a short time in the Zürich jail, and the next month made his way to N i k o l s b u r g where we shall meet with him again.

When Disputations and lesser compulsions failed to produce conformity, a wave of expulsions spread out into the countryside from Zürich and the other cities. In March, 1525, Grebel, Manz, Blaurock and many others had been imprisoned for life on bread and water; they were released only through the instrumentality of Jakob Grebel, (father of Conrad, and a town leader) and exiled. On the same day, drowning was announced for re-baptism, without trial or hearing. On August 11,

1527, a meeting was called by the Zürich Council, with representatives of Ulm and Augsburg as well as Bern, Basel, Schaff-
hausen, Chur, Appenzell and St. Gall. The delegates agreed
upon a policy for suppression of the radical movement. To enforce their commitments, the cities gradually took up the policy
of using special police (*Täuferjäger*). By the time Roman
Catholic (Imperial) policy was formulated at Speyer, (1529),
most Protestant lands were already enforcing exile and death
against the Anabaptist movement.

In the meantime the movement was spreading rapidly
throughout Switzerland and South Germany. Persecution of the
groups and killing of the leadership did not halt the expansion.
The gathering of small congregations by believers' baptism
went on apace, and Anabaptism spread in many areas closed to
the state-churches by their acceptance of the principle of terri-
torialism. The Anabaptists represent thereby an early Protestant
vision of a world mission unrestricted by territorial limitations,
and in a unique fashion fore-shadow the later concept of the
Church as a community of missionary people.

"Their presupposition is the little band of elect, which is something quite
other than a conventicle. It is the first understanding which encompasses
the whole world, pressing on to the true church at the end of time. This
little band shall tomorrow give the whole earth a new order. The Anabaptists (*Schwaermer*) believe in the totality of their church."[70]

At this time the Roman Catholics and Reformers were still
thinking in terms of the Church pattern of the Middle Ages:
religion was a certain phase of a civilization, controlled and bor-
dered by the agreement of princes. The Reformers generally held
that the Great Commission was binding only upon the New Testament Apostles, while the Anabaptists (*Täufer*) made it fundamental to their whole attack.[71]

In South Germany and Strassburg.

The Swiss radicals declared that the true church was to be
gathered in spirit and in truth, "and shall not be bound, as Israel, by proof texts and ceremonies."[72] From the early meetings
the free spirit revealed by this passage was contending with
the Biblicism which we have seen on other occasions. Individuals
and groups were not immediately clear as to the implications of
such conflicting positions; all weapons were welcomed in the
fight against the standing order. In a comparatively short time,

however, the tensions were resolved in most quarters and an Anabaptist congregational life of discipline and integrity was established. The focal center for many of the conflicting tendencies in the radical movement was S t r a s s b u r g.

Students of the Swiss Brethren have noted their strong expectancy of the end of the world,[73] an atmosphere in which certain types of prophetism and spirit possession could easily flower. With savage persecution loosed against them, the chiliastic tendencies were augmented; revivalist symptoms showed on occasion, with dancing, acting like children and speaking with tongues.[74] In the South German cities the preaching of Hans Hut also made itself felt, and added to the already electric atmosphere. There was a vigorous Karlstadt/Müntzer circle at N ü r n b e r g in the fall of 1524.[75] Later the prophet Augustin Bader gathered a little following, looking toward the coming Kingdom on earth; his short-lived effort, reveals the chiliastic note which became fairly common in certain groups:

With the new age "the new understanding of the Scriptures would be spiritually revealed through Christ, as he had previously done in the flesh. Then would all outer sacraments be rooted out, and there would be no baptism but affliction, no altar but Christ, no church but the community of believing men. And all that would come and be fulfilled by him, who had revealed and opened that (fact) to the prophet previous to the (written) word. And in this revolution Christ would spiritually teach what one should do or not do."[76]

For a time also A u g s b u r g was the center of Anabaptism in South Germany, during the time when Hans Denck was the most forceful leader. On August 20, 1527, the famous Martyr Synod was held there, with most of the prominent leaders present.[77] Denck apparently presided, although his dependence upon the Inner Word led him back into individual radicalism in a few months.[78] The ideological incoherences among the early leaders and groups all showed themselves during this period: pacifism and revolution, quiet eschatology and chiliasm, inner word and Biblicism, anti-Trinitarianism and orthodoxy, prophetism and synodical discipline.

Because of its generally liberal policy S t r a s s b u r g became the meeting-place of Left Wing leaders, the point where the several issues were joined between the Anabaptists and other radical movements. Not only was it a "bridge" between the Lutheran and Reformed teaching, but also between the several early groupings in "Anabaptism."[79] Storch was there in 1524, leaving a little group of chiliasts. Others who met and worked in Strassburg included Gross, Marpeck, Sattler, Denck, Servetus, Hetzer, Hofmann, Joris, Franck, Schwenckfeld, Bünderlin, Widemann.[80] Jakob Kautz of Worms and Wilhelm Reublin cooperated in a Disputation against the authorities on January 15, 1529, and other noteworthy debates marked the city as a forum.

Of men who made Strassburg their headquarters none showed more clearly the centrifugal factors in early Anabaptism than M e l c h i o r   H o f m a n n.[81] Hofmann was with Nicolaus Amsdorf at Wittenberg; there he impressed his colleagues by his concern for the strife over the supper between Luther and Karlstadt, and also became attached to Thomas Müntzer. On leaving Wittenberg, he went as Lutheran preacher to Stockholm (with Knipperdollinck, later a leader in the Münster "kingdom"), and Kiel (where he split with Amsdorf after a bitter polemical exchange).[82] But during this time several heretical doctrines had already appeared in his writings to cut him off from the Reformers: he disputed repeatedly against the doctrine of the Real Presence in the bread and wine, he proclaimed strongly millenarian views of the coming Kingdom, he expounded an heretical Christology (that Jesus passed through Mary like water through a tube). For a time Hofmann worked beside Campanus and then Karlstadt; his wide travels and prophetic fervor brought together many little groups, awaiting the signal for the New Age. The time never came, although he set a date for it. When his followers in the Netherlands were persecuted he instructed them to "stand still" for two years (*Ezra* 4:24), and himself turned southward to Strassburg. There he was greeted as a prophet by a little inspired circle, but in a short time was called for a Disputation (June 3-15, 1533) and imprisoned for life. By the time he was released, sick and forgotten (1540), the Kingdom which he had forecast had come and gone and left a trail of broken dreams and bodies behind it. The New Jerusalem (Münster, 1533-35) owed much, in both ideology and personnel, to Melchior Hofmann and the "Melchiorites."[83]

Strassburg circles were associated, therefore, with the revolutionary accent which was found among certain leaders and groups generally called "Anabaptist." It was also in Strassburg that another centrifugal tendency in the movement was resolved: the authority of the Inner Word. The men of the Inner

Word (*Spiritualisten*)[84] take their place with other leaders of Anabaptist thought during the inchoate period. They could appeal to Luther, who in his early days made much of the way Paul and Augustine pitted the spirit against the letter. Yet for Luther the inner is impossible without the outer. He vigorously rejected the Zwickau prophets for their separation of inspiration and the historic revelation. The theme of the Wittenberg radicals was taken up again by later Anabaptists, with interpretations of the Inner Word ranging from an identification with the mystics' *Fünklein* (Hans Denck) to dreams and visions (Hofmann). Among the more notable Spiritualists were H a n s D e n c k[85] (considered the leader of South German Anabaptism during the first half decade), L u d w i g H e t z-e r,[86] J o h a n n e s B ü n d e r l i n,[87] S e b a s t i a n F r a n c k[88] and C a s p a r S c h w e n c k f e l d.[89] The *Spiritualisten* shared the general vision of Early Church, "Fall" and Restitution which marked most Anabaptist thought. But their vision of the Restitution was not the gathering anew of the Christian Community of New Testament discipline and integrity, at least not without special commission to a prophet from God. Rather, looking to the New Age of the Spirit, they condemned all sectarianism and compulsion (including the Ban).

"We pray (God) also for all good-hearted men, who hunger and thirst after thy divine righteousness."[90]

They were non-sectarian (*parteilos*) and worshipped the tolerant (*unpartheyisch*) God.

"The true inner word is one eternal and almighty power of God, identical in men and God, and accomplishes all things."[91]
"But what man preaches is only the sign or symbol of truth. The Eternal word will not be read or preached; the solitary man will be assured of it in the abyss of the soul by God, and it will be inscribed on a human heart by the finger of God."[92]

Jakob Kautz said at Worms:

"The word that we verbalize/ read/ write is not the living/ eternal Word of God/ but only a symbol and sign of the inner by which it makes outward appearance. No outward word or sign or Sacrament/ also no outer office has this power/ for it strengthens and comforts the inner man. . . ."

Therefore Gottfried Arnold, not unsympathetic, judged that Kautz was guilty as accused of saying that

". . . man must hear not only God's word (the Bible)/ but also the special revelation of God (*sonderbare Offenbarung*)/ and of course man must recognize and listen to the Voice of God himself. . . ."[93]

This was ths doctrine which moved Luther to fear and condemn "*die himmlischen Propheten*"; what Luther never realized was that the doctrine here expressed came to be feared and condemned by responsible Anabaptist leaders also.

The testimony of the men of the Inner Word was never to produce a coherent church life in their generation. Essentially, they have neither doctrine of the Church nor practice of its life. Their uneasiness concerning the increment of the ages might produce a general renunciation of institutional life, or it might produce indifference to "forms" (as among many who never left the state church); they hung in the middle world "beyond good and evil," in which they neither made nor had to justify the sort of choices which beset any group living in the world. Denck is reported to have regretted at the end that he had ever given enough importance to outward form to re-baptize.[94]

"All true 'Christians', that is all men who are inspired in truth by the Spirit, 'are one in God with Christ.' "[95]

Although Bünderlin was baptized and participated in the Augsburg Synod of 1527, under Denck, he came at the last to oppose Anabaptism and all other "forms."[96]

"For him even the Church is an inner, purely spiritual collection of men who may be a thousand miles and further from each other."[97]

Franck and Schwenckfeld both believed that the True Church was lost unless a prophet appeared who was especially commissioned to gather in the faithful. Although they both had little bands of followers, Franck and Schwenckfeld are therefore to be strongly distinguished from those groups which undertook the responsibility of making a new beginning in Church life, and piloting it through the whirlpools of historical existence.

The radical individualism of the Spiritualists constituted, in fact, a fundamentally different view of the Church from that of the *Täufer*.[98] Nevertheless, the evidence does not warrant cutting them off from our discussion of the Anabaptists. On the contrary, it appears that in every center of Left Wing significance there was an early tension between those whose uneasiness regarding historic "forms" led them away from community in a concrete sense, and those who were moved to go on and gather a people. At first level the revolutionaries and *Spiritualisten* have the same relevance to the emerging Anabaptist congregations. As peripheral groups and centrifugal forces in the movement they competed, in the name of a general world change, against those who viewed the world with pessimism but the "True Church" with hope. The Anabaptist view of the Church was shaped not only by external pressures (persecution), but in a mortal struggle with those internal tendencies which would have forbidden any organized life at all. This situation is a marked parallel to that in the Early Church, where also the compulsion of a fresh spiritual experience produced in its extremes a type of prophetism which had to be suppressed to save the life of the organized congregations. Or, to put it another way, *the reversion of various radical groups to the life of the Early Church was at first a return to its eschatological atmosphere as well as to its ethical disciplines.*

The revolutionary and independent tendencies went spinning ahead through the years, and to a certain extent represent permanent challenges to effectively organized sectarian Protestantism. But among the dominant Anabaptist groups these tendencies were challenged and defeated. To a goodly extent that joining of issues and final victory was the contribution of P i l-g r a m   M a r p e c k, who has been termed "the greatest of the South German and Swiss Anabaptist leaders. . . ."[99] Marpeck was an engineer, and managed the city wood-supply in Strassburg for a time; banished after a dispute with Butzer (December, 1531), he adopted Augsburg as his headquarters and for decades labored among the South German Anabaptist congregations. Marpeck's view of the True Church was vigorously covenantal, continuing the Biblical insistence given first in Michael Sattler's Seven Articles of Schlatten am Randen (1527).[100] For long his work has not been properly assessed, for the writings in which he expressed his church-view were early suppressed and only recently re-discovered in part. With a strong sense of the meaning of history, Marpeck became involved in a dispute with Schwenckfeld's independent opinions. The polemical exchange ran from letters into books over many years, and resulted in the *Vermanung* (long lost, but recently re-discovered),[101] the *Verantwortung* (three copies extant, in Zürich, Munich and Olmütz),[102] and the *Testamentserläuterung* (lost, partially pieced together by Loserth).[103] On Schwenckfeld's part we have a number of letters and *Judicium de Anabaptistis* (1529),[104] *Uber das neu Buechlin der Tauffbrueder* (called "Juditium," 1542) ;[105] Schwenckfeld had already been banned by the Brethren for refusing to adopt Believers' Baptism, which he termed a new captivity of the conscience.[106] About June, 1529, Schwenckfeld wrote *Das noch heut kain Apostolische kirch seie von den Paulinischen und Apostolischen Christen,*[107] and this theme continued in his writings throughout the years. Marpeck and his associates replied that Schwenckfeld wouldn't have been satisfied with Christ's Church if contemporary with Him,[108] and maintained Believers' Baptism and spiritual government were Biblical ordinances given by Christ for the maintenance of His Church. They not only repudiated the vision of a New Age of the Spirit, but they felt that "standing still" in the face of persecution was moral cowardice. The *Spiritualisten* were as dangerous to the existence of a vigorous voluntary association on the one side as the state-church Reformers were on the other.

It is worth noting that Anabaptism had its own effect upon the Reformers in Strassburg. The leaders of the Reformation in that city did not represent the same hard hostility to sectarian ideas as did the men of Wittenberg and Zürich. Nor did they persecute as quickly. For a time the city leaders, especially Matthäus Zell and Jakob Sturm, stood for a broad and tolerant policy. Cellarius, won away from Luther by Storch, had considerable influence upon his friend Capito—whose writings show Anabaptist tendencies. Capito also was friendly to Marpeck, and opposed Butzer's harsh dealings with the radicals. Martin Butzer himself at first doubted infant baptism, but finally accepted the magistrate's orders. In his attitude to the Supper Butzer leaned toward the Swiss,[109] however, and he wanted a stronger congregational discipline. These were tendencies only, for three times he held open disputation with Marpeck; he defined the policy against Hofmann; and he succeeded in winning back Peter Tasch and two hundred Anabaptists for the establishment. Butzer's attack was slow and moderate, but persistent.[110]

Mass was not abolished in Strassburg until February 20, 1529, and complete re-organization of the church was postponed until 1534. Although there were mandates against giving shelter and food to Anabaptists in 1527 and 1530, banishment was not ordered until 1538. It was the experience with Melchior Hofmann and after that the Münster episode which put iron into the situation, and gave Butzer a lever for persuading the more reluctant Capito against the various radical groups. Although the South German Brethren (like the Swiss, Hutterians and Dutch) vigorously protested that they repudiated the violence, especially in the Peasant Revolt and at Münster, they were made liable to drowning if they returned a third time to the city. It should be said in conclusion that the law was more stern than the policy, for important Anabaptist synods met in Strassburg in 1555 and 1557.

Revolution

In tracing the Anabaptist experience in South Germany and in Strassburg we came naturally to speak of those centrifugal factors which threatened in the first decade (1524-1535) to break the movement into ineffectual fragments. We have seen how religious individualism constituted a real threat, in the *Spiritualisten* and perhaps "pre-Pietists."[111] The prophetic and chiliastic were also noted, and these elements grew to tragic proportions in the latter half of the first decade.

There are various ways in which the creative tension between the "church" and the "world" may be reduced. The fashion in which the Münsterites, with their foreshortened eschatology, resolved the matter is instructive in the history of the gathering of Anabaptist congregations.

The Münster episode has, it is true, only secondary significance in a history of "Anabaptism" (we refer to it in parenthetical fashion); but there were other revolutionary attempts in the North German and Dutch strongholds of Melchiorite teaching,[112] and the revolutionary motif is a logical outworking of certain enthusiastic tendencies we note among several significant leaders—especially in H a n s   H u t and Melchior Hofmann.[113] Hofmann we have reviewed. Hut also stands as a significant bridge between revolutionaries and *Stille*.

The chiliastic note which marked Müntzer's call to revolution did not die with him. Hans Hut,[114] a book-peddler, had been won to the revolutionary party of Wittenberg and became a prophet of the last times.

". . . they also held that in a short time Christ would come again to earth and institute an historical rule and would bestow upon them the sword of righteousness (as they call it), to root out and destroy all magistrates and those who did not accept re-baptism and were not related to their Band."[115]

Thus it was reported of his followers. Hut travelled widely in South Germany, baptizing thousands and proclaiming the speedy invasion of the Turks, time of persecution and revolution, followed by Christ's reign upon earth.[116] The ideas took different phrasing among different groups, but the tone and intention remained constant. At the time of His coming the dead are to rise up and

". . . establish the reign of God here on this earth; but heaven and earth will at the same time be made new."[117]

Another said of the end of the world

". . . then would the righteous who yet remained, come together from all the ends of the earth in the twinkling of an eye, and slay all the godless who yet lived; one would slay a thousand and another ten thousand; such triumph would be given by God to his own. . . ."[118]

After the collapse of the Peasant Revolt, Hut met with other leaders in Hans Denck's house in Augsburg (May, 1526); there he pledged to repudiate the sword,[119] but did not change from the excited eschatology and wide missionary preaching which marked his work throughout. In May of 1527 he participated in a dispute with Hübmaier at Nikolsburg,[120] which helped initiate the split between *"Schwertler"* and *"Stäbler."* That fall Hut was burned to death in attempting an escape from the jail in Augsburg, but in three short years he had left a permanent mark upon the thinking of the South Germans and Hutterians.[121]

The eschatology represented by Hut and Hofmann took concrete expression in the stand and fall of the Davidic realm at Münster. The incident demonstrated the tremendous pull upon all highly expectant movements:—to release the tension, to press ahead bitterly and at whatever cost to realize the dream.

J o h a n n e s   C a m p a n u s has been termed the father of the Münster restitution.[122] Campanus was a follower of Hofmann and the head of "the Wassenburger preachers." It was he who put in dramatic fashion the vision of the "fall" and restoration of the church; the ideas were then championed in Rol's *Die Slotel van das Secreet des Nachtmaels* and Rothmann's *Restitution rechter und gesunder christlicher Lehre.* Bernt Rothmann, who had received Humanistic training and represented the Lutheran cause for Münster in the Schmalkaldic League, was moved first to adopt a Zwinglian view of the Supper[123] and then to repudiate Infant Baptism.[124] Shortly thereafter one of Hofmann's missioners, Jan Matthysz, arrived in the city, and assumed as prophet an increasing authority in town affairs. The split of Lutheran and Anabaptist parties widened beyond repair, and Rothmann joined the latter in determination to gather "the believers in a holy community separated from the unbelieving godless."[125] This meant that those who didn't join would have to be expelled from the city, introducing a new element not faced by a voluntary congregation as such; the fact was recognized—"The Lord God would here rule the city and the godless would be thrown out. . . ."[126] At this point we see in Anabaptism the possibility of a combination of Church as voluntary association and yet coterminous with the community. The idea spread throughout North Germany and the Lowlands that Münster was the Key City of the New Age; the communism which began *"unter Freunden"* in imitation of the Early Church assumed a larger significance in the following January (1534). The second prophet (Jan of Leyden) had meanwhile arrived, and the city was proclaimed the New Jerusalem.

The word spread rapidly throughout the northern cities that the time was at hand which the prophets had declared. The 144,000 were to be gathered in.[127] A book of baptisms was kept, probably the first Covenant-book of believers.[128] From many Melchiorite centers—Deventer, Zwolle, Amsterdam, Leiden— groups started out by land or water.[129] Colporteurs and missioners travelled to the North German and Dutch cities. In October the Book of Wrath (*van der Wrake*) was released to arouse all neighboring fraternal peoples to usher in the New Age, overthrow the Babylonian tyranny, slay the godless. They should let fall the mild weapons of the apostles and seize the armor of David![130] Under Jan of Leyden ("King" David as of August 31, 1534) the crest of the city displayed a globe.[131] The prophet proclaimed that after the time of suffering and revolution, the messianic age was at hand. Thus the preaching of Hofmann and Hut led to concrete though transitory results. The kingdom was beset by combined Roman Catholic and Protestant troops, betrayed from within, and destroyed with the most ferocious cruelty. The iron cages in which the bodies of "King David," Knipperdollinck and Krechting were placed after torture still hung on the tower of St. Lambert's Church into the last century.[132]

Two radical departures were taken during the time of rapid social movement at Münster, deserving special attention— C o m m u n i s m and P o l y g a m y.

German Social Democrats have suggested that the economic policy in Münster was occasioned by the siege, and should be considered as parallel to rationing in the Paris Commune.[133] This will hardly bear analysis, however, for the practice was begun six months before the siege; it was an expression of religious conviction rather than economic necessity.[134] Communism in Münster resulted from a combination of admiration for the Early Church, and a radical interpretation of the Love Feast.[135]

In the matter of Polygamy, the problem is more obscure. Considering along with the system at Münster the bigamy of Philipp of Hesse and of Henry VIII, we might be led to suppose Protestantism was remarkably indecisive in the matter. Remember, however, that they had just dealt a mortal blow to a most general adjustment on sex—monasticism. Men who had made such a break might falter in shaping a new ethic. There were two noteworthy Scriptural arguments for polygamy: *first,* the New Testament forbids divorce but is silent on polygamy; *second,* by special revelation God permitted it to the patriarchs, and might under similar conditions approve the institution among later servants.[136] The Münster attitude is a curious combination of asceticism and laxity. Extra-marital relations were strongly condemned and within wedlock sexual relations were restricted to propagation. But marriage was expanded to permit more than one partner. This solution may have been precipitated by the large plurality of women within the city, but no doubt Old Testament influence was paramount. The command to be fruitful and multiply must be given maximum obedience.[137] The orthodox Reformers who on occasion condoned bigamy were scarcely in a position to cast stones.

A Covenantal People

The struggle with the religious individualists on the one hand and the revolutionaries on the other left the main line Anabaptists with a vigorous community of discipline. The persecuted groups of the early years had little opportunity to work out their complete vision of the True Church, and less to live it. Their leaders were cut short and their meetings were constantly harrassed. In perpetual tension between forces without and within that would have destroyed them, they only suggest in an atmosphere of expectancy the manner of life which they might have elaborated if permitted. But their attitude and teachings were eager with anticipation of a Good Life to come.

The congregations of the later period, which had withstood the inroads of prophetism and violence, represent a fruition of the New Testament radicalism which marked their point of departure from Luther and Zwingli. By the second decade, inspired leadership and novel interpretations had largely disappeared; both organizational and credal conformity were strictly enforced according to the fashion of vigorous voluntary associations. Elders and synods were the effective enforcement agencies for the New Testament disciplines of the Church of the Restitution.

The growth of effective discipline, which has been marked throughout this historical exposition, reached culmination in the strength of the Hutterian colonies and the Dutch Mennonite congregations. The Swiss and South German Anabaptist movement did not attain full maturity until the settlements blossomed in America.

The communistic Anabaptist colonies in Moravia were founded by refugee Swiss Brethren who did not find in Hübmaier's great church at Nikolsburg the discipline which they read about in the New Testament. In 1529, under pressure to take the oath to the princely family which had given a place of retreat to the fleeing Swiss, a little band of two hundred followed Jakob Widemann out onto the land. There they laid all their belongings on a cloak, resolved to live the life of sharing depicted in *Acts* 2 and 4, and chose seven Stewards (*Diener der Notdurft*) on the authority of *Acts* 6:3-5.[138] It was the duty of a steward to enforce the rules of community, seeing that all sought the common good and none betrayed it by self interest. This was the unpropitious beginning of the "communism" of the Hutterian Brethren, an economy which persists to this day in the north central United States and central Canada, and in Paraguay.

Under the brief but vigorous leadership of J a k o b H u t e r,[139] in the years 1533-35, the communism of consumption thus introduced was made a coherent social system. During the early decades the Hutterians were blessed with a remarkable series of able leaders: besides Huter, we may mention Wolfgang Brandhuber, Peter Ridemann and Peter Walpot. Brandhuber built up a strong economy, teaching those skills and crafts by which the Christian brethren could avoid contamination by war and commerce.[140] Ridemann perfected the emerging communism of production, and gave it a confessional grounding.[141] Peter Walpot headed the greatest missionary organization of that epoch, maintaining an extensive correspondence and guiding a large and effective corps of lay missionaries.[142] The Hutterian economy, and the contributions of these remarkable leaders, will be discussed later in connection with the Anabaptist teaching of Community[143] and the Great Commission.[144] As gathered churches, the Hutterians are remarkable for representing a kind of "realized eschatology"; they are the one continuing section of Anabaptists who were able at an early date to resolve the tension between Church and society. The Church became a *societas economica* in itself. Throughout the centuries the Hutterians kept this pattern by following the frontier.

In the Dutch congregations the matter was resolved in quite another way. Anabaptist eschatology included two emphases which might be supplementary to each other or might compete. In time both tendencies fulfilled themselves. In the first place, there was a compelling drive to make their life a total authority, economic as well as religious (to be unspotted by the world)—in a kind of "realized eschatology." The Hutterians settled in this pattern. And on the other hand, there was also a missionary world-view (to go to all the world), which from the earliest years sent Anabaptist missioners throughout the German-speaking lands and beyond. The process of aculturation and compromise which established communication with "those of the world" reached its final stages among the Dutch Mennonites.

In the years following the debacle at Münster all called "Anabaptists" were under suspicion as revolutionaries. The independence of their small meetings, the refusal to take the oath and give military service, seemed subversive to the state-church authorities. Further, the *Stille* in North Germany and the Netherlands ("Obbenites") owed their origin as well as the revolutionaries to the energetic preaching of Hofmann and his associates. Obbe Philipsz was a disciple of Hofmann[145] and Menno Simons' own Anabaptist ordination came through Obbe from Jan Mathysz. Menno's Christology continued to be the Docetism of Hofmann, and although they did not follow him there his followers were always questioned at this point in court.[146] Prophetism persisted for decades in non-violent form as well as chiliastic, and the more conservative leaders had to contend repeatedly against this factor in shaping up the congregational life of the faithful. Sebastian Franck had a large following in the Netherlands;[147] there was a party of his name, and Henrik Niclaes, David Joris and Adam Postor show the effect of his writings. It might appear that the northern Anabaptist ranks would be hopelessly frustrated by inner incoherence and external pressures, following the collapse of the New Jerusalem. That this did not happen is due in part to the fact that for some years Hofmann and his followers were the major representatives of "Lutheranism" in the Netherlands; Anabaptism was not there a radical split off the major parties, but *the* Protestant party. But further, the survival and greatness of Dutch Anabaptism is in large measure a tribute to the rugged and tenacious leadership of M e n n o   S i m o n s.[148]

Even during the most excited days at Münster the majority of Dutch Protestant congregations did not go over to the revolutionary position. They remained as they had begun, voluntary associations of baptized evangelicals in a Roman Catholic land, determined to fulfil the New Testament ordinances in the restored apostolic church. As a priest, Menno was first moved by the reading of Luther to doubt the Mass (1528); he decided to follow the Bible. Then he was stirred by the Scriptural Command for Believers' Baptism (1530). In March of 1535 a little band of Evangelicals (including his own brother) died defending themselves at the Old Cloister at Botsward; Menno realized that the opinions for which they suffered were his own,[149] and he pitied their tragic and misguided condition without responsible leadership. About a year later he gave up his protection as a priest and began to pastor among the people who represented what he had come to regard as New Testament life. From that time until his death in 1561 Menno lived the life of a corner-preacher, travelling secretly from town to town with a price on his head, binding together the shattered fragments of a great movement and building of them a Church.

The memory of apostolic Christianity was strong in many of the Dutch cities,[150] and Menno's leadership meant a return to old evangelical principles.[151] Even more than among the South Germans the simple New Testament teachings were made central, and paramount among them was the inner and personal *re-birth*—which in the individual believer parallels the break of the Church of the Restitution from the fallen period and condition of the Great Church. For both individual believer and the Christian Community, Christ alone is the true foundation.[152] The dark passages of Scripture, in which the chiliasts searched eagerly for the hidden promises, are to be shunned; the Sermon on the Mount is plain enough.

"As Luther defined his position against the 'enthusiasts' (*Schwaermer*), so Menno took his stand against a like aspect of 'Anabaptism' (*Taeufertum*). Indeed his very first writing waged this battle, in which he placed himself directly against the kingdom of Münster—which was a product of the allegorizing of Scripture and chiliastic prophetism. He comes forward boldly not for truth through a 'revelation or heavenly inspiration' but rather through the 'expressed, written word of the Lord.' He wants to know nothing of 'his own opinions, dreams, and visions.' He angrily cried out in a defensive writing that he was neither an Elias nor an Enoch nor a 'third David' nor yet a seer or prophet."[153]

The ethical emphasis (Synoptic) was first, and the evangelical/missionary second.[154] When the End comes it will be sudden and by God's act; the faithful are not preparing the way in any programmatic sense.

In Menno's first book to John á Lasco he wrote:

". . . as before God who knows our hearts, we are clear of all their abominable doctrine, power, uproar, mutiny, bloodshed, plurality of wives and the like abominations. Yea we hate and from all our heart oppose them as acknowledged heresies, as snares to the conscience and deceit, as deception of souls and pestilential doctrine. . . ."[155]

Menno's weight was thrown on the side of authority in the church as well. The fight against the Great Church tended to obscure the difference between laity and clergy, for some spoke with more authority than others and these gained a hearing. But in reaction against Münster and to control the enthusiasts a strong policy was developed in regard to ordination and commissioning of Elders.[156] Menno also adopted a more conservative attitude to the Magistrate than some Anabaptist leaders: he is ordained of God, and may even be a Christian. For our purposes Menno's leadership may mark the final elaboration of a mature Anabaptist church-view. By the time of his death (1561) all necessary lines had been drawn. The Anabaptist church view had attained its historical and sociological maturity.

During the time when the Dutch Anabaptists were missionary minded and persecuted, their discipline was strong and the tension with the "World" maintained. By the time Holland became a center of toleration, however, the "Mennonites" were a powerful commercial class. All restraint toward government and the sword broke down in time, along with other special ethical disciplines. Today the lineal descendents of the Dutch Anabaptists are alert in matters of profit and investment, vigorous in politics and war. Long ago the government of the Netherlands, in permitting voluntary religious association, removed the main area of conflict between their congregations and the society surrounding them. Since they were closely tied to industrial society, and did not fasten upon any cultural behavior-pattern, the Dutch Mennonites are today rather more like other representative Protestant connections than like American Mennonites and the remaining Hutterian colonies.

The Problem of Classification

The preceding survey is based on the latest source materials. In so far as previous treatments have been deficient due to inadequate use of documents, their lack here stands corrected. But the problem of classification, the quest for the essence of Anabaptism, still remains. The difficulty is that there were certain very serious incoherences in the movement itself, and these incoherences are reflected particularly in the oldest documents and earliest years of the movement.

With the first-hand evidence before us from the leaders and groups of the Left Wing, we are impressed by the wide diversity of teaching and practice. This was especially true in the first decade, while the impulse was fresh and uncritical. Both doctrinal and institutional problems were treated very freely and with great originality by some of the early Anabaptist leaders. The persecution which drove them underground also added to the wide variety of life in the congregations. The basic problem of the radicals, we may safely conclude, was in gathering and disciplining a movement, in effecting a reasonable balance between the strong individualism of a fresh spiritual experience and the hard decisions facing a community living in the world and in history.

Many of the incoherences have been observed in our descriptive survey. The problem lies not only in these factors, but in the very diversity of views on organized Christian life on the part of the leaders. Robert Friedman has shown in a stimulating article that if different schemes of classification are used, various points of origin for the ideas must be admitted and different groupings appear.[157] Various classifying principles which may be used are the attitude to tolerance, the use of different books of the Bible, the view of the state-church relations. The early movement was very diverse, and by taking different approaches we find some groups may be called "Anabaptist" and others may not; but the lines shift with the issues at hand. The Italian scholars have usually mentioned the doctrinal issues, and the orthodox associated the radicals with social revolution. To Rufus Jones they were a movement of inspired faith which broke through the encrusted patterns and rituals of centuries, while to John Horsch they were Bible Christians who pursued to logical conclusion the teachings of the Reformers. Actually, Friedmann concludes, they were *sui generis,* and must be treated as such: they took their departure from Luther and Zwingli upon no single idea or practice, but upon a general discontent with the compromises of "the half-way men."

All of this indicates that the movement is not susceptible to a facile interpretation, and it may be possible to term it a "movement" in the earliest period only by reading back into that decade certain resolutions of conflict which later authenticated themselves. *Although certain teachings concerning the Church appear strongly from the beginning, it took a decade to winnow out competing concepts and make the main teachings concrete in the life of disciplined congregations.* For general purposes, "the Left Wing of the Reformation" may be a better term for those generally termed "Anabaptists,"[158]unless we understand that "Anabaptists" has precise meaning only by limiting it to include only those numbered among the Swiss Brethren, Hutterians, South Germans and Dutch Mennonites. "The Left Wing" counts all the vari-colored individuals and groupings associated with the movement at first and later hanging on its periphery: the groups following Franck, Campanus, Denck, Bünderlin, Schwenckfeld, Joris and Pastor— as well as the more centrally significant leaders and congregations. The radical protest of the Left Wing asserted itself in a wide fashion, and coherent congregational life eventually emerged in some quarters, only by throwing off certain centrifugal tendencies. At first it was not clear what might eventuate in the Anabaptist movement as a whole, although certain centers of discipline like the Swiss and Hutterians have a fairly consistent record throughout. The initial stress upon individual conscience and congregational autonomy ran its course before this disciplined life was established. This mixed picture, which we see through conflicts between various leaders and groups, is itself a large part of the problem of giving meaning to the term "Anabaptism." Does it mean (assuming that we cast off the traditional tendency to use it with complete abandon) those congregations which eventually emerged, or should it be used to cover all of those diverse tendencies which characterized the early years (1525-35)? In brief, we may state that the problem of later historians to define and classify "Anabaptism" is not far from that one-time problem of the radicals themselves.

CHRISTIAN PRIMITIVISM:
THE FALL OF THE CHURCH

Our descriptive survey has revealed the concept of the Church as the essence of Anabaptism proper (without quotation marks). This is to be understood in the "concrete" and historical sense as well as in terms of the teaching of the Anabaptist leaders. Two notes stand out from the rest:

1) The Church must be a voluntary association.

2) The Church must follow the New Testament pattern.

With the exception of Münster and the Hutterian colonies the Church of the Restitution did not become coterminous with the community. But the distinction needs to be made, for under toleration a voluntary church may not differ markedly from a state-church in its social outlook. Continental Mennonitism has remained a voluntary association but has lost the "primitivist" marks of the New Testament community. The ethic, the attitude to the world on the part of the Anabaptists, has often been called a new monasticism. The common element is the attempt to realize in the concrete the radical ethic of the Sermon on the Mount. But the Anabaptists went further: the whole membership of the "True Church" was pledged to re-live in studied fashion the life of the New Testament community in all of its phases. *The Anabaptists proper were those in the "Left Wing" who gathered and disciplined a "True Church" (rechte kirche) upon an apostolic pattern.*[1] We return to the definition proposed in the Preface.

There is something deeper than mere Biblicism in this social program. It is part of an outlook on life which can best be described under the concept of Primitivism. If we inquire as to the goal of these Anabaptist groups we are driven at first not forwards but backwards. Their objective was not to introduce something new but to restore something old. "Restitution" was their slogan, a Restitution grounded in the New Testament. And surrounding their groups was a certain atmosphere, an atmosphere whose precipitation point was a certain vision of the Early Church. In the earlier period, before institutional and ideological discipline had given ideological coherence to certain groups, and especially before persecution and the necessary defensive organization had weeded out the "centrifugal" tendencies, the single thread running through the Left Wing was this dream of the Early Church. This is the thread which ties together *Spiritualisten* and *Täufer,* Swiss Brethren and Polish Brethren, Schwenckfeldians and Hutterians, Mennonites and the followers of Sebastian Franck and Adam Pastor. The final pattern was to be the restitution of this Early Church, and its coming triumph on earth.

This was essentially an attitude of Religious Primitivism, and as such is but part of a special manifestation of a widespread and recurrent aspect of "civilized man's misgivings about his performances, about his prospects—and about himself."[2] The concept is both cultural and chronological. It is Christian and it is classical. For the Anabaptists and other Left Wingers it involves a philosophy of history: an Eden in the past, a partial Restitution in the present, a divine restoration in the future. Various ingredients of this attitude are discernible in previous movements.

In classical antiquity Cynics and Stoics believed in a Golden Age without war, slavery and property. Jews and Christians looked back to Eden as a garden devoid of strife and exploitation between both men and animals. The theory of a "Fall" runs throughout them all. In the early Fathers classical and Christian themes are sometimes fused. The classical-Christian ideal of the communism of a Golden Age was picked up again by Sebastian Franck and through him transmitted to Anabaptism.[3]

This might at first seem to be a purely speculative discussion about the past, until we recall that the use of the primitive as a norm involves not only myths but manifestoes. Primitivism is a fertile source of ethical concern, as well as a familiar device in historiography. The projection of Eden into the future was the work of apocalyptic Judaism, from which the concept passed into Christian eschatology. In the time of the Reformation and pre-Reformation groups there were variant forms of primitivism; frequently this centered in a type of Adam-mysticism which glorified the simple, unlettered and unspoiled man. In argument, the appeal is made to the plain man's judgement, unspoiled by institutions and less corroded by speculation than the scholar's. Those who work with their hands (craftsmen) or close to the soil (peasants) are presumed to be more receptive in spirit, and their minds have not been addled by the folly of the wise and learned.[4] The exaltation of "primitive" cultures is another form which flourished in the sixteenth century, in connection with the discovery of primitive people in the New World. Various Humanistic circles spread the tales of simple living and savage nobility. On the one hand there was a high idealization of the simple life and the man of Nature; and on the other

". . . what is even more significant, . . . not the discovery that savages can be noble, but that civilized people can become good savages and can be regenerated by a natural life."[5]

Secular and Religious Primitivism sometimes fused, in that the primitive man was regarded as fertile soil for the primitive gospel. Bartholome de las Casas gave wide currency to this theme in his *History of the Indies,* and established a Utopian colony to implement it.[6] A group of Anabaptists at Zürich announced that they were going "to the red Indians over the sea" when their evangel was greeted with hostility and persecution at the hands of civilized men.[7]

The man of the Reformation epoch was thus profoundly uneasy about the manner of his social life and the pattern of his own formal thinking and worship. He thought that his own age was "decadent;" a three-fold fall (*triplex discessio*) had occurred—national, in the Church, of the age.[8] The historians of the Renaissance and Reformation frequently rejected the historiography of Orosius. The thinking man of the period was conscious of a renewal to come, a new birth of spiritual vigor following the long decline. A new periodization was introduced, with a fall both political and religious in Imperial Rome, with a restitution of old virtue in the present. This became the framework of much of the historical thinking of the Renaissance and Reformation.[9]

Religious Primitivism in the Left Wing

Among the radical thinkers there was a frame of mind remarkably parallel to classical primitivism, and reflecting in good part the melancholy of the age. When we consider the detailed structure of Anabaptist life we find many evidences: their normative view of the Early Church, the historical expectancy implied in use of "Fall" and "Restitution." With independents like Franck and Schwenckfeld it is not so difficult to trace the effect of certain pre-Reformation ideas. But with the more Biblically centered groups, who rarely cited any non-Biblical authority, it is a speculative if not futile effort. We may, however, mark certain centers of ideology which affected their intellectual climate and, largely in indirect fashion, their ideas.

Before persecution destroyed the educated leadership of the Anabaptists the men at the head of the movement were university trained. Among the South Germans and Hutterians there were several converted priests, highly educated. Other leaders were trained in the literary circles which everywhere marked the spread of Humanistic learning, among them Hans Denck and Leonhard Bouwens. In Westphalia and the Valley of the Yssel, the schools of the Brethren of the Common Lot supplied a number of the most able leaders.[10] To point up the discussion we may take two great figures: Erasmus and Zwingli.

Desiderius Erasmus (1466-1536)[11] was educated by the Brethren at Gouda, Deventer and s'Hertogenbosch. He was greatly influenced by their regard for simple living and simple Biblical truth; from Wessel Gansfort, Alexander Hegius and Rudolph Agricola he learned concern for apostolic Christianity and its manner of life. Pacifism and tolerance were articles of faith. He knew the English Humanists (Colet, More, Warham), worked in Venice with Aldus Manutius (the friend and fellowstudent of Pico), and corresponded with all of the leaders of thought of his day. The Anabaptists admired him greatly for his ethical insight and accent upon sincere and uncompromising New Testament truth. In his writings the return to Gospel simplicity was the way to rejuvenate the faith and the Church. But Erasmus, who also influenced the Reformers more than any other single author, was the despair of both Catholic and Protestant parties. If he would not accept Roman Catholic preferment by denouncing the Reformation, he would not declare for the Reformers either. He did not believe in the rancorous partisanship which characterized both sides. He believed change should be reasonable and enlightened. His last days were embittered by von Hutten's attacks and the accompanying break with Zwingli, and he died with one faithful disciple by his side: his executor, Bonifacius Amerbach.[12]

Ulrich Zwingli (1484-1531)[13] was educated in the Latin School, then at Bern under Lupulus; following two years at the University of Vienna under Conrad Celtes and Cuspinian, he returned to Basel where Wyttenbach taught him the Bible. He also became acquainted with Pico's work and corresponded with Erasmus. At Einsiedeln he read the Church Fathers—Jerome, Origen, Ambrose—and also Stapulensis and "Dionysius." He copied out the Pauline letters from Erasmus' New Testament, and was moved to the attitude which permanently marked his churchmanship: "Back to Christ!" He never broke, however, with the cultural and political life of the Swiss city-states, but the radicals (Grebel, Manz, Blaurock, Reublin) who left him and went beyond him were following the logic of his message.

The direction of Humanism was away from speculation and dogma to pious ignorance (*pia ignorantia*), away from ecclesiasticism to the simple ethic of the Synoptics (*Nachfolge Christi*), away from the hierarchy to the elemental lay brotherhood of the disciples' democratic band. There was, furthermore, a certain attitude to the origins which is most significant: just as return to classical forms was the purifying principle for their beloved Latin, so a return to the life of the early Church would revitalize the corrupted faith.

Because primitivism is not essentially a theory of origins but really a device for passing judgment on contemporary society it is closely linked with views of the future. Eden is also Utopia. The imagery of the lost Paradise reverberates through the apocalyptic visions of the book of *Revelation*. Primitivism leads straight into eschatology. The man who represented this combination in the age preceding the Reformation was J o a- c h i m   o f   F i o r e.

The Abbott Joachim had been significant in one way or another for the radicals of pre-Reformation and Reformation from the time when the Fraticelli appropriated the Eternal Gospel in their fight against the papacy.[14] Joachim's periodization of history is especially relevant, with seven ages culminating in the *Restitutio ecclesiae*. His followers were far more radical than he, and marked history by his own person or that of Saint Francis. He taught that, through the prophet of the last times justice and peace were to be re-established in all of the Roman provinces. The prophet was to be a spiritual Constantine, freeing the Church from the trammels with which the Imperial Constantine had bound her. For with Constantine all heathen had streamed into the Church, polluted and compromised her. The Fall of the Church which followed the time of the Apostles would soon be ended, however; the recovery of the Church in the present would precede the last things. Whereas in the middle period salvation was linked to the institutions and sacraments, in the Age of the Spirit these lost their meaning; as Simeon took in his arms the child Jesus, so should the Curia act to fulfil the *ordo spiritualis* (the "withering away" of the Church).[14b] The Great Church was near to death (following the Fall) and would be renewed by a re-appropriation of the relationships in an earlier and more vigorous period (*institutio fidei Christianae*—"the people of faith were of one heart and soul," in *Acts*).[14c] At the end of time there is a secret unfolding, in the revelation that the oppressed, the humble and anonymous are those who carry history.[14d] At the end of time the absurd, dark, obscure passages of Scripture will be revealed as the greatest mysteries;[14e] hidden within the outward is the inner Church, slowly revealing itself.

"The history of this church leads from the apostles through the martyrs, the hermits and monks of the Greek Church to the Benedictine monasticism of the Western Church, to the Canons Regular and their effort to make the poor life of humility and submission binding upon all clergy, to the Cistercian reform, to the Cluniac monasticism, and expresses itself conclusively in the Franciscan reform movement." [14f]

When the old forms opposed the New Age, then the old Church was recognized as the Anti-Christ; its efforts to hinder the revival of apostolic Christianity were the proof of its diabolical character.[14g] The moving power toward the New Age was to be martyrdom, the willingness to suffer without stint for the Gospel without glosses.[14h] The whole teaching was bound together with a sense of world mission, of ultimate triumph at hand.[14i]

In the radical groups of the Reformation these ideas constantly recur. Anabaptism was primitivist and eschatological. The norm is the past, the hope for the future was the Early Church. The idea of Restitution represents a studied effort to reverse the verdict of history, to shed the accumulated power and intellectual sophistication which seemed to corrode and obscure the pure and inspired faith of the founders of the Church. In the Anabaptist "Restitution" there was the same agitated historical expectancy which we find in Joachimitism and in the Early Church itself: a keen sense that the end and final reckoning are close at hand; and conjoined with it a vigorous missionary outlook which embraced the whole world in its sweep. And it was a suffering Church, whose changing patterns were ever cast in the shadow of the Man upon the Cross.

These were the main elements which went into the intellectual atmosphere of the radical Reformation, and which form the back-drop for the emergence of a type of Religious Primitivism in a radical view of the Church and its place in history. As we move on to consider the relation of Primitivism to Anabaptist thought, and the various factors which make it evidently a type, we do well to make certain distinctions to avoid serious error. The attitudes which we were considering formed an intellectual climate for the various groups of the time, bound together the Left Wing especially, and are to be considered along with the records of their actual historical experience. Our discussion has attempted to deal with "concrete'" groups rather than only with ideas. The view of the Church which the Anabaptists championed will be repeatedly tested by the actual experience of the groups.

In total perspective, the evidence from classical Primitivism and similar streams of thought in the Reformation has only relative value. In spite of suggestive eddies to mark cross-currents, and a few instances of streaming together, the evidence as a whole is circumstantial. It gives us a good deal of help in understanding the general climate in which Anabaptism emerged, but we shall find few quotations or other evidence of direct influence. While doubtless the Zürich Anabaptists such as Grebel were familiar with the classical ideal, the prevalence of religious Primitivism in Anabaptism is due more largely to the fact that Christianity is an historical religion with a sacred book in which all reforms seek their inspiration and confirmation. Since the norm provided by the book was itself diverse, it was in turn selectively applied in the light of the real problems of the age.

We may return to our original concerns: to discover what it was certain groups hoped to be, and to what extent they were successful. We shall draw mainly upon their own testimony in elaborating their church view, testimony now generally available in usable form. In judging to what extent the Anabaptists succeeded, we shall consider the problems they faced, both from without (persecution) and from within (centrifugal forces, both doctrinal and organizational). And we shall speak from a footing in free church life which is the eternal memorial to those who championed voluntary religious association and vigorous congregational life at a time when Christianity was for most simply the religious aspect of a civilization, indeed frequently only the tool of government. It is only from such vantage that Anabaptism can be truly understood, and its importance properly assessed.

The Fall of the Church

The idea of a general fall of man has been adapted by Christian reformatory groups to the history of the Church. There are two falls: man fell and the Church fell. The whole idea of the recovery of New Testament Christianity is tied up with the thought that at some point in Christian history the pattern was lost. A very prevalent contemporary opinion is revealed by the approach taken by Hobhouse in the 1909 Bampton Lectures:

"Long ago I came to believe that the great change in the relation between Church and the World which began with the conversion of Constantine is not only the decisive turning-point in Church History, but is also the key to many of the practical difficulties of the present day; and the Church of the future is destined more and more to return to a condition of things somewhat like that which prevailed in the Ante-Nicene Church; that is to say, that instead of pretending to be co-extensive with the world, it will accept a position involving a more conscious antagonism with the world, and will, in return, regain in some measure its former coherence."[15]

We see here the familiar teaching of a "Fall," coupled with the hope of an eventual Restitution. It is not surprising to find that at the present time a book on *The Fall of Christianity* by the head of the Dutch pacifist organization[16] is being distributed in quantity by the American office of the Fellowship of Reconciliation. The Constantine Myth is an essential part of the discussion:

"When he was converted to Christianity (in 312), and when he exalted this faith into the State religion (in 324), Christianity began to turn toward the State for support, and became reconciled to war and the soldier's calling."[17]

For Heering this is the turning-point of Christian history, and the pivot of the discussion. The pattern of thinking is well known; what is not as familiar is the fact that this is Anabaptist thinking. The Anabaptists were among the first to ground the Church in a total and systematic application of this historiography.

Elements in the Idea of the Fall

When we break down the various ideational associations into their constituent parts we find several different themes customarily linked together: glorification of the first three centuries (the "Golden Age" of the faith), a lamentation for the decline in association with the Empire (the "Fall" of the Church), a vigorous sense of new beginnings (the "Restitution"). The latter theme will be treated in the next chapter, in a discussion of the constitutive elements in the church-view. We shall consider now the attitude to the Early Church and its subsequent decline.

In true primitivist fashion the Anabaptists considered the earliest times the Age of Heroes. True, there had been before the sixteenth century a conscious glorification of the life of the Master and His Disciples, buoyed up by a general feeling that the men of the first centuries were spiritual giants after a fashion not equalled by later generations. The imitation of Christ (*Nachfolge Christi*) was a familiar medieval theme, of special importance to the Brethren of the Common Life—whose house at Deventer first instituted the practice of community in deliberate imitation of the Church at Jerusalem.[18] There were other anticipations, notably among the radical Franciscans and the Hussites. But a well-defined primitivist periodization of Christian history—with the "True Church" beginning to re-live in careful fashion the life of the early heroes—was a major Anabaptist contribution.

When we review the cardinal points in Anabaptist thinking about New Testament times and the primitive church, the parallels with the classical "Golden Age" become immediately apparent. There were certain personal virtues and social practices which characterized the good society in both schemes of thought, and we may consider them briefly.

P a c i f i s m was a prime principle in the classical "Golden Age."[19] It was accented also in the Anabaptist vision of the Early Church. For them, pacifism was intimately tied to the testimony of the non-resistant martyrs: as the early Christians had won the Roman Empire by suffering, so should the martyrdom of the followers of Christ in the later age lead on to the final triumph.

The Anabaptist repudiation of violence was especially related to the integrity of the believing community. Above all it it was wrong to compel religious submission and use force in matters of conscience. As David, the man of war, was not permitted to build the Temple, and as Solomon built it without hammer and axe, so the Church of Christ was first created by voluntary association without force or compulsion.[20] The law is to go out from Zion and the Word of God from Jerusalem, and a people gathered without weapons.

C o m m u n i s m characterized the classical "Golden Age," and de-humanization through the advent of private property marked the "Fall."[21] Viewing the Early Church, Leonhard Schiemer wrote that the "Communion of Saints" was most clearly seen in *Acts* 2.4.5, and true disciples should live as men did in that glorious time of the faith.[22]

"One Christian should buy nothing from the other, but give freely. (read Acts 2.3.4., whether the Christians at Jerusalem didn't have all things common!)"[23]

They were real Christians then, and the people of God most plainly seen! The Hutterians wrote to the Moravian Lords (1545) that their communism was modelled for that of the Early Church.[24] The Holy Spirit visited the Jerusalem community, and they were a people of power. The actual Anabaptist practice differed in various congregations according to the time and place; but the insistence upon Community (whether communism of consumption only, or of production also) remained constant.

Sometimes a more general historical understanding entered the picture. Thus Peter Ridemann taught in his *Rechenschaft* that everything was in the beginning created common (I *Moses* 1:26-29), and property entered by sin[25]; presumably the Early Church was returning to the life of Eden by practicing communism. Ulrich Stadler showed a strong historical sense in his treatment of the subject, pointing out that only the Church at Jerusalem had communism and at the other centers Christians were left alone in their own houses. Communism came to the Hutterian Brethren, then, because they were driven together with no other place to go and no other life to lead.[26] But over against these historical observations we may place dozens of normative statements concerning the first age of the Church; Communism was generally considered authoritative simply because it was the life of the heroes of the faith. Give all to the poor (*Matth.* 19:21)! Consider the widow, who gave

all she had! There is an apocalyptic quality in it: as time is tele-
scoped between their groups back to the "Age of Heroes," so
it is shortened between them and the end of history. Some felt
the end was already begun in themselves. When asked their
trade and location in court many replied, "no Master" (*kein
vorsteer*), for in the New Age only Christ was Master. An
economy had been introduced in which all were equal and all
were to share according to need.

A v i g o r o u s s i m p l i c i t y was the mark of the
man whom the world could not victimize: his wants were well
controlled, his tastes directed to the truly essential.[27] Like the
classical Hero, the man of spiritual power in the Early Church
was also cut loose from personal display and absurd convention.
By vigorous enforcement of spiritual discipline (including the
Ban), unethical and immoral practices were avoided—not to
mention frivolous clothes and strong language. A congregation
of spiritual athletes was trained. In his testimony before the
court Julius Lober said:

"Luther and other Christian teachers do not preach nor teach baptism as it
was taught at the time of the apostles. . . Saith further, that Luther and
others promote no true Christian order (in it), that they suffer and permit
whoredom, avarice, usury, blasphemy and other depravity in the community, which the apostles did not bear so far, but had the ban among them."[28]

The enforcement of heroic virtue by the group enabled the Hero
to perform wonderful deeds; he was able to fulfill the testimony
of suffering, and occasionally to perform miracles.

A c e r t a i n a t t i t u d e t o A r t (technology)
might be linked to this vigorously cultivated simplicity.[29] The
agriculturalist, close to Mother Nature, was thought to be more
wise than he whose spirit was corroded by the artifices of civilization. The craftsman, who worked with his hands, was said
to learn more by his craft in the spirit of humility than ever
the Scribe with his multitude of books. Hans Hut and his disciples preached the *euangelion aller creatur,* pointing out that
Jesus made clear to the Common Man by his trade the great
wisdom to which the theologians were blind.[30] The radicals never
tired of pointing out that the men who knew Jesus were simple,
unlettered, anonymous; they asserted that the poor and depressed and naively literal were those who carried the Gospel.[31] The
unsophisticated were said to believe that Jesus meant just what
He said, without any glosses. In the great time of the faith, so

the radicals claimed, neither doctrine nor church life were bound and corrupted by "forms," by dangerous inflections and compromises.

When we speculate how such marked parallels could exist between classical primitivism and Anabaptist thought, since it is difficult to prove direct classical influence upon the radicals—who rarely cited any book but the Bible, we may remember their debt to Erasmus, Zwingli, Oecolampadius, and especially Franck. And, although the most educated leadership was martyred during the first years, the early leaders—Grebel, Hübmaier, Denck, Hetzer—were men of marked accomplishment in the university world weighted with the new Humanistic studies. The devotion which the Renaissance directed toward the origins and the eager quest for the origins of the Faith were related phenomena. It was not a program nor detailed content that carried over, but a certain method and attitude toward antiquity.[32] This method and attitude, when related to distinctly Christian concerns, became the hall-mark of Anabaptist thought.

In their portrayal of history, after the "Age of Heroes" life declines and a definite "Fall" occurs. This is an old theme, but given special content by the radicals. In secular primitivism also the Fall marks a turning point in society. The Fall has cultural aspect, indicated by the loss of simplicity and "natural" living; there is also a chronological aspect, revealed in a definite periodization of history and the hope of an eventual restoration. There is almost always a detailed theory of "Fall" in primitivist thought.[33]

"It is incumbent upon the servants of the Lord to teach, to instruct and to warn to that end (i.e., spiritual pilgrimage, martyrdom) with all patience and neither spoil nor condemn, as we have a model in Paul. Decay had scarcely any power to hold those (who were) free, unencumbered, resigned. In the beginning they were living in the Lord. But now, because prosperity is sought, they nestle comfortably back into the world. And consequently they don't see themselves leaving the world, yes, they would far rather live than die."[34]

Lydia Müller has noted the fascination which the Eusebian history of the power and triumph of the Early Church had for the Anabaptists.[35] Here they saw the record of power in apparent weakness, growth in martyrdom, triumph out of persecution. Here was shown the way of the Church from Christ to Constantine

". . . . in a certain sense . . . as a peerless Passion-way. The Eusebian church-history is the history of the Church under the Cross. The Imperial-church and later the papal-church were no longer martyr-churches. So after Constantine (it was) above all the communities of heretics who took over and furthered the traditions of the true and precisely for that reason persecuted community of Christ."[36]

The growth and victory of the Early Church against incredible odds was a mysterious thing, a sign of the secret workings of God. *But more mysterious still was the fact that in the very hour of her apparent triumph and well-being the Church fell into disgrace.* The Anabaptists concluded, only a little household (*ein klaines heuflen*) has gone the right way since creation.[37] The "True Church" and a Land-Church or State-Church were two different things.

The Uses of the Idea of the Fall

The idea of an Heroic Age from which later generations have fallen away is a useful concept for polemicizing the existing scene in its many phases. The attack of the radicals was comprehensive, embracing many social issues in terms of the Christian way. The Anabaptists, who were the groups of radicals most concerned for the Church, employed the idea in both chronological and cultural aspects. They adopted the historical framework, and upon it hung a vigorous critique of contemporary Christendom.

The dating of the "Fall" is a significant clue to an understanding of what was meant by the term. Among the Polish Brethren we find a reference to Eusebius, dating the "Fall" with the death of Simeon, the last of the grand old men who had known Jesus and the Twelve, who died as Bishop of Jerusalem in 111 A.D. at the age of 120;

". . . . up to this time the church remained a virgin pure and incorrupt. . . ."[38]

Related to this is a feeling that those who had personally known the Master would not miss the meaning of his simple and straight-forward words. Those who came later, having neither the impress of his personality nor inner inspiration, corrupted and compromised the purity and simplicity of the Gospel. Thus the Anti-Trinitarians commonly maintained that early Christianity was non-dogmatic and inspired. In the best times there had been no scholastic disputing over the Trinity, nor defining of "heresy" on dogmatic grounds. Nor was force used to compel intellectual conformity, for the concern of true religion was then ethical and moral. The "Fall" is then dated with the Council of Nicea, 325 A.D., when the crystallization of the Trinitarian formula put an end to charismatic leadership and inspired congregational life.[39]

Menno believed the decline began early, was accentuated by Constantine, and culminated in an Edict of Innocent I, 407 A.D., which enforced Infant Baptism.[40] But among most Anabaptists the "Fall" is usually dated during the reign of Constantine the Great. The Christian Emperor seemed to them the very culmination of worldliness and power-consciousness. Among the Anabaptists the special mark of the "Fall" was the union of Church and State, and use of the civil arm in matters of faith.[41] True religion is inward and may not be compelled by any.

"But later, when Sylvester the 34th Pope paid tribute and prevailed upon Constantine the Great, who was the 43rd Emperor, with many flattering, sanctimonious words, (having) accepted him as a Christian in baptism, the Emperor provided throughout his whole realm great peace, with good intention to do thereby a service to God, to the Pope as Roman bishop, and to all who called themselves Christian. That is the disease of craftiness, which slunk in the window, and the corruption which perverted at High Noon. Crowding in with power, the Cross was conquered and forged to the sword. All that happened through the slyness of the Old Serpent."[42]

It, was thus with Constantine that the voluntary religious association of the true believers became the Church of the Land, with authority resting upon outward compulsion rather than upon the Sword of the Spirit which is the Word of God (*Eph.* 6:17).

It is notable that the radicals, both Anti-Trinitarian and Anabaptist, largely agreed in dating the "Fall" with the powerful administration of Constantine the Great. This is but another evidence that the ground of initial dissent was not a single issue but rather a general discontent with the formalizing and crystallizing "outwardness" of the Great Church. At first there were many leaders and groups free in both doctrine and ethical emphasis.[43] But after a decade and more of persecution and internal discipline some groups shaped a congregational life concerned chiefly with ethical issues, whereas others went on to emphasize the doctrinal concerns.

The Reformers were less anti-historical than the radicals, but they still found the concept of the "Fall" useful. Luther

dated the "Fall" with Sabianus and Boniface III, who immediately followed Gregory the Great in asserting the temporal
claims of the papacy.[44] For Luther, the Church was never totally corrupted and the reign of Constantine was the summer-
time of the faith.[45] For Zwingli, the "Fall" was dated with Hil-
debrand and the assertion of hierarchial power.[46] For Calvin,
the Bible rather than any evidence from history gave authoritative opposition to the Old Church. Nevertheless, he stated
different dates of the "Fall" on different issues, emphasizing
especially the papal arrogation of authority under Gregory I.[47]

The Church in her fallen estate seemed to the Anabaptists
far different from the community of true believers, the brotherhood of spiritual athletes. We must remember that they counted
the fallen condition of the Church *from the days of Constantine
until the beginning of their own movement*.[48] The Anabaptists
said that the revival began with Luther and Zwingli, but the Reformers clung to the old concept of Christendom and are reck-
oned in the Church of the "Fall." The criticisms directed against
the imperial Roman religion are the criticisms directed against
the Reformers: Church and State were amalgamated, empty
formalism and spiritual slackness prevailed, infants were baptized into Christianity before their understanding could give
the association any content. The Anabaptists wanted a thorough-
going Restitution of the Church before the "Fall," and they
criticized the nominal Christianity of the middle period in suggestive terms.

What did the Anabaptists consider the marks of the fallen
church? What did they list as the compromises and corruptions
which set the fallen church off against the True Church as it
had been in the Heroic Age?

The Anabaptists felt most strongly about the u n i o n
o f C h u r c h a n d S t a t e. It was here that the Anabaptist
vision of voluntary religious association conflicted irreducibly
with the amalgamation of worldly and ecclesiastical power dating from the reign of Constantine the Great. The Hutterians
said the proof that the authorities of the so-called Christians
(*vermainten Christen*) were not truly Christian was in their use
of compulsion in religion.[49] In the youth of Jakob Huter the
"religion" of the Tyrol switched five times according to political
change of fortune. This seemed to him the most crass denial of
that faith which is engraven upon the heart of the true believer,

which is a secret thing and not conformed to the pattern of the masses.[50] When the so-called Christian magistrates attempted to enforce conformity they resorted to various compulsions and in the end to persecution. Thereby the Spirit passed from them and was given to the brotherhood movements which were persecuted, the "heretics" who walked the way of suffering and humility (*die geistlich Armen*). The authorities became "Turks after the Spirit," against whom the Anabaptist pacifist would rather fight than against the real Turk.[51] The Anabaptists, on the other hand, were among the first consistently to champion religious liberty in the modern sense. They believed that no individual might rightly be compelled by the magistrate in the matter of faith,[52] and *they distinguished between political sovereignty and those controls of the Church which belong to its internal discipline and integrity.* According to a great American historian, to Hans Denck (Nürnberg, 1524) goes the honor of the first modern enunciation of the principle of a man's right to private religious interpretation.[53]

The Anabaptists asserted that political compulsion in religion was the denial of spiritual government and affronted the spiritual power of the Church; the *potestas ecclesiae* of the Christian congregation was not possible in a union of Church and State.[54] Therefore the true Covenantal Community could not exist in such a situation. Luther and Zwingli were no less tyrants than Constantine, because they also enforced religious conformity by the civil power.[55] An Anabaptist testified before the court that he did not attend communion in the church of the land for two reasons: 1) the church was not worthy, for good and evil were together (no spiritual government, Ban); 2) the magistrates coerced with prison, whereas they have no true authority in matters of faith.[56]

"The right, the true community compels no one, but rather is itself always suffering under another. And they seek to kill no one."[57]

The free congregation may exist anywhere a little band of faithful meet and covenant together to walk in His ways; the Ban is their only "sword."[58]

The separation of Church and State which they represented thus involved at least two positive affirmations of vital religious significance: the right of a free man to private religious interpretation, and the right of the voluntary association to enforce a strong internal discipline. Far from being contradictory, these are two closely linked aspects of healthy congregational life.[59]

Another mark of the "Fall" of the Church was the widespread w a r r i n g i n C h r i s t e n d o m. Holding office and taking the oath were condemned not only on the Biblical injunctions but in a program involving total separation of the religious and political authorities. Carrying and using the sword, taking the oath of allegiance and serving to enforce political and economic controls were all part of the feudal system. The constitutive aspect of the non-resistant position will be discussed later,[60] but it is here important to note that conscientious objection to war and killing was closely related to their interpretation of history and the historical hope of the movement. That "Christians" should kill "Christians" was thought one of the sure signs of the fallen Church. This and other sins of violence belong to the middle period which the Anabaptists believed they were leaving behind.

When the Church was no longer the free association of those who have been inwardly moved and were met together for mutual improvement, religion d e c l i n e d i n t o d e a d f o r m a l i s m. In both dogma and ecclesiastical organization an empty "outwardness" obtained, a mere sham of religion which the Anabaptists scorned. They made no distinction between the Roman Church and the Reformers in their condemnation; perhaps dominant Protestantism gave a greater freedom in "forms," but it still exaggerated the significance of the outward expression. [61] Anabaptism was in its rise a conscious reassertion of inspired religion, and this gave issue to certain problems as well as producing a vivid attack upon the dead wood of old ways of doing things. The restitution party said strength lay in true inwardness, in the perfect simplicity of the Common Man. Sectarianism was itself a mark of concern for outward matters, since true believers are to be drawn together by inner power and magnetism rather than observance.[62] Beginning with the imperial pomp and display of Constantine a type of personal ambition entered the Church which was the precise opposite to the submissive humility (*Gelassenheit*) which marked the saints of the Lord. Some writers have claimed that the Anabaptists depended on the medieval virtues and were therefore a return to monasticism. The Anabaptist attitude was not, however, a return: rather the priesthood of all believers was taken to mean

the application of the *consilia perfectionis* to all Christians instead of only a special class. They pitted these counsels against
the ambitious personality produced by formalism, and looked
for another type of leader who would re-live the virtue of the
Early Church men.

Of special significance was the Anabaptist d e n i a l   o f
t h e   M a s s,   and it must be comprehended in terms of their
general reaction to display and formalism. The radicals refuted
the objective merit upon which the Roman Church rested, and
denied the real presence which Luther and Calvin retained.
For them the Supper was a memorial and a symbol of their
corporate union with each other in the Risen Lord.[63]   A n-
d r e a s   K a r l s t a d t   (c. 1480-1541)[64] played a large part
in the sacramental discussion, and during the short-lived radical revolt in Wittenberg he celebrated the Supper in both kinds,
without motions or ceremonies and in civilian clothes.[65] His writings influenced Hübmaier and were known in Zürich,[66] but the
Swiss Brethren seem to have taken their figurative understanding of the Supper primarily from Zwingli and Oecolampadius.[67]
The Anabaptists said that Christ was not in the material, but
sat on the right hand of God the Father Almighty.[68] For them,
to worship the physical bread and wine was the most awful
idolatry and materialization of the spiritual truth of the presence
of Christ. It was blasphemy, wherein Christ was martyred
again.[69]

Following Luther, the Anabaptists said that with the rise of
Rome the heart of organized Christianity became rotten with the
pomp and display of w o r l d l y   p o w e r.   In its prime Christianity was a lay religion; under the imperial authority there
arose a swarm of professionals, who did not comprehend the
democratic simplicity of Christian brethren. The rise of the
hierarchy was a sign of the "Fall."[70] It is far better to count
upon Christ and His simple Gospel than upon the pope and all
the councils. Not only did the organization show the corrosive
effects of power-consciousness, but the very buildings indicated
the concern for outward show. Great stone structures were piled
up where once two or three had gathered together in His Spirit,[71]
and now no sincere and simple spirit could feel at home there.

"Instead of the Church of Christ that is the community and congregation
of believers they have built and erected stone Temples, called them churches to deceive men thereby. Instead of the Saints and pious men who are
sanctified by God they have placed in their churches pictures—wooden,

stone, silver likenesses and dumb saints. And to show honor and service to them they have robbed living Saints called for the service of God."[72]

In their portrayal of history, during the dispersion of the middle period the True Church met in the woods, forests, fields and private dwellings. And the Anabaptists testified that they did not enter the great buildings, but gathered informally in two's and three's.[73] In every case they opposed the externalization of the faith, the compromise with worldly standards of "success" and well-being.

On the matter of I n f a n t   B a p t i s m the State-church rose or fell,[74] and the Anabaptists were quick to repudiate the rite. They maintained that there was no indication of such practice in the Bible or Early Church.[75] The baptism of children was not from the Master,

". . . . but established after the Age of the Apostles by the popes through their cunning in their Christian churches."[76]

Neither were sleeping adults baptized, as they pointed out when Luther said the faith of the congregation justified the act.[77] The "Fall" was indicated in the promiscuous use of the rite to bring into the Great Church all kinds of pagans without inner reformation; when this happened the moral life of the community harmonized with that of the world. There came to be no difference between Christian and non-Christian; indeed, the non-Christian might walk closer to the path He walked than the professing man. They felt that the corruption of the Church was precisely this: that she *took in masses of people who had no understanding of what the Gospel meant, and then completed the compromise by taking in generation after generation of children who had not reached the age of understanding.* "For a Christian life is no child's play,"[78] but a matter of stern spiritual discipline and vigorous ethical living.

When the radicals at Zürich began to condemn Infant Baptism, Zwingli saw that it meant a Church separated from the State, and clarified his own thinking against them. At first they only refrained from baptizing infants. But January 17, 1525, a Disputation was held and the leaders of the "root and branch" movement were expelled from the city. Shortly thereafter Adult Baptism was introduced, at Zollikon, and Believers' Baptism became a spiritual sword aimed right at the heart of the State-Church system.[79] The baptism issue became more important during the time of persecution than it was among the various early groups,[80] but from the first it implied a significantly different view of the Church which the Reformers could hardly miss.

With the addition of large numbers of nominal Christians at the time of the "Fall," and successive centuries of admission of all the people of the land through infant baptism, the Church was no longer the congregation of the elect. The Anabaptists condemned the triumph of s p i r i t u a l   l a x i t y;   they told how the spiritual athletes of the heroic age were followed by men and women whose lives conformed to the world rather than to the Kingdom. Not only were New Testament truths not emphasized in the fallen Church but there seemed to be no consciousness that mere observance of ritual and professional procedure could not substitute for true inwardness. The nominal Christians met in great crowds and maintained confession and fast-days, but no admonition of brother for brother prevailed. The Anabaptists were convinced there could be no spiritual government in a State-church.[81]

It especially offended the Anabaptists that the relation between brethren meant no more than the general social relationship. Rightly living, Christians were accountable for each other, and Christ had given the commands for true believers who lived together in the bonds of brotherhood. Cupidity and self-interest were not only condemned in the clergy, but also in the lay Christians. According to the Brethren, Christ threw the thieves out of the Temple, showing that he didn't want traders in his Church.[82] The man who lived by rents and tithes upon the toil of another was no true Christian brother, whether clergy or lay. Andreas Castelberger of the Swiss Brethren said such a man was no better than a thief or murderer.[83] It is impossible to be friend of both God and the world![84] Perfect fraternity demanded submission to the needs of the community; personal display and aggrandizement were to be strongly condemned and vigorously curbed by spiritual government.

During the centuries of her fallen estate the Church was so thoroughly corrupted and compromised that a thorough-going revolution in her life was necessary. The Anabaptists demanded that she return to the life of the Age of Heroes. Similarly, the nominal Christians must go through a spiritual revolution, like a new Noah's Ark setting sail from all earthly things.[85] Having submitted to empty observances and half-hearted ritual for so long the Church must be purged with the Spirit and baptized into a new life of Christian discipline. The inflections and shadings were to be sloughed off, and the new law of Christ to obtain without any glosses.

Analysis of the Idea of the Fall

In the primitivism of the radicals we find a definite mixture of chronological and cultural elements. The glorification of the Early Church, the "Fall," the restoration of lost virtue— all represent a heavy weight of ethical judgment as well as an historical framework. It must be understood that these elements cannot be disentangled, and different themes are interwoven with varying degrees of emphasis in the groups and leaders. The historical framework is not explicit in all recorded teachings, and it would appear that even the most common ethical understandings (e.g., pacifism, spiritual government) were not shared by all leaders and groups. However, during the time of clarification the main outline became evident and has persisted in various ways in radical Protestant groups to this day.

We may well ask in what way this framework of Christian history is related to more g e n e r a l   c u l t u r a l   c o n c e r n s a n d   s e c u l a r   h i s t o r y. On occasion there may be associated with the "Fall" of the Church the theme of recurring falls in history. A religious revolutionary fifty years before the Reformation epoch expressed the occasional inter-weaving of religious themes with social expectancy: in the coming restoration the Church and the world would both be set right by the Prophet King. The worldly power of the papacy is the foremost evil, and Kaiser Frederick was the prophet's heroic type for politico-religious reform. He taught that Communism was the true order and Roman Law marked the "Fall" in both Church and society:

"All evil is established by the Latins; they set forth *jus Quiritum militare,* this is mine, that is yours. Thereby they broke all friendliness and the love of God, because that (Roman) law is against the natural Godly law; thereby inferiority and enmity were established. . . ."[86]

The coming politico-religious Messiah whom this revolutionary proclaimed was the *König vom Schwarzwald,* who will be the Lord of all Christendom.

"The King of the Black Forest . . . will make a reformation with pious Christians, kill the blasphemous, wipe out the drunken, root out the lecherers, cut off the lustful, take power from the frivolous, banish the clergy from the land, who needlessly distort the work of the Lord—to put to work all the orders, who seek more their own than the common need, and also to imprison the prelates who buy them with friendship."[87]

Among various radicals of the Reformation certain old themes recur. The attitude of Sebastian Franck has already been noted.[88] At Münster the revolutionaries destroyed the old historical records in the cathedral to clear the air for a fresh beginning in both church and world. Occasionally the religious primitivism is mixed in this way with general cultural primitivism among the more significant Anabaptist teachers and groups; and the expectation of a purification of Church life may lead on to a broad social reform at the end.[89] Broadly speaking, however, the Anabaptists proper avoided general social issues. The experience of persecution was so vivid in their first years that they looked for little in the world and its renewing; only in the final age would the fulfilment of the Church restoration lead on to a general social renewal, and they remained somewhat vague as to how this was to occur.[90] Eventually, however, the primitivist strain expressed itself in cultural patterns also; today the most direct descendants of militant Anabaptism reside in *cultural enclaves* in America. Like the Continental Mennonites, they have "gone over to the world," but in another way; they have "gone over to the world"—of a past age. The Hutterian Brethren and some American Mennonites today represent an archaic social organization strangely out of place in the twentieth century. The original heightened tension between the "Church" and the "World" has deteriorated into a tension between the eighteenth century and the twentieth century.

The idea of the "Fall" is only part of a general periodization of history, and various classifications reflect the view of the thinker involved.[91] In a prophet like David Joris, who saw three ages—each introduced by a "David," the scheme is fairly obvious![92] In Bernt Rothmann's *Restitutio* there were a number of successive falls and restitutions, as also in Sebastian Franck's writings. We find in them the thought of a last age, a millennial reign shortly to be introduced or which was already begun in the congregations of the Restitution. There have been various "falls" in the past, but this is the last Restitution—to be followed by the eternal restitution of all things (*Acts* 3:21).[93] In the Anabaptists proper, the periodization seems to have involved the Church in the main, although there is the suggestion that the

Restitution of the True Church will lead on to the millennial reign.

What happened to the True Church during the fallen estate of the Great Church? There was a gathering of God's people in the beginning of history and they were being established again; but the Anabaptists said that in the middle period the faithful were in dispersion—like the Israelites in the wilderness. The radicals were accustomed to trace their succession back to the Early Church, usually identifying the faithful during the dispersion with the "heretics" condemned by the Great Church: John Scotus, Waldo, the Fraticelli, Wyclif, John Hus.[94] There were also those who said that the succession was totally broken off with the "Fall." In the marginal "Anabaptist" movement at Münster they said there had been no true Church for 1400 years.[95] Sebastian Franck, Caspar Schwenckfeld and David Joris believed the continuity was broken and only a prophet with divine commission could gather again a community of believers—introducing thereby the New Age.[96] But the more historically minded groups elaborated their primitivist historiography, in which the small brotherhood groups were the bridge of evangelical faith between the "Fall" and the "Restitution." Among the Anabaptists this was the familiar interpretation: *during the middle period the True Church was in dispersion, among those called "heretics."*

From their cultural attitudes and periodization of history it is clear that understanding the radicals involves a large concentration upon their eschatology.[97] Their attitude was no pale historiography, but involved a doctrine of *the moving power of history itself.* There is some difference of opinion as to how closely the Reformers and radicals followed the same historical patterns in their interpretation, but it becomes clear that the Anabaptists conceived of themselves as the secret meaning and bearers of the New Age: we find in their church-view an eschatological accent not found as prominently in the dominant groups.[98] The "Fall" is reversed in the New Age and the old corruptions and compromises are left behind by the community of believers.

Origins of the Idea in the Left Wing

The contributions of Humanism and Joachimitism to the primitivist church-view have been previously suggested.[99] The paired ideas of Early Church and "Fall" have seen the light in various group records since Joachim and the Fraticelli. But we may fairly conclude that the total and systematic application of such historiography to the life of the Church was a major work of the Anabaptists.

"Which is the true (Church)? The ancient, apostolic. My wish, my yearning is that the world may go back to a true apostolic church. The *Acts* and the writings of the Great (Church) Fathers and ancient Bishops show the way on which we must go back to it. The apostolic church flourished to the time of Constantine. From then on it was perverted, because the Bishops went over to the world. . . ."[100]

In these words G e o r g W i t z e l stated the feeling about the "Golden Age" of the Faith which came to be distinctive about Anabaptism. Witzel wanted to see an ethical Reformation, had a great vision of the purity of the primitive community in Jerusalem,[101] and when Lutheranism failed to produce the desired fruits he broke with it. Eventually he returned to Rome, but not before having a great influence on early Anabaptism. Johannes Campanus was for a time his friend and associate and took the historical framework from him; and through Campanus' lost masterpiece—*Contra totum post-Apostolos-mundum*—the primitivist motif found wide circulation among the radicals. Campanus greatly influenced the Wassenberger preachers, whose advent in Münster was of such a fateful consequence for that city. In Bernt Rothmann's *Bekenntnisse van beyden Sacramenten* (1533)[102] we find the influence of Campanus' book, to which Henrik Rol had called Rothmann's attention in 1529.[103] Sebastian Franck was also among those who liked Campanus' denial of all authoritative teachers since the apostles, and is accredited with being the first to promote the theme of *restitutio* among the historians of the Reformation.[104] The praise of life in the Heroic Age leads readily to the concept of restoring the lost virtue; primitivism and the idea of perfectibility are frequently confused and entertained in the same material, according to a student of Primitivism, and such proves to be the case with Anabaptism.[105]

It is not far from the idea of the "Fall" to the hope of an eventful Restitution, nor from the hope to the practice of a new life in the New Age. The Anabaptists pressed forward to those positive disciplines which gave permanent form to their congregational life, moving on from the fallen church to the new in-gathering.

THE RESTITUTION

The dominant theme of the mainline Anabaptists was the recovery of the life and virtue of the Early Church. The ordinances which had marked the True Church (*die rechte Kirche*) in that heroic age were to be made a program for thorough-going reformation. The Reformers were not willing to make so radical a break from the past, but those whose key concept was *restitutio* rather than *reformatio* were determined to erase what they considered the shame of centuries and recapitulate the purified church life of the golden age of the faith. In reviewing the records, the reader is struck with the Anabaptists' acute consciousness of separation from the "fallen" church—in which they included the Reformers as well as the Roman institution. Some writers have therefore concluded that Anabaptism is not merely a variant form of Protestantism, but is an ideology and practice quite different in kind from those of both Rome and the Reformers. The present writer is moved to suggest that in distinguishing the church types of state-church Protestantism and the sixteenth century "free churches" we may properly speak of "the Church of the Reformers" on the one hand and "the Church of the Restitution" on the other.

Where did the Restitution Begin?

For some in the Left Wing, especially the revolutionaries and independents (*Spiritualisten*), the separation from the "fallen" Church was conceived in most specific terms. The place where the truly spiritual life was restored, and the names of those found faithful, were very serious considerations. The revolutionaries believed that the End was begun in their movement. They believed in the totality of their church and in its world mission. Even the more quiet groups faced a parallel problem in interpreting historical events.

"The Reformation hopes for a coming heavenly revelation of victory. But the *Schwärmer* believe that there is yet only a little stride to make in order to be *ecclesia triumphans* on earth."[1]

In spotting the origin of their movement, some looked to Nikolsburg or St. Gall; Nürnberg was favored by certain groups—

Some declared ". . . . that there should be a great battle about Nürnberg and whoever was baptized should not be slain. Thereupon there would come to be a new rule and all would be alike."[2]

Groups in Middle Germany looked toward Mühlhausen, others to Strassburg and then toward   M ü n s t e r.[3] Captured missioners and many who never joined the Hutterians frequently declared M o r a v i a the place where true Christian order had been restored. But the *Stille* generally accepted the Reformers' doctrine that the True Church might be anywhere; also, they apparently held merely to the quiet principle that the True Church could not be destroyed, which is different from the pragmatic power-consciousness of the revolutionary wing. Thus the precise moment or point where a pure Restitution is effected seems of no fatal consequence to the mainline Anabaptists. But what seems apparent is not absolutely true. The *Stille* also treasured a social hope; and among the most vigorous groups that hope was expressed by vital internal discipline and outward evangel. Certain it is that the creative state of tension which marked the early Anabaptists was far from the cultural and religious resignation of many of their descendents.

All wings of the movement were agreed in a strong attack upon the standing order. Some called for a strict return to what they considered the New Testament pattern.

"For it is better and more certain to build on Christ and His teaching than to rely on Fathers and Councils. Behold Christ the Lord will judge on the Last Day and not pope, fathers, councils."[4]

Others cried aloud for the inspired leadership which might deliver them from dry formalism and deadly institutionalism.

"Therefore, my beloved brethren in the Lord, if you will learn in truth the judgment of God and the testimony of Holy Writ, then do not listen to the clamor of the professionals (*geltprediger*), but search out the poor who despise the world and become enthusiasts and demon-possessed, according to the example of Christ and the apostles. Listen to these. For no one may obtain the truth unless he follows in the footsteps of Christ and His elect in the school of all affliction, or has in part at least determined to follow in the justification of the Cross of Christ according to the Will of God. For no one may learn in the dens of assassins or nests of all knaves, as we have them at Wittenberg or at Paris."[5]

After a short period of general protest a strict Biblicism triumphed over prophetism and Chiliasm in large sections of the Left Wing, and the restored True Church began to assume definite proportions. The pattern was defined in terms of a strict adherence to certain ordinances defined in the New Testament.

What was the pattern, as the Anabaptists re-read it from the New Testament?

Believers' Baptism (Erwachsenentaufe, Spättaufe)

Infant Baptism was challenged by many dissenting groups on Scriptural ground, and it came early to the fore in discussions at such various points as Wittenberg, Zürich, Strassburg, Münster, and among the Hutterians and Dutch. The radicals were convinced that the practice was introduced after apostolic times, in spite of the classic rejoinder that the baptism of households must have included children (I Cor. 10:2).

In defining the classical Anabaptist positions we can rely heavily on the important statement known as the Sleitheim Confession. The first of the Seven Articles of Schlatten am Randen (Feb. 24, 1527), the Sleitheim Confession, condemned the practice as non-apostolic:[6] the rite would not be used, therefore, in a congregation seriously trying to re-live the life of the Early Church.

"A great mass of men is without God's word and command in today's world with its infant baptism—a trickery to the simple and an insidious shame to all Christianity, a brassy pretence of all godless; for in all the Bible not a single quotation can be brought forward to justify it."[7]

The Great Church said it was necessary to baptize children lest they die in sin; but if children were in mortal sin in their natural state would Christ have said, "suffer the little children to come unto me and forbid them not, *for of such is the kingdom of heaven*" (*Luke* 18:16)?[8] According to the Anabaptists, the children were restored by His sacrifice from the depths of Original Sin, and remained so until able to distinguish between good and evil.[9] When Menno Simons questioned the practice of Infant baptism and turned toward the apologists they could not allay his doubts: Luther justified it by the child's appropriation of faith from the congregation, Butzer called it a guarantee of godly training, Bullinger—following Zwingli—said it was the Christian parallel to the Old Testament ordinance of circumcision; Menno said, no one spoke from the New Testament.[10]

By the very example of the Master, baptism must be an adult matter. At the age of 30 he went into the Jordan to observe the approved custom at the hands of John; thereby he became a sign of the New Covenant.[11] Those who would walk in His way of submission and martyrdom might thereby know that the Christian life requires mature dedication and discipline. Such commitment requires a degree of understanding (*Vernunft*) which only mature persons can possess.[12] According to the Anabaptists, such commitment begins in a thorough-going repentance; Repentance was the key word in the oldest baptismal liturgies.[13] The new member must be deeply aware that he has foresworn the world, sin and the devil, and in whole heart and soul and body set out to live for God and His Church.[14]

The Baptism is a symbol of sinking in the death of Christ, being raised to a New Birth in His resurrection.[15] No one can come into the Kingdom unless he be born again (*John* 3:3), and this was the spiritual event symbolized by water baptism into the community.

" 'Marx, you have been before now a light-hearted young fellow, and must become another man, to put the Old Adam from you and take on a newer and better self.' Marx answered, he would do his best. Then Blaurock asked if he longed for the Grace of God and when he answered yes Blaurock spoke: 'come here, and I will baptize you!' Then Marx went and at that Blaurock baptized him."[16]

In Anabaptist teaching, the New Birth has Christ alone as foundation, and must occur radically in the history of both individual believer and the True Church; it was this constitutive element which distinguished the Anabaptists from both Roman Catholic work-righteousness and Lutheran *sola fides*.

". . . . the Scripture speaks of Perfection, which will be initiated through the Holy Spirit when one lives according to the command of God."[17]

This is the ground of the Anabaptists' uncompromising integrity in working out a Christian witness.[18]

"Therefore the baptism is a battle with sin, to kill it throughout the whole of life."[19]

The real issue was the restitution of a vigorous congregational life, as it was thought to have been lived in apostolic times, and the argument between Infant Baptism and Adult Baptism was a vehicle for the prior issue.[20] The preaching of the Gospel, often carried on the Great Commission,[21] was an open invitation to any man to make personal absolution and covenant with God and the community. The idea of a covenantal relation to God and one's fellows became the foundation of the Anabaptist community, and through it came use of the Ban (spiritual government).[22] The Anabaptists said repeatedly that true Baptism was that submission to the Divine described in I *Peter* 3:18-22, the responsibility of a good conscience toward God.[23] They saw that this couldn't be easily done, but required brotherly admonition and exhortation, the practice of intentional fellowship. By baptism the believer came under the discipline of a Biblical people, and if the door of entrance was closely watched a strong and true Church could be maintained. They noted that the Master worked long with a small group, and then one of them betrayed Him. A long time of training was required for membership in the Early Church, and the True Church in Restitution would not add members promiscuously.[24] The Church covenant was undertaken at baptism and was thought to be the highest expression of religious voluntarism short of martyrdom; the balancing authority was the power of the community to forgive sins.[25] This was the Key of David (*"schlüssel Davits"*), which in the inchoate Anabaptist circles had resided in the primary religious experience of the individual.

"The Father of mercy will establish the Key of David in our hearts so that we may open thereby the closed Book, the secret of His will."[26]

In the quest for final authority the Key of David and the Keys of Peter became identical.[27] Group-consciousness became a dominant force in baptized life. Among the rules of the Hutterian community (1529) was this: the internal admonitions exercised under the authority of the baptismal submission were not to be revealed outside the church.[28] For all practical purposes, the power of the esoteric group was final in spiritual matters[29]; neither the unbaptized selfishness of the Old Adam nor a larger social control might invade the spiritual dominion thus mapped out.

Spiritual Government (*Bann, Ehemeidung, Hirten*)

Spiritual government rests, at the end, upon the threat of expulsion from the congregation of believers: the Ban. Those unwilling to be so harsh complained—

"They blame us especially because we don't have the Ban. They mean to separate good from evil as was frequently done at the time of the Apostles."[30]

In some cases this might mean social ostracism, but generally it meant the loss of privileges within the brotherhood. There is no compulsion in a voluntary association but this breaking of fellowship.

"And if thy brother sin against thee, go, show him his fault between thee and him alone: and if he hear thee, thou hast gained thy brother. But if he hear thee not, take with thee two or more, that at the mouth of two witnesses or three every word may be established. And if he refuse to hear them, tell it unto the church: and if he refuse to hear the church also, let him be unto thee as the Gentile and the publican." (*Matth.* 18:15-17).

This New Testament ordinance was the beginning of every Anabaptist elaboration of the problem of government within the Church,[31] and it is obvious that it presupposed a freely acting congregation who did not depend upon any worldly power but upon their own spirit of fellowship.[32] They said of the table of the Lord:

"23. It is not to be used without the rule of Christ in Matt. 18, otherwise it is not the Lord's Supper, for without that rule every man will run after the externals; the inner matter, love, will be passed by, if brethren and false brethren approach or eat it."

"Go forward with the word and establish a Christian church with the help of Christ and his rule, as we find it instituted Matthew 18 and applied in the epistles. . ."[33]

The secular government was quite outside the discussion.

The most famous Anabaptist confessions concerned themselves very largely with the matter of spiritual government. The second of the Seven Articles (Feb. 24, 1527)[34] dealt with this agreed practice of the congregations, and the fifth of the Five Articles of the Hutterians (c. 1547)[35] dealt with a special application of spiritual government: divorce between believers and unbelievers. In Anabaptist thinking, the majesty of the Church paralleled the power of the magistrate in the world, and the sovereignty of the Church rested upon their loyalty.

"After the people have received the Word of God and through water baptism in the presence of the church have put themselves under obligation to God to live according to the Word, and if they are ready to walk in newness of life and henceforth not to let sin reign in the mortal body, they still have need of medicine, because men are by nature children of wrath, evil and incapable, whereby the foul and stinking flesh together with the poisoned members may be somehow cut off, in order that the whole body may not be dishonored and corrupted."[36]

Hübmaier elaborated the theme extensively in two works: *Von der bruderlichen Strafe* and *Vom christlichen Bann*. He went into some detail to describe the process:

" 'Leonard: What is fraternal discipline?

'John: When one sees his brother sin, he should go to him in love and admonish him fraternally and privately to leave off such sin. If he does leave off, his soul is won. If he does not, then two or three witnesses should be taken, and he may be admonished before them a second time. If he yields it is well,—if not, the church should hear it. He is brought before her and admonished a third time. If he leaves off his sin the church has won his soul.

'Leonard: Where does the church get its authority?

'John: From Christ's command, given in Matt. xviii. 18, John xx. 23.

'Leonard: By what right may one brother use his authority over another?

'John: By the baptismal vow, which subjects every one to the church and all its members, according to the word of Christ.

'Leonard: Suppose the admonished sinner will not correct his course?

'John: Then the church has the power and right to exclude and excommunicate him, as a perjurer and apostate.

'Leonard: What is excommunication?

'John: It is exclusion and separation to such an extent that no fellowship is held with such a person by Christians, whether in speaking, eating, drinking, grinding, baking, or in any other way, but he is treated as a heathen and a publican, who is bound and delivered over to Satan. He is to be avoided and shunned, lest the entire visible church be evil spoken of, disgraced and dishonoured by his company, and corrupted by his example, instead of being startled and made afraid by his punishment, so that they will mortify their sins. For as truly as God lives what the Church admits or excludes on earth is admitted or excluded above.

'Leonard: On what are the grounds for exclusion?

'John: Unwillingness to be reconciled with one's brother, or to abstain from sin. . . ."[37]

Hübmaier was not, however, able to attain any high level of spiritual discipline in his Nikolsburg congregation. Nevertheless, there were those who carried through elsewhere and left spiritual progeny organized in disciplined congregations. These were the Anabaptists proper.

The Ban was not, then, the final word. Nor was even the Scriptural rule the only ruling power. In the instruction of the Master the Anabaptists beheld a certain concept of what His Church should be like: a community of saints.[38] They said the Great Church was apostate, for there was no moral earnestness exercised in it by the power of the Ban.[39] The True Church was a strong band of ethical discipline and integrity.

' Thus saith the Lord: I have drawn you out of the world. Thus the world hates you. Thereby he shows plainly that there is a clear distinction between God's children and the children of the world."[40]

The True Church must be separated from the evil and wicked; Israel must go out from Babylon and Egypt.[41] Said Huter:

"Furthermore, we have sundered ourselves from worldly society and its loathsome life and have gone out from it."[42]

"Thereby God makes us free and purifies us from the world and all its creatures through affliction. . . ."[43]

The Hutterians criticized their Anabaptist confreres, the Swiss Brethren, because they mixed with the world and made no Christian distinctions regarding war taxes, woodwork on images, and "close practice" in commerce.[44] In similar terms the Polish Brethren later criticized the Dutch Mennonites on their ethical life:

"In which respect the Mennonites err not less than the others, who will not walk proudly themselves (and) yet make for others proud clothes, paint pictures, make vases and more of such things, which the world should not have for the lust and pomp of its life."[45]

Concern for a vigorous internal ethic was to them of paramount importance, a quality of life to do honor to God and the high calling in which they were set apart. As free associations they felt themselves on Biblical ground in expecting all who stayed in good standing to concern themselves for the good name they bore in common. Within the pattern of authority of which the Ban was the outer limit there was a whole fabric of common concern and mutual aid.

Before the decades of savage persecution the Anabaptists were sometimes men of some substance, but during these years they lost all rights before the law. Even under the rule of Philipp of Hesse, more mild than most Protestant statesmen, the Anabaptists were treated as Jews before the law and forbidden to hold land.[46] This gave rise to special problems in property holding and within the family. Anabaptist goods were commonly confiscated if there were no orthodox heirs, and holding to a heresy was sufficient ground for a spouse pleading divorce in the courts. This general social situation was countered by rules within the congregations and especially within the Hutterian communities: provisional approval was given for divorce from an unbelieving partner.[47] Christ brought not peace but a sword. And in all congregations counsel was given against marrying out into "the World."[48]

"Thus the church of the *Schwärmer* took release from all bonds in order to separate itself from the godless. For the people of God would be spotted by relations with the godless."[49]

Only the Swiss Brethren attempted a moderate policy based on St. Paul's advice for the winning of a non-Christian spouse to Christ. What should be done in the case of a partner who refused to come into exile for the faith? In the Hutterian society the most strict policy was evolved, for family life was organically related to the spiritual power of the congregation. In any thorough-going communism the family affords a problem of special significance, and the Hutterians were the Anabaptist wing most vexed by the conflict of sovereignties involved.

The place and function of the Elders are also worthy of special discussion. The radicals were strong for lay religion at the beginning, and did not view too favorably any professional workers—certainly not those supported by rents and tithes.[50] In their oft-mentioned letter to Thomas Müntzer (Sept. 5, 1524), Grebel and his group made a point for voluntarism and asked him if he still accepted a salary. At first there were no paid clergy anywhere in the movement, nor were there regularly constituted governors of community life. Christ's office as High Priest (*Hebr.* 10:14 and I *Peter* 2:9) was thought to be exclusive.

"XVIII. They have no rulers, one is like the other, all equal in the service of one another.
XX.   When they are together it is their custom to speak of the Word of God and to admonish one another in a brotherly fashion."[51]

As has been seen in the case of Menno Simons,[52] this informal picture was altered during the struggle against religious individualism and prophetism, and in the effort to survive persecution. Like the Early Church, the Anabaptists had their Montanists; and they were hardly more successful than the early church in maintaining the principle of charismatic leadership within the movement, after they suppressed prophetism. The conflict between Jakob Huter and Simon Schützinger was primarily this: whether "inspired" or "elected" leadership should prevail.[53] Other wings of the movement had to deal with prophetic leaders and groups from time to time, but the leadership chosen by the community customarily prevailed.

Peter Ridemann wrote back from prison that they should honor one another and especially the *"Dienner"* (1540).[54] These leaders were laymen, chosen by the congregation on the authority of the New Testament example of *Acts* 14:23, *Acts* 20:17 and 28, *Titus* 1:5, I *Tim.* 3. 5:17, I *Cor.* 9:14.[56] And they were chosen on the basis of piety and dedication for the shepherding of the community—to read, to warn, to teach, to punish. There were various offices; among the Hutterians the most notable were the "Shepherds" (*Hirten*), Missioners (*diener des Worts*) and Stewards (*Diener der Notdurft*).

The leaders were never supported by more than voluntary collections, and at a late date it was Menno Simons' proud boast that he had lived for years from brother to brother and never gone hungry nor in want. There were some who claimed a minister should support himself—by hand work as did Paul. Hofmann and Rinck and some other earlier leaders did so, but voluntary support was most commonly practiced. Despite the presence of variant practices it is evident that the Anabaptists as a whole shared certain prejudices rooted in the New Testament and opposed to a salaried hierarchy; the community of believers was to be sovereign in all cases.

Community (Gemeinschaft)

The suggestion has been made that there was pooling of goods at the time of the revival in Zollikon, but even if the fact is sustained we may conclude that there was never a closed economy among the Swiss Brethren as a whole.[56] There was throughout the entire Anabaptist movement a pledged communism of consumption ("community" might be a better word), but the creation of a total communistic economy was the work of the Hutterians.

There were various Biblical injunctions which served to enforce the surrender of acquisitiveness and self-interest required for vigorous community. The Anabaptists recalled a favorite text of the medieval mystics:

"In the 5th of Matthew Christ says: 'Blessed are the meek (*die geistlich Armen*), for theirs is the kingdom of heaven.' They are also those who, excused from the world, given over and abandoned for the sake of Christ's will, have no more ownership; whoever is driven by the Spirit into this poverty and submission, the same shall be blessed. But whoever stands in opposition shall be wretched."[57]

The argument sometimes rotated around *Matth.* 19:29—"sell all thou hast," of *James* 1:17—"every good and perfect gift is from above," or another passage of similar significance. The widow gave all she had—

"See: all her wealth! . . . . Therefore we shall practise all Christian community which is nothing more than (did) this evangelical widow."[58]

And occasionally there appeared a general argument belonging to the early years of the movement—". . . the animals in the wood and the birds in the air are free"—reflecting the old peasant movements.[59] But above all and most frequently we are referred to *Acts* 2.4.5., the vision of the Church at Jerusalem.[60] For the Church of *Acts* was a "covenant toward perfection," a model for the true fellowship of Saints.

"In conclusion, *ain* and *gmain* builds the Lord's house and is *rain*, but *aigen, mein, dein, sein* rends the house of the Lord and is *unrain*."[61]

> "Gottes Wort Wär Nit so Schwär
> Wan Nur Der Aigen Nutz Nit Wär."[62]

Thus, even the nursery rhymes taught the children community along with the alphabet. The practice of Biblical communism was basically for the revitalization of the Church; it was a "vocational" witness and directed to that end rather than any general social hope.

"When true Christianity was permitted to wane and depart, the community life became an unbearable burden, it failed utterly. Twice in their history the community of goods was abandoned by the Hutterites through religious decline, to be taken up again through a revival of religion."[63]

The opponents of the Anabaptists learned fairly early to distinguish between their communism and revolution, and the Hutterians strongly dissociated themselves from the events at Münster. The questions directed toward travelling Missioners in court would indicate the authorities' knowledge of the difference between communism by voluntary submission and communism by force (Münster). The sum of Anabaptist teaching was that a Christian should not have anything apart from his brother: both were pilgrims and walked the martyrs' way, and their citizenship was in another city from the city of this world. If any will not share, then the Lord's Supper may be closed to him.

"Item: our Christian faith says, a holy Christian church and a communion (*Gemeinschaft*) of saints; whoever now recognizes the communion (*Gemeinschaft*) of saints with the mouth but does not maintain Community (*Gemeinschaft*), he is false."[64]

It is important to add that there was a heavy note of restraint in the Hutterian writing about Community. There was none of the joy in poverty and simplicity which we remember in connection with St. Francis. The Hutterians left their accustomed ways with pain and heavy hearts, recognizing that the path was the path of suffering and martyrdom. But they thought individualism was a sin against God; the union was not a positive and hopeful program of economic intention, but an inescapable religious mandate.

The stress upon sharing characterized all groups among the Anabaptists, although the communism of the Hutterians was unique to them. Hans Hut said he didn't teach men to sell all their property, but to share with the needy.[65] Hübmaier said he stood for sharing, but not communism.[66] This was the familiar interpretation during the first decade of Swiss domination of the movement and continued in all groups except the Hutterians and the "fringe" community at Münster. It was a communism of consumption, quite thorough-going at times, but without much system and without compulsion.[67]

"But whoever eats and drinks alone, the same has fellowship with Judas, who (it is true) ate and drank with the other disciples from the bread and drink of the Lord. But he would not have community in the common brotherly love. . . ."[68]

Wolfgang Brandhuber related the Hutterian communism to a historical necessity, and said that it might not always be fitting to have it;[69] for him, the command of Jesus to share was what was important, not the particular external organization of it. Yet the Hutterians became, through the years, very critical of those who were not as thorough-going in their submission of individualism as they.

"19. He answered: a true Christian, who would be a Christian in name and work, shall have nothing of his own, and to the extent that he already has wife, children and goods, he shall limit himself and conduct himself as if he had none."[70]

Jakob Widemann debated with Hübmaier's successor, Spital-maier, and complained especially that the loosely defined congregation at Nikolsburg was neglecting its duty to the refugees of the faith.[71] But all wings of Anabaptism started at the same point: in time of need, following the model of the life of the time of the Heroes of the faith. Only historical circumstance and and cultural adaptation made the difference between the Hutterians and other Brethren.

The Lord's Supper (Abendmahl)

The Lord's Supper became an especially important symbol to the Anabaptists. They took the description of the remembrance as given in *Matth.* 26, *Mark* 14, *Luke* 22 and I *Cor.* 11, and interpreted the event in the most straight-forward and simple fashion. In the third of the Seven Articles (Feb. 24, 1527),[72] and in the second of the Five Articles (1547)[73] the Mass was treated as a memorial only.

"He had taught the flesh and blood of Christ not transformed in the bread, only, as Christ had demonstrated it bodily they should understand it spiritually. The bread which he had broken was the Gospel; if he had not broken it it would not have come into the whole world. If they took and appropriated the word and clasped it in their hearts, as Christ had taught, they were benefited in spirit by the body of Christ; and the cup, which Christ had given his disciples, meant his suffering, the blood in the cup was the blood of Christ in the flesh of men; and, if the man was a Christian, he had the blood of Christ, and to the degree that suffering becomes flesh the cup was in blood."[74]

John 6:32-35—"I am the bread of life"—appeared very frequently during the course of the discussions,[75] the implication being that the Master was speaking in figurative fashion at the time of the Supper as well. They saw that the materialistic interpretation was not needed to give the true meaning. There were other Scriptural arguments commonly used as well: Christ could not be many thousands of times in the bread and also on the Cross.[76] He could not be "at the right hand of God the Father" and also in the bread;[77] the simple understanding of the Supper was the proper one. In a Swiss disputation, one of the priests gave proof for the Mass when he was accused of lying in saying the true flesh and blood were there in the bread and wine; his Anabaptist opponent shouted,

"We won't have the argument from philosophy; you shall argue through the Gospel!"[78]

The opposition of the radicals to the Mass was, after all, in the line of the Swiss Reformation.[79] But they also denied the special office of the Clergy which gave the rite its meaning and objective character, and tied the ceremony to the general concern for a purified and perfected community. Baptism had been the center of debate in the first days at Zürich; in Wittenberg, where the Reformers held to the Real Presence, it was the doctrine of the Supper over which controversy raged. Throughout the entire movement, however, the symbols became linked to the drive toward a rigorous internal ethic. As with many sectarian movements from the time of the Donatists,[80] the moral and ethical character of both celebrant and partaker were discussed strenuously. And many who were called into court for abstaining from the communion services of the church of the land said that they could not attend because they were not worthy.

The Anabaptists believed that an unworthy person might do great hurt to himself by taking part in the remembrance,[81] and defined unworthiness in ethical and moral terms. It was an important matter for the brethren to admonish each other and exercise the spiritual government which would prevent such disaster. And the Anabaptists thought it especially vital that the entire congregation should be worthy of the Supper; no one should take part in a "mixed" celebration, where the evil and good were not separated. Therefore they condemned the congregations of the land-church, where no spiritual government obtained and the people nevertheless went to the Supper.

"If one refrained from sins, made penance and led a pure, improving life, he still should not go to our Supper, for the flesh and blood of Christ were not literally in our Supper as we maintain. But whoever was pure from sin might break the bread as Christ broke it. Wine and bread are only a remembrance."[82]

In this fashion one of the orthodox reported the Anabaptist attitude.

In this doctrine, as in the others, we find that the cornerstone was the concept of the true community of believers. In court one of them said that Christ was in the community of faithful, and not in the bread and wine.

"The Christian community is his living temple, wherein he dwells and remains, O brethren, in that and not in stone houses. Because Christ will dwell in this (economy) he may not be in the baked bread."[83]

In any case, the sacraments were only symbols of a certain relationship within the community or between the True Church and Her Lord. The metaphor of the Didache re-appeared frequently, being related to the working of God in a suffering and martyr people. Luther's *Von dem hochwürdigen Sakrament des heiligen wahren Leichnams* (sermon, 1519) told the story of the working of the corn and grapes to become bread and wine, and was popular among the radicals.[84]

"As the bread which I give you, brought together from many kernels, is fused and united through the water, so will we be united through the faith that Christ died for us."[85]

The Anabaptists spoke of this as the kneading and working which marked the martyr people, who were worked and formed by the Master of history according to His plan. It was not a material partaking,

"But he had thereby instituted the cup of the New Covenant, which is Suffering."[86]

The Authority of Civil Government
(Apostolic Nonresistance and the Oath)

The relation of the Anabaptists to the magistrate (*Obrigkeit*) is the most difficult problem in any study of their ordinances, and it is an area in which there is still much dispute. Most probably the controversy is still current because the refusal of some of their descendents to bear arms is a very practical problem to a government which attempts to wage total war and still tries to respect conscientious objection. There is further difficulty in analyzing the evidence from the early groups due to the existence of the state-church system at the time: certainly a good deal of the restraint toward government was due to the Anabaptist denunciation of "official" religion. Further, the question of cooperation in a free society was not faced by any of the early leaders and groups for long; for the sake of their very existence they kept as far from the persecuting authorities as possible. In submissions it was customary to require the recanting Anabaptists to swear to carry the sword and fulfil their bounden duty to the authorities. Conscription did not then exist, but it is plain that the radicals were striking at the very heart of feudal civilization when they refused sword duty to the lord or magistrate, and attacked the union of Church and State. By their negative attitude they were just as dangerous to the establishment, in a certain sense, as the more obvious revolutionaries.

"Concerning the worldly magistrate, we recognize indeed that it was established and ordered to chasten the evil, but it is not given that a Christian can or may be it, for Christ commands one shall not resist evil. Item, we shall love our enemies."[87]

If, as some have claimed, the early Christians brought about the collapse of Rome by their restraint, then just as truly the Anabaptists fore-shadowed the collapse of feudal Christendom. It must not be inferred, however, that this was their intention; they took their stand purely upon the Biblical ground that Jesus

said, "love your enemies and pray for them that persecute you"
(*Matth.* 5:44).

"We wish and desire well for all men and would also do evil to none,
whether pope, monk or priest, whether emperor or king, yes, whether any
creature."[88]

God, in His good time, purposed to give them the Kingdom,
and the *Stille* did not plan to force the issue from any strategic
considerations.

There was a general scepticism about waging war among
all the Swiss, derived in part from their relation to the mercenary system.

"The pope, the emperor, and the king of France were the chief employers
of Swiss troops. The mercenary system was not morally elevating either
to the soldiers themselves or to the influential citizens who were pensioned
by the foreign powers in consideration of their good offices. But it un-
doubtedly had the effect of destroying superstitious veneration for the
church whose carnal battles they were hired to wage and of fostering
freedom of thought. When in 1518 the pope asked for twelve thousand
Swiss troops to fight against the Turks, they somewhat reluctantly prom-
ised ten thousand, adding that if he liked he might take in addition the two
thousand priests."[89]

Zwingli revolted against the mercenary system, and in the first
flush of his evangelical faith appeared to be a pacifist.[90] Bonifacius Amerbach so strongly disapproved of taking up the
sword for the Gospel in the Second Cappel War that he avowed
open sympathy for the Roman Catholics.[91] But the objection of
the Brethren was not Humanistic and cultural. They were concerned first of all with the purification of the Christian witness,
separating the True Church from power and imperial interest.
Their attitude was primarily "defencelessness" and not "pacifism."[92]

For the Anabaptists, the magistrate as policing authority
was of historical origin, given by God as a necessary control of
men's drive to sin. Hübmaier dated the origin of government
right after the fall in Eden, *Genesis* 3:16. Ridemann dated it
right after the deluge; until that time God ruled men directly.[93]
Both revolutionaries and *Stille* were agreed that the power of
the magistrate did not reach within the Christian community,[94]
but the latter made the distinction on a vocational basis. They
had no hope of bringing into being a society without coercion.
The duty of the Christian community was spiritual perfection.

". . . . you shall not participate in strange sins. Therefore we don't carry sword, nor lance nor guns nor any kind of arms or weapons."[95]

As Jakob Huter put it,

"They must put away all outer and iron weapons . . . . and arm themselves with spiritual (weapons)."[96]

The attitude of restraint toward the magistrate's calling and various functions related to it was based upon the thought that there were two different worlds, and the things pertaining to life in one were not proper in the other.

All warring, upheaval, concern for worldly good, killing and hating were now forbidden within the new dispensation.[97]

"Yet further it was noted that the Christian was not permitted to be a magistrate. Wherefore? The world regime is after the flesh, but the Christian regime is according to the spirit. Their house and dwelling is physical, in this world, where the Christian's dwelling place is in heaven. The world citizenship is in this world, but the Christian's citizenship is in heaven. Their warfare and armaments are fleshly and according to the flesh, but the Christian's arms and warfare are spiritual against the sovereignty of the devil. The worldly are equipped with armor according to the flesh, but the Christian's arms are the armor of God, that is truth, righteousness, peace, faith, sanctity, and with the Word of God. . . ."[98]

There is an eschatological note in such teaching, as though the things of the last age are different, and a small minority is already living the last age in the midst of a society of force which is already passing away. Wars in the Old Testament were permitted—

". . . . for servitude was not yet separated from childhood and the way to dominion was not yet revealed. . . ."[99]

The Christian was said to be fighting a different battle with different weapons from those of the world.

The angel with the sword in mouth indicates "that for us Christians also the sword doesn't belong in hand, but in the mouth—namely, the sword of the Spirit."[100]

The authority cited for this restraint toward government and civil functions was the New Testament command and example of Christ. Andreas Castelberger, the earliest to emphasize this testimony, considered the warrior no better than a murderer.[101] The Sermon on the Mount was enough for him, and the command of Jesus against the oath (taken by vassals and soldiers): "Let thy words be 'Yea,' 'Yea,' and 'Nay,' 'Nay.' "[102] The master forbade all swearing (*Matth.* 5:34 and *James* 5:12).

And as for executing the office of judgment and wrath, "we shall love our enemies." The Anabaptists observed that the magistrate can't forgive enemies; his was "an office of wrath" (*ain ampt der raach*).[103] One confessed his doubts—

"5. The Magistrate shall not kill, that was against the 5th commandment, yet he had doubts therein, as in Just Wars (*in billichen kriegen*)."[104]

Thus it was not always clear at what points the line might be drawn by various Anabaptist groups. Some said that they would support only the magistrate who obeyed the Bible: to put down evil and aid the good.

"Also we pray for all worldly government, that thou wilt bless them, that they may use thy sword which thou hast given them, for protecting the good and punishing the evil ones; and watch, that they stain not their hands in the blood of thy saints."[105]

But the more general rule was that the magistrate was given for the sins of the world and should be obeyed in all things favorable or adverse except those of conscience. The Swiss Brethren refused to bear arms but paid taxes, for which the Hutterians criticized them on the war tax.[106] The magistrate's office was generally enough to ban a person from the congregation, but Menno permitted such to remain members.[107] Among the Anabaptists only the revolutionaries seemed to have much social concern; the *Stille* had almost no mind for questions of public policy. A more general pacifist note seemed to enter with the saying of Grebel that Christian should not kill Christian; and a case of non-cooperation occurred among the slaves in the war galleys at Trieste (1539), who refused to put their hands to the oars although beaten for their non-cooperation.[108] But these incidents were rare departures in an otherwise Bible-centered and church-centered nonresistance.

In reducing the various emphases in the peace testimony to a scheme of logical outline, we note three prominent accents in the Anabaptist view of the magistrate: *first,* their opposition to compulsion in religion; *second,* their opposition to revolution; *third,* their sense of destiny as the church of the martyrs.

The Anabaptist o p p o s i t i o n t o c o m p u l s i o n i n r e l i g i o n grew out of their sense of the incongruity between the Early Church pattern and the establishment. When they were persecuted they grew even more rugged in condemnation of the state-church. The whole matter has been reviewed in another connection,[109] but it is useful at this point to call attention to the way in which it is tied to their nonresistance. The only power recognized within the congregations was spiritual government.

The Anabaptist o p p o s i t i o n t o r e v o l u t i o n grew out of their pessimism regarding power and the possibilities of social betterment. After the Münster episode, all branches of the *Stille* reacted strongly against ethical concern outside the True Church, and vigorously asserted the authority of the magistrate.[110]

"Our will and mind are not, however, to do away with worldly government nor not to be obedient to it in goods and sanctions. For a government shall and must be in the world among men just as the daily bread and just as the schoolmaster must have the rods among the children. For because the great house of this world will not admit and let rule the Word of God, the knaves and rascals or children of this world who pursue no Christian piety must yet have a worldly and gallows-piety. . . Therefore the magistrate is an institution of God."[111]

But the Anabaptists would not serve in the Magistrate's capacity themselves; the calling of the Christian is to other work. They reported that the ban was exercised within the community, and their law-abiding quality was to be such that their restraint at this single point of faith should not lead any to think that they were not whole-heartedly for good order and sound government.

The Anabaptist s e n s e o f d e s t i n y a s t h e C h u r c h o f T h e M a r t y r s is of highest importance. The Bible, which tells of the Good Shepherd, frequently calls His flock "the sheep."

"By sheep Christians alone were meant. A sheep is a meek, weaponless, submissive beast, that has no other defence for itself than to run as long as it can and may. And it resembles the governance of the sword not at all, as little as a sheep resembles a wolf or lion."[112]

The Anabaptists taught that Christians must expect persecution and exile, for this was the inevitable lot of those who submit and will not wrestle for political control; and it was also the martyrs' testimony which validated their Christian authority in the baptism of blood.[113]

In most quarters of the Mennonite movement today the peace testimony has lost all eschatological content. On the Continent the testimony itself has been generally abandoned, but in America it is associated with an agrarian economy and has survived. Dutch and German writers have attempted to show that the early Anabaptists were not really nonresistant in the complete sense, but rather opposed to revolution and restrained toward government because persecuted.[114] This interpretation has been combatted by the Americans,[115] who sometimes combine the traditional testimony and cultural primitivism in a strictly "vocational" and certainly also in a non-evangelical way. It is hard to deny that the early New Testament literalism of the Anabaptists cuts through most of the differences, and a review of the Anabaptist vision of the church as it was in the age of heroic witnessing makes such later disputes seem quite pragmatic and historical.

When we survey, both historically and dogmatically, the ways of "nestling back into the world," we are forced to the conclusion that cultural enclaves which have lost their missionary passion and sense of a new world to come are hardly more true to original Anabaptism than those who have acclimated themselves to commerce and warring. For the "evangelical *Täufer*" linked their suffering nonresistance to the evangel of Him who commanded "Go ye into all the world . . ." (*Matth.* 28:19), and they had great expectations concerning a time to come. They were certain that after the long centuries of the Dispersion they were gathering together again the faithful people of the Lord, to be His blessed community and to live the life for which he gave precept and example. And in that restored community there dwelt the promise of great things to come on earth.

THE GREAT COMMISSION

Myr ist geben alle gewallt ynn hymel vnd erden/ dar umb gehet hyn/ vnd leret alle volcker/ vnd teufft die ynn den namen des vaters vñ des sons vnd des heyligen geysts/ vnd leret sie halten/ alles was ich euch befolhen have/ vnd sihe/ ich byn bey euch alle tage/ bis ans ende der wellt.—*Matth.* 28. *Das Newe Testament Deutsch* (Wittenberg, 1522).

Gehet hyn ynn alle wellt/ vnd predigt das Evangelion/ alle Creaturn/ wer do glaubt vnd taufft wirt/ der wirt selig werden/ wer aber nicht gleubt/ der wirt verdampt werden.—*Mark* 16.

Die erde ist des HERREN vnd was drinnen ist/ Der erdboden vnd was drauff wonet.—*Ps.* 24. *Biblia/ das ist/ die gantze Heilige Schrift Deudsch* (Wittenberg, 1534).

The Anabaptist Understanding of the Command

The Restitution of the True Church was full of meaning on the world map. The Anabaptists believed that they were fore-runners of a time to come, in which the Lord would establish His people and His Law throughout the earth. Both revolutionaries and *Stille* had this vision of approaching fulfilment, although their understandings of the details differed greatly.[1]

No words of the Master were given more serious attention by His Anabaptist followers than His final command:

"Go ye therefore, and teach all nations, baptizing them in the name of the Father, and of the Son, and of the Holy Ghost:
Teaching them to observe all things whatsoever I have commanded you. . . ."

The words seemed to point up His whole teaching in a glorious program comprehending the whole world. The pilgrim, familiar seeker of the Middle Ages, was transformed in the fiery experience of the "evangelical *Täufer*"[2] into an effective evangelist and martyr. His wandering foot-steps and shedding of blood were a determined if not always systematic testimony to the influence of a lay mission which counted no cost too dear to him who would walk in the steps of the Crucified.

According to Anabaptist understanding, in right faith the Great Commission was fundamental to individual confession and a true ordering of the community of believers. The proof text appeared repeatedly in Anabaptist sermons and apologetic writing. Confessions of faith and court testimonies gave it a central place and the series of questions prepared by the authorities for use in court indicates that the authorities expected it to be of prime importance in Anabaptist argument.[3]

"Our faith stands on nothing other than the command of Christ (Mat. 28, Mark 16). . . . For Christ didn't say to his disciples: go forth and celebrate the Mass, but go forth and preach the Gospel."[4]

The very order of the words conveyed His intent for His followers:

"Firstly, Christ said, go forth into the whole world, preach the Gospel to every creature. Secondly, he said, whoever believes, thirdly—and is baptized, the same shall be saved. This order must be maintained if a true Christianity is to be prepared and though the whole world rage against it. Where it isn't maintained there is also no Christian community of God, but of the devil, and thereby of the whole world and all false Christians who alter it in their topsy-turvy order, and fight perversely."[5]

The evangel comes first, and then faith, finally baptism; a failure to respect this scriptural sequence indicated a lack of respect for the Mind of Christ for His disciples:

"Go forth into the whole world and preach the Gospel; whoever believes and is baptized the same shall be saved; for the preaching of God's word shall go before and not after the baptism. . . . etc."[6]

Baptism of those in whom faith was stirred by the preaching of the Gospel was the logical culmination of the mandate which begins, "Go forth . . ."

The article on Believers' Baptism in the Five Articles (1547), Confession of Faith and second most important document of the Hutterians, found its cornerstone in *Matth.* 28 and *Mark* 16.[7] Hans Hut baptized, telling his followers to obey the commandments, preach the Gospel, and baptize in the Great Commission.[8] Other evidence is of a kind. For the Anabaptists, the freely spoken evangel was the moving force in a complete re-working of the Old Man, whose crucifixion and rebirth in faith were sealed by the sign;[9] only those of mature judgment passed through a crucial and transforming adult experience, and could rightly be let through the door to a responsible covenantal relation to God and one's fellows. The strenuous life of a Christian is "no child's play."[10]

Not only was the missionary mandate obeyed most seriously, but it was given sweeping application. It applied to all Christians at all times. By traditional exegesis the words were directed only toward His immediate audience, the Apostles, whose travels to the far corners of the earth had been long a part of Christian legend.[11] There had been from time to time vocational groups in the Great Church which strove to fulfil the Master's world view, notably the Franciscans.[12] *But the Anabaptists were among the first to make the Commission binding upon all church members.* In their organization, the promise to go where sent was part of the ceremony of admission to the "True Church." They "went freely under the cross" where the representatives of the state-churches dared not go, and for the Gospel's sake were made pilgrims and martyrs throughout the known world.[13] If, as a great historian of the missionary movement has described it,[14] the expansion of the faith has in modern times for the first time become the concern and activity of the total membership rather than the princes, it is not too much to call the *Täufer* fore-runners of the modern missionary movement.

Not only was a new historical significance given to the Great Commission, but it was made relevant to the life of the Common Man. It applied to the most simple believer and claimed him for an evangelist. Until this time the ordinary Christian had looked largely to the higher authorities, both secular and religious, to make decisions of policy and carry the weight of Christian statesmanship. In the Church of the Restitution the world view was no longer restricted to the powerful and educated. In Anabaptist opinion, the craftsman might make a better missioner than the cultured man. Jesus himself preached to men in terms of their trade, not with many books.

"For the common man can be better informed by (lessons from) the creatures than through writing."[15]

When the missioner Hanss Schmidt was asked about his studies, he told the authorities:

"I study with pick and flail."[16]

For the Brethren that was honorable and sufficient, and better equipped him to go forth into all lands "in order to gather the sheep to the Lord" and "to fish for men" than the wranglings of the philosophers.[17] There lies a deeper meaning as well: from the peasant who plows his field for the planting the faithful were to learn how God works his people in fulfilling His purpose.[18] In suffering and travail His faithful are plowed for the Kingdom's sake. And the Common Man can best proclaim the Gospel to Common Men. The domination of the outward, the material, the powerful, will give way before the calm speaking of the simple Christian whose only authority is the Gospel. And it will be the babes, the naive, who will come through where those wise and understanding "after the flesh" will fail.

The party of the Reformers resisted the "wandering" of the Anabaptists. Lutherans taught that each calling has divine blessing, and condemned the irresponsibility of those who cast loose from family and job to be missioners. They came, in their resistance to the corner preachers and radical congregations, to enforce tight authority in the parish. Orderly ordination and calling to the ministry was vigorously championed against the Anabaptists,

". . . . for they cannot establish their calling."[19]

Such separatists were the devil's apostles, for

". . . . no one can have a ministry outside and without command or calling."[20]

The Reformers made no sharp break from the relation of Church and State previously known in Christendom. They were familiar with the Anabaptist teaching, however:

"No one shall be baptized before he learns and believes, because Christ has said—in the last of Matthew—go forth, teach all peoples and baptize them. Item, the last of Mark: Who believes and is baptized, the same shall be saved. But children can't be taught anything/ therefore they also can't believe/ therefore man shall also not baptize them."[21]

And in reply the Reformers challenged the whole Anabaptist interpretation of the Early Church and the recapitulation of its life:

"God sent only the Apostles into all the world. . ."[22]

"Therefore the Apostles gave command, not only for themselves but their disciples/ and in their writings, teachings and examples they left precedent as to how servants of the Gospel should be called in the church— to wit, that the servant of the Gospel does not travel here and there in the land,—and shall not preach in one church today, another tomorrow— white in one, black in the other. But each servant stays with true constancy by his assigned church/ leaving the other churches to peace and quiet. Each church has thereby its own constituted servant, and avoids and excludes strange unaccredited wanderers—as is seen in *Acts* and in Paul's Epistle I *Tim.* iij and *Tit.* j."

The Reformers knew well the mobility of the Anabaptist leadership and congregation, and they opposed it ideologically and in practice. Their criticism serves to establish further the fact that the Anabaptists conceived of the Church as a voluntary association of committed pilgrims.

Characteristically, the Anabaptists believed that the Early Church was the time when the missionary command was obeyed most faithfully. Indeed, those called by Jesus were known as "missioners" (*Evangelisten*) ; *Matth.* 28 was the first order, and *Luke* 24 the second.[23] Christ did not conceive of winning by iron or prison, but by the glorious and contagious forthgoing of the inspired community.[24] The Anabaptists felt that the winning of the world by free evangel was the denial of the compulsion which had controlled the Great Church's fallen estate. The community organized about an evangelical purpose, like the Church of the first centuries, was to be a standing testimony to religious liberty.

The Early Church ideal was re-capitulated in the Left Wing of the Reformation. It is notable that the Schwenckfelders and Anabaptists were frequently thrown together in proscriptions; and their meetings faced many of the same problems. Both of these evangelical groups were threats to the authorities of the establishment, and in some respects they had a common strategy. When Luther held fast to the medieval parochial system, Schwenckfeld defended the Pauline missions-method of letter-writing and visitations.[25] A definite pattern of charismatic organization emerged in the former time of free evangel,[26] and the same development would characterize the church of the New Age. Schwenckfeld's contention with the *Täufer* was because they established Biblical rule, notably governance by Elders and the Ban (*Matth.* 18); he considered this coercion of free movement of the Spirit as wrong as any by secular government.[27] His conception of the restitution was limited to the free preaching of the Gospel; the Anabaptists also affirmed the evangel but built upon it a New Testament community. Both Anabaptists and Schwenckfeld dreamed of the Early Church.

The gathering of voluntary religious associations[28] by a freely and comprehensively conceived evangel, sealed by Believers' Baptism, constituted in early times a challenge to the Imperial power and in the sixteenth century a threat to the state churches which sought to offset the winning power of the broadly conceived and energetically pursued mission by Infant Baptism. This bulwark of the standing order was introduced in the Roman Empire, according to Jakob Huter, as a blunt reaction of tyranny to the power of the Great Commission.[29]

Its maintenance by the state-churches of the Reformers placed them in the period before the Restitution, in the fallen time of the Great Church. The words of the New Testament were clear enough, and the example of the Early Church could hardly be misinterpreted. The Anabaptists looked out upon the known world as a great missionary territory, and they sought to evangelize on the comprehensive scale of the Great Heroes of the past.

The Heroic Prototype

In the life of the radical congregations the man of the Early Church re-appeared. He was a Hero with one supreme loyalty, to Christ His Master. He performed miracles. His persecutors sometimes died terrible deaths.[30] He strove to obey literally the counsels of perfection which were now binding upon every believer, and he "lived loose from the world" as a p i l g r i m, m i s s i o n e r and m a r t' y r.

From prison a pilgrim of the faith wrote of his condition:

"I am cut loose from all the world, from wife, from father, and mother and sister according to the flesh, and from all men; but that is right; Christ was also cut loose from all men and from his disciples; it is enough that I be as He was. . . ."[31]

This ascetic emphasis led to a glory in pilgrimage and a triumph in martyrdom. Scores of missioners travelled from Waldshut throughout Switzerland, from Zürich through the Tyrol and Southern Germany, and finally, from Moravia as far as Venice, Amsterdam and Krakow. Lay evangelists moved among corner-congregations, threading all central Europe, and a chain of synods and free gatherings tied the movement together. Occasionally we find rather startling evidence of the wide holding of Anabaptist opinion. An Hutterian missionary was martyred at Aachen, October 19, 1558. And when Hans Beck was in prison at Passau, delegates came from Salonica in Greece and held fellowship with him.[32] Missioners were bound by Scripture to travel and carry the word, and by church organization were bound to be pilgrims for the faith wherever sent.

"Blessed is the man whom the Lord finds watching when he comes. First he speaks of gathering up—in this, we have to understand with this gathering up, that we shall lift up our countenance and thanks to heavenly things so that the earthly will not spot us."[33]

The preacher was also instructed to maintain his vigorous ethical testimony against the corruptions and compromises of the world:

"Furthermore we shall light our light; that is the light whereby they see our good works and glorify our father who is in heaven. . . ."[34]

Matth. 5:14! The Anabaptists felt that God Himself showed them where to go and bring their testimony of word and act, and the land should not be forbidden them: for the earth is all the Lord's (*Psalm* 24:1).[35]

The deliberate strategy which was so marked at the later stage was hardly a part of the early picture. Anabaptist leaders at first wandered as pilgrims, seeking peace from persecution and shepherding from time to time the little groups of the faithful. As persecution grew more savage, hundreds of families took to the road, moving slowly eastward toward the land of the Bohemian Brethren's settlements. A whole people thus became pilgrim, exiles for Christ. Hutterian missioners such as Wolfgang Brandhuber worked among them and helped many to make the trip. Others applied to the Brethren directly for aid in migrating, and a "Servant of the Word"[36] was sent to investigate and make recommendation.[37] That their judgment was not infallible is evidenced by the watering down of vigorous internal discipline due to the advent of economic refugees,[38] as well as by the number who later went home and made submission;[39] but the Moravian colonies became through the devotion of the great leaders and the discipline of their people one of the greatest missionary centers of the sixteenth century. The pilgrim people became a great intentional power for the spreading of the Gospel to every creature.[40]

There was a definite transition from the Anabaptist pilgrim, who evangelized and taught where driven by the hounds of the established order, to the missioner whose trips were assigned as part of a grand strategy of spiritual conquest. Generally speaking, the establishment of the economy in Moravia may be used to mark the line of crossing from one dominant type to the other.

For an example of the early itinerant evangelist, committed to spiritual independence from the things of this world and destined to early martyrdom, we may consider the Swiss leader,

Georg Blaurock.[41] Blaurock was outstanding for his wide travels, and noteworthy because he linked the circle at

Zürich with the colonies in Moravia. Blaurock and Stumpf were those who pressed Zwingli most energetically for the gathering of a purified "community of all things as also the apostles (had it) in Acts 2."[42] Blaurock led the little band on to the first adult baptism and the vigorous simplicity of his life and witness won many common people to the movement. A powerful preacher, and utterly fearless in commanding a hearing for the Word, he was popularly called "the second Paul," "sturdy George." At Zollikon a crowd of 150 persons was swept into mass baptism by his preaching, and at Hynwyl he entered the chapel and preached to 200 people before the regular minister arrived.[43] When imprisoned, he said Christians should go out as missionaries as Paul indicated, and the magistrate was not necessary in matters of faith. "The earth is the Lord's . . ." He was driven into exile and wandering, and in May of 1529 began his great work in the Tyrol, laying the foundations there for the life of a people who reached their perfected Christian economy in Moravia.[44] Among those who watched his heroic death at the stake was a boy, Peter Walpot, who became later the greatest missionary executive of the Hutterian Brethren.[45]

The "evangelical *Täufer*" carried on extensive missionary cultivation, rotating around several centers of the new life. Even before the Moravian settlements grew powerful there was some centralized planning. The original circle at Z ü r i c h scattered widely and on an apparently spontaneous basis: Blaurock, with Manz erecting a community in the Grisons, went on to the Tyrol; Reublin and Sattler went to Alsace and Swabia, Hetzer to Nürnberg and Augsburg, Gross to Strassburg and Augsburg. W a l d s h u t, center of a great reformation under Hübmaier, was the source of concentric circles of influence: Ulrich Teck and Jakob Gross were especially active in trips from this base of operations.[46]

Recorded planning began with the famous Martyr Synod of August 20, 1527, which could as well be termed a Missionary Synod.[47] This Synod not only effected cooperation between the parties led by Hans Hut and Hans Denck, but divided the land on a grand map of evangelical enterprise; brethren were sent out from it to centers in South Germany, Switzerland and Moravia. Those attending numbered the outstanding leaders and missioners— Denck, Hut, Jörg von Passau, Hetzer, Gross, Dachser, Salminger, Langenmantel, Gall Fischer—most of whom died as missionary martyrs within a few years. The fate of an Anabaptist missioner ("agitator" in Christendom) was usually sealed without trial or hearing. But the answer of the heroes of the Restitution was the gallant testimony of the cup of blood. Persecution only changed them from wandering pilgrims to missionary strategists, ready when the time came to be martyrs also.

The cost in trained leaders was tremendous in the early years, before semi-permanent bases of operation had been established and the means of operation and communication worked out. Only two or three of the Martyr Synod (1527) lived to see the fifth year of the movement. A long list of those martyred, 1527-31, is still extant.[48] In Switzerland and Southern Germany the leadership and supervision of the congregations fell into the hands of laymen, with the occasional supervision afforded by visiting missioners.

The unarmed knight of the faith, whose chief virtue was long-sufferingness (*Gelassenheit, lijdsaamkeid*), became the character type of the movement. The knightly symbol was revived to describe the weaponless defender of truth, God's champion against the powers of this world's darkness.

"In place of the athlete the knight is at the point of conflict . . . in place of the arena, the tourney or field of battle is entered. In this sense the Anabaptists speak of the battle of the Cross which must be fought. For martyrdom is no case of laziness, but of strength . . . only the Hero can go the martyr's way."[49]

This spiritual warfare has run through all history, from the dualism of Cain and Abel through Judas and Jesus to the present time.

"All Biblical writing speaks entirely of the suffering of the elect from Abel up to the apostles. Therein is the lamb slain from the foundation of the world."[50]

"I pray to God. . . that in carnal souls Christ will create and illuminate the eternal fire of his love, the sole courtrobe of all Christians. Even if today there is no Abel without a Cain; no Jacob without an Esau; no Peter without a Herod; no Paul without a Nero; God loves us just the same:—yes, the old God of Israel—the ruler of the earth—will not let us be overcome. He gives to all of us a free, constant, spirit and an unflinching heart in all trouble. May this remain true."[51]

In a certain sense, then, Christ's example was made a type of all suffering in the world, and the fact of suffering itself achieved Divine significance.

"Even as you contend in knightly fashion for the truth, so will the Lord God contend for you. . . ."[52]

Economic Factors of Importance

No ideology can survive, nor can it even come to birth, except "in the fullness of time." In particular, the theoretical pattern must be related to large historic forces which give the atmosphere in which the intellectual movement can live and give concrete form to its tendencies. At the time of the Restitution there were certain given factors, largely economic, which favored the emergence of a new solidarity and which joined forces with the Anabaptist vision of religious reform.

The sixteenth century was a time of social unrest and economic upheaval, of revolutionary dreams and attempted reform. Craftsmen and peasants found themselves displaced in an economy made fluid by commerce with Asia and wealth from America. These were the chief classes to produce programs and centers of revolt, to respond most readily to the intense eschatology of the Melchiorites, and to go in large numbers to the Christian communist villages in Moravia. Though court records show that many who joined the colonies had some substance, the Hutterian mission found ready response from the hungry and depressed.[53] Journeymen without fixed place of residence or master were a common sight in this age; if they were also Anabaptist they added to their testimony that Christ alone was "Master" (*vorsteer*). The Anabaptist craftsmen transformed social circumstance into a religious vehicle, and glorified in "living loose from the world."

Groups disjointed by a changing economy became wanderers in the land. On the social side they were torn loose and dispossessed; on the religious side they were seekers. Women imprisoned at Erlangen in 1527 reported that their husbands left, seeking the word of the Gospel and consigning the children to their care. One journeyman had said,

"I will go and will search out the old and new faiths (to see) which is the true and best."[54]

The savage persecution loosed on the Anabaptist congregations threw hundreds into the currents of economic and religious unrest. Poor relief records show the travel of families toward Moravia. Most of them were like Veit Frick,

". . . a poor, unpromising people, what have to do their daily work and have many children. . . ."[55]

Standard processes for confiscation of property and goods were worked out in the courts, and affected the most able farmers and craftsmen as well as those cast adrift by economic circumstances.[56] Whole families were uprooted, and many men travelled from city to city leaving families to fend for themselves.

Those who were able agriculturalists or handworkers, who were displaced from their former station by religious persecution rather than by unrest, constitute a somewhat different phenomenon from the individual wanderers. But displacement for religious causes became increasingly important with the years. Such displacement was a permanent function of religious territorial agreements such as that of Augsburg (1555). In the years of preparation and early gathering of groups the wanderer was common. Later, under the impact of a strict discipline, the community responsibility loomed large in meeting the economic need. The more responsible parties were concerned to maintain a family economy, and within the Hutterian communities real honor was tendered craftsmen in terms of their work. But in the larger society there was a looseness of relationships toward job and family which the Reformers considered thoroughly irresponsible.[57] The Reformers could not understand the apparent instability of one who

". . . had a wife and four children, no home place and was the citizen of no city."[58]

They were concerned to carry over from medieval civilization those relationships which made for a stable society. But to the religious radical, driven by persecution and the Lord's Commission, such relationships were "worldly'" concerns. We can hear the Anabaptist say to the authorities of Church and State who tried to hold him fast in his "natural" responsibilities:

I no longer live but Christ in me and the world crucified in me![59]

Just as economic displacement joined forces with the religious drive to make pilgrimage common, so the establishment of a planned economy in Moravia became the cornerstone and the surety for a consistent and planned missionary effort. The practice of Christian Community established in Moravia was intimately tied to Anabaptist evangelical operations in the German-speaking lands. The Great Commission itself seemed to argue for the kind of selflessness best expressed by a strong discipline of community or communism.[60] In all groups a communism of consumption functioned for the evangel, and the

Hutterian communities saw their strongest internal discipline during the days of ardent missionary passion.[61] A base of operations was built which served the entire movement, and the most missionary minded were the congregations fraternally related to that economy.

Congregational communism was introduced when the pacifist wing under Jakob Widemann separated from the followers of Hübmaier after the Nikolsburg Disputation,[62] establishing themselves on the apostolic disciplines at Slávkov. They were joined in 1529 by Jakob Huter, who had been working with Georg Zaunring in the congregations founded in the Tyrol by Blaurock, and who saw in their new religious economy "the communion of saints" of his ideals. Huter worked as a missioner until 1533, when he brought the last group from the Tyrol,[63] and took responsibility as leader[64] in the Auspitz community which Reublin and Zaunring had established in a 1530 succession from Widemann's autocratic leadership.[65] In three years of extremely able leadership Huter left an indelible mark on the communities which came to bear his name,[66] concentrating on the practices of Community (*Gemeinschaft*) and Separation (*Ehescheidung*—a special type of spiritual government),[67] and laying the groundwork in the discipline of a missionary people who reached out from Venice to Aachen to win men to "community" in Christ.

The strength of the Hutterian missionary economy was evidenced not only by acquisitions from "the world," but from the more loosely organized Swiss Brethren[68] and the Gabrielites and Philippites, whose leaders had originally resisted Huter's energetic program.[69] Through the years the finest Hutterian leaders approached the erring brethren for union,[70] and the last group came in about 1565. When a man such as Ulrich Stadler, leader of the "Austerlitzers" was gained (1545), the vision of "the pilgrim of the Lord" was accented among the Brethren.[71] In Stadler's mind pilgrimage for the faith requires a strong discipline: there are some who say all should be by free will, but the Biblical requirement of communism and rule by elders is plain.[72]

In P e t e r R i d e m a n n, who came to Moravia in 1531,[73] after succeeding Brandhuber in the groups in the land of the Ens, the Brethren found a most powerful leader. He was author of the 1540 *Rechenschaft,* which became the basic document of the movement.[74] He was the Hutterians' outstanding hymn-writer. He served for years as missioner to Gabrielites in Franconia and Nürnberg, and in the loosely knit *Täufer* groups in South Germany.[75] After a long life of service in bringing groups in ten's and twelve's to Moravia,[76] and in other positions of community leadership, Ridemann died a natural death on December 1, 1556. Ridemann's most notable contribution was in organization and discipline, but his importance as missionary teacher and executive must be underscored. As for other leaders and the movement itself, the tight community life was a function of his world-view.

The Hutterian Brethren developed one of the most perfect missionary organizations of the time, and strongly under-wrote the work in the Tyrol, South Germany, and even in the Netherlands, with personnel and place of refuge. The original Anabaptist impulse survived most vigorously in those congregations which were most missionary.

"Quiet Eschatology"

"However be comforted in your pious Christian hearts, realizing and accepting indeed that it has been so for all the prophets, Christ the Lord, his apostles, and in fact all saints from the beginning of the world, yea all them whom the Lord God has loved. Such is plainly and frequently demonstrated for you without gloss, namely, that all lovers of divine truth will be elect saints and all will be driven and hounded until the Judgment, as the Bible gives us sufficient evidence and shows in all places."[77]

At the core of the formal organization of both revolutionaries and *Stille* there was a missionary mind. Even the radicals at Wittenberg sent out twelve missioners to proclaim the day of wrath and judgment, quoting the Great Commission and calling for moral reform.[78]

We recognize Hans Hut as the bridge in the early period between the revolutionary wing and the "evangelical *Täufer*,"[79] a large percentage of those called up by the authorities in central Germany reported that Hut baptized them, dipping his hand in a water pitcher and making a cross on their foreheads.[80] No missioner travelled more widely, and Hut won so wide and enthusiastic a following that he was accused of drugging the multitudes with a potion.[81] When held by the authorities before his death he testified in significant terms:

"The word which stands on Mark 16 had moved him to preach, namely, that preaching was first, afterwards faith, and thirdly baptism. And man must let the word of the Lord stand. (He is) not to do anything apart from it, (and) also shall depart neither to the right nor the left, according to the last of Matthew that one shall first teach and afterwards baptize. Item, also in Acts 19 it is written that John called some to repentance and baptized those whom the Apostle Paul himself later permitted to be re-baptized."[82]

Hut was first a book peddler associated with Thomas Müntzer, and in Jörg Haug's church at Bibra called upon the peasants to take the sword against the Magistrate.[83] In the summer of 1526 Hans Denck won him to the non-resistant position, and the following year Hut debated Hübmaier in several meetings at Nikolsburg which led to the split-off of the radical groups and establishment of pacifist/communist communities. In preaching and winning thousands[84] he would begin by citing the Great Commission, and pass on to a fiery proclamation of the coming again of Christ.[85] The structure of his message did not change when he repudiated a violent ushering in of the Kingdom. In fact, the chiliastic mood stayed with the *Stille* after revolution was repudiated. Some said that Armageddon occurred whenever a Christian bore persecution.[86]

When the New Jerusalem was established at Münster, ten years later, missioners were sent forth to gather the people of the new age, and all north-west Germany contributed.[87] March 24, 1534, was set as the day of mass migration, and although the authorities stopped most large groups, Münster continued to be even during the siege a center of the most excited evangelism. As the siege intensified, evangelism gave place to prophecy and the New Zion looked forward to world revolution, the slaying of the godless, the restitution of all things.[88] They proclaimed that in that very generation Christ would come again, His Kingdom would come on earth, and all the ends of the earth would bow before Him.[89]

"God's people, who remain eternal . . . must inherit the earth and establish Christ the king to rule over the whole world."[90]

The Restitution of the true apostolic church and the gathering of the Church of the Dispersion were to lead on directly to the restitution of God's law in the world. Unbelievers wondered at the calm assurance with which the faithful faced their unlikely prospects, as for instance when Jan Matthysz led a futile sortie of 200 hymn-singers to disperse the besieging forces. Even after the revolutionaries "let drop the apostolic weapons to the earth and seized the armor of David,"[91] their spirit of certainty was a marvel to the sceptical. Through "special revelation" and not through lack of expectancy they took up the sword.[92] The missionary passion and eager world-view of the revolutionaries never flagged, and in both significant social explosions (in the Peasant Revolt and at Münster) constituted an essential part of their eschatology.

We have already seen that among the *Stille* the missionary personality and congregation was of primary importance. They interpreted the very meaning of history in such fashion. In Anabaptist teaching the True Church of the Restitution was a pilgrim church, a missionary church, a martyr church. Throughout history it has been both forbidden and persecuted.

"It is solidly packed in God's word and the three words: the first, many are called but few are chosen; the second, the way of God is narrow and straight and few there be who find it; the third, not all who cry unto me Lord Lord shall enter the Kingdom, but those who do the will of my heavenly father, they shall enter the Kingdom. . . ."[93]

Although the authorities were sometimes capable of making the distinction between those who actively opposed the magistrate and those who only refused to obey on matters affecting the faith, they generally regarded all corner-meetings as hostile to ecclesiastical and political order. The radicals in return justified their small meetings.

"The gospel is not to be preached openly in churches, but only in secret byways and privately in houses."[94]

The True Church is where two or three are gathered together in the Lord's name and not in the "idol-temples."[95] Indeed, since creation only a little household has gone the right way, and this has been anonymous and persecuted. For them, the forbidden church was the True Church.[96]

"For the Babylonian harlot who sits on the seven hills, I mean the Roman Church, a synagogue of the living devil, only spits out all children of God and drives them into the wastelands, into their byways. . . . ."[97]

They believed it was God's plan that His people should be strangers and pilgrims in the world, and as citizens of a better city persecuted and hounded in this.

"For power is given to the beast to fight against the saints and triumph over them—not in spirit but in the flesh. For the suffering of Christ must also be fulfilled and made concrete in their limbs."[98]

The martyr church was to be able to establish its place in history in terms of its suffering. It is the wolf which drives others; the sheep is a poor, defenseless beast. The Anabaptists made much of the struggle and suffering in *Hebrews* 11:33-38, and the analogy between baptism and death ("blood-baptism"), in restoring the martyr-theology of the Early Church. Martyrdom was their carrying power, their triumph beyond obvious defeat, their final long pilgrimage free from the world and its controls.

The Anabaptists saw themselves living again the painful persecution of the apostolic church, hounded by cruel political and religious lords who had no mercy for the defenceless, the sick and helpless.[99] They knew what it was to invite new members to "take up their cross." In this trial by fire and water, where their faith was tested as gold in the furnace, they were fortified by the memory of Christ's suffering and by the hymns and records of other brethren of the cross.[100] The first hymns were from prison,[101] and the finest records were stories of the martyrs who

". . . . have sealed in knightly fashion the truth of God with their blood."[102]

The full Believers' Baptism, of which Water was the first order, was according to I *John* 5:8:

"And there are three that bear witness in earth, the spirit, and the water, and the blood: and these three agree in one."[103]

The true follower of Jesus will not hesitate to drink the cup he drank (*John* 18:11), indeed he will expect it.[104]

"For whoever will not suffer with Christ also will not rule with Him, and whoever doesn't have this holy spirit is no Christian."[105]

Thus the Anabaptists developed a theology of suffering, transforming the persecuted remnant into a triumphant Church, both in historical significance and present salvation.[106] It became their moving power and hope in the Third Age, a refined and non-violent parallel to the revolutionary conquest as thought at Münster.

"Suffering is the way, the door, and the means to God, the door into the sheep-stall."[107]

In baptism the believer learned that he was to leave all selfish concern, including private ownership, and through the cross and suffering come to salvation. The internal significance of suffering is revealed in their records in the use of communism and the ban. When threatened by the authorities, Hanss Schmidt said, Let God's will be done; he had suffered all his life as a pilgrim loose from the world; and his brethren would take care of his wife and children.[108] (Here again communism's utility as a base of operations for the missionary work is clear.) *"Creutz christy"* and *"gemeinschaft der heilligen"* are the key ideas in Anabaptist testimony at this level. Good and evil must be separated by vigorous use of the Ban so that the individual hero and the heroic community will be able to stand in time of trial.

"For a Christian without suffering is like an untrained doctor, and like a house whose beam has not been hewn."[109]

The internal organization of the community was a function of their capacity as pilgrims, missioners and martyrs.

There is no doubt that the *Stille* consciously repudiated the revolutionaries' shift from weaponless warfare to the taking of the sword, but it is questionable whether all chiliastic thinking was repudiated.[110] And certainly there was a great surcharge of eschatological thinking, in which the missions-method came to play the dominant part. The teleological necessity of suffering remained, and with it the sense of participating in the last scene of a Great Drama. When the last cup of blood has been shed, they might look for the Day of Victory. The quiet eschatology which triumphed after Münster did not change the world view nor the expectation of a Kingdom on Earth; *it changed the attitude to power.*[111] And the manner of the coming of the Kingdom was for the *Stille* through the Pauline missions-method rather than by the "slaying of the godless" and revolution. The willingness to suffer martyrdom[112] for the Gospel was their strength.[113]

The expectation of a coming Kingdom of God on Earth, to which the faithful come through a welter of blood, can be seen to link the revolutionaries and the *Stille*.[114] The lack of historical concern which is frequently noted in Anabaptist thinking[115] was not truly non-historical, but rather stemmed from a contempt for the traditional things upon which God had already passed judgment and which were soon to pass away. Their unconcern with present matters was rooted in a great expectancy. Hübmaier said that those who deny a visible church and say his Kingdom is not of this world are faced with the prayer,

"Thy Kingdom come. . . . . ."[116]

The Hutterians expected the wrath to break out over the world, and eschatology blended with the theology of suffering in such manner as to blunt its harshness; but they retained confidence in the "restitution of all things" (*Acts* 3:21) to follow upon the Restitution of the Church.[117] The precise character of this impending finale was not clear. Some said that it would bring the return of created things, and others, only those things of which the prophets speak (*Isaiah* 66).[118] The revolutionaries expected the taking of the sword to herald His coming; the *Stille* replaced this act with the pilgrimage—mission—martyrdom method. For the *Stille* as well as revolutionaries the restitution of the True Church leads into a restoration of justice and peace in the world, but suffering, rather than violence, was the cooperative act of God and man which acted as the moving power of history. This was explicit in Menno:

"But the martyrdom of Stephen, in which there appears the Christ-pointed situation, is today relevant and primary. It shows not only that the disciple must undertake to follow the vision of Christ's suffering and death, but *how* he must do it. He cried in the way and manner of his Master on the Cross, Father do not count these sins unto them! That is according to Christ's mandate the new concept with which the elect conquer their fate, their opponents."[119]

The simple missioner, who went forth in obedience to the Lord's command, assumed thereby a significance as social strategist which never occurred to him in the period of our study.

The Verdict of History

We may find it fruitful to consider briefly at what point the spirit of renunciation ceased to be identified with a naive evangelical concern, and became instead the cultivated manner of a sectarian community. What happened in the years toward which the Anabaptists looked with such eager hearts? We are now in a position to assess the movement and its statesmanship, both in terms of internal discipline and in terms of the broad impact made upon society at large. What message and Christian testimony did the Anabaptist movement carry into the ongoing stream of Christian history, and over the world?

The problem has been put before in our discussion of the Restitution,[120] and it remains with us. In Biblical living the tension between "the Church" and "the world" is progressively overcome by the evangelical outreach of the community. The people of the Covenant is a special people, a royal priesthood (I *Peter* 2:9), with a special mission and responsibility for those who dwell in darkness. Judging from the subsequent history of the Anabaptists, which takes us into a period later than that involved in our study of the developed church view and indeed involves a basic transformation of it, two changes may occur which are prejudicial to a continued evangelical passion. 1) The adaptations accepted as necessary by those who determine to live responsibly, accepted at the time as new insights, become in fact a "going over to the world" which cancels out both special witness and missionary passion. This is the experience of the Dutch and Prussian Mennonite groups, who became in time opulent in economy, proud in intellect and effective in competition and war. 2) A strong internal discipline and agrarian economy at first developed in frontier flight from persecution, may lead in time to a completely self-centered religious and economic community, in which the inevitable egotism of a group living in history is translated into a genuine technological and cultural as well as religious primitivism. With the decline of the missionary passion, the latter fate is what overtook those groups which followed the frontier into Moravia, Transylvania, Russia, America and Paraguay.[121] In these apparently opposite resolutions of the tension there is a common factor: both later wings of the movement have lost in large degree the creative tension, the eager expectancy, the catalytic effect upon Church and society which was the original genius of Anabaptism.

But there is another and broader basis on which the significance of the Anabaptists may be judged: in terms of their early testimony for certain New Testament ordinances now widely taken for granted among Free Churches. Until the comprehensive history of sectarian Protestantism is written, we can only suggest the indebtedness of large sections of twentieth century Christianity to these early champions of Religious Liberty.[122] Certainly the true importance of the churches of the Restitution goes far beyond those communities which today admit lineal descent from the Anabaptist movement.

REFERENCES

PREFACE

1 Cf. for instance the comments of the religious sociologist, Joachim Wach, "Caspar Schwenckfeld, a Pupil and a Teacher in the School of Christ," XXVI *The Journal of Religion* (January, 1946) 1:1-29, 3.
2 Evans, Austin P., *An Episode in the Struggle for Religious Freedom: The Sectaries of Nuremberg, 1524-1528.* (N. Y., Columbia University Press, 1924), pp. 14-15.
3 *Infra*, p. 77.
4 Bainton, Roland H., *David Joris: Wiedertäufer und Kämpfer für Toleranz im 16. Jahrhundert* (Leipzig, M. Heinsius Nachf., 1937; Erg. Bd. VI *Archiv für Reformationsgeschichte*, p. 11.
5 Documents printed in Schornbaum, Karl, ed., *Quellen zur Geschichte der Wiedertäufer: Markgraftum Brandenburg* (Leipzig, M. Heinsius Nachf., 1934); XVI:2 *Quellen zur Reformationsgeschichte*. pp. 1-5 (Hereafter, *WtQ1934*).
6 The term "Bolshevik" is actually applied to the "Anabaptists" by partisan historians. See Smith, Preserved, *The Age of Reformation* (N. Y., Henry Holt & Co., 1920), ". . . . those Bolsheviki of the sixteenth century . . .", p. 154. Also, Dosker, Henry Elias, *The Dutch Anabaptists* (Phila., Judson Press, 1921), p. 66.
7 *Infra*, pp. 47 et seq.
8 Heyer, Fritz, "Der Kirchenbegriff der Schwärmer," 59 *SVRG* (1939) 156:1-108. p. 3. Perhaps worth noting is the fact that John Baillie, writing recently on *What is Christian Civilization?* (N. Y., Charles Scribner's Sons, 1945), settled upon the church view as the essential matter,—and especially cited the doctrine of baptism as the dividing point between traditional land church and sectarian views. pp. 34-35.

FORMER TREATMENTS OF ANABAPTISM

1 Whitney, James P., *History of the Reformation* (London, Macmillan Co., Ltd., 1940), First edition, 1907.
2 Smith, Preserved, *The Age of the Reformation* (N. Y., Henry Holt & Co., 1920), p. 244.
3 Lindsay, T. M., *A History of the Reformation* (N. Y., Charles Scribner's Sons, 1941), 2 volumes. First published, 1907. The chapter on Anabaptism is II of Book V in the second volume.
4 *Ibid.*, p. 431, footnote. His notation on the difference between articles on Anabaptism in the second (1877) and third (1896) editions of Herzog's *Realencyclopädie für protestantische Theologie und Kirche* is revealing.
5 *Ibid.*, p. 443. "The Anabaptists would have nothing to do with a State Church; and this was the main point in their separation from the Lutherans, Zwinglians and Calvinists. It was perhaps the *one* conception on which parties among them were in absolute accord. The real Church, which might be small or great, was for them an association of believing people . . . ."
6 *Ibid.*, p. 441. "For the whole Anabaptist movement was medieval to the core . . ." "The Swiss Anabaptists were in no sense disciples of Zwingli. They had held their distinctive principles and were a recognized community long before Zwingli came from Einsiedeln, and were the lineal descendants of the medieval Waldenses." p. 445. For discussion of this classification, *infra*, p. 112.
7 For a more competent treatment of the radicals in a general survey, see Chapter VIII of Williston Walker's *The Reformation* (N. Y., Charles Scribner's Sons, 1917); volume IX in *Ten Epochs of Church History*. "But though in many things thus representative of earlier tendencies, these extremer movements were even more children of the sixteenth century Reformation. They were called into

being by it. They were not demonstrably in organic continuity with the medieval anti-Roman sects . . . .'' p. 337.
Chapter XXXIX in Henry S. Lucas' *The Renaissance and the Reformation* (New York and London, Harper and Bros., Publ., 1934), is the most reliable textbook treatment of the Anabaptist movement.
Volume II, ''The Reformation,'' of *The Cambridge Modern History* (N. Y., The Macmillan Co., 1918), adds nothing to the discussion.

8 N. Y., The Macmillan Co., 1914, p. 345. Chapters X-XIII in Vedder's *A Short History of the Baptists* (Philadelphia, Am. Bapt. Publ. Soc'y., 1907), are much better done.

9 London, Methuen & Co., Ltd., 1928. For discussion of this idea, *infra*, p. 98.

10 *Infra*, p. 88.

11 *Infra*, p. 43

12 *Infra*, p. 65.

13 *Infra*, p. 16.

14 *Infra*, p. 20. For another discussion of the various schools of thought in interpreting and classifying Anabaptism, see Smucker, Donovan E., ''Anabaptist Historiography in the Scholarship of Today,'' XXII *MQR* (April, 1948) 2: 116-27.

15 Published in Wittenberg by Nickel Schirlentz; microfilm from the Columbia University Library (UTS). Found also in *Der Ander Teil/ der Bücher D. Mart: Luth:/* (Wittenberg, Georg Rhaw Erb, 1551), pp. 302f. Hereafter cited as *ML*1551.

16 *ML*1551, pp. 350f. Also at Union Theological Seminary.

17 Melanchthon in a letter of September 29, 1559, printed in *CR* IX, 926-30, 927. In 1551 appeared a less well known writing, *Von den Blutfreunden aus der Widertauff*, printed by Gervasius Sthürmer in Erfurt.

18 Of special importance is *Ein Bedencken/ der Luneburgeschen, ob/ einer oberkeit gezime die Wiederteuffer, odder andere Ketzer zum rech/ten glauben zu dringen* . . . . (Hamburg, Fr. Rhodum, 1537). There is a small item of importance in the President White Library at Cornell University, annotated by George Lincoln Burr—*Das welt/liche Oberkeit mit/den Widerteuffern mit/leiblicher straffe zu / wehren schueldig / sey / Etlicher be-/dencken zu Witeberg* (n. p., 1536).

19 In the same exchange, *Ein Sendbrieff Hans Huthe,/ etwa ains furnemen Vor/ steers im Widertauf/ferordenn* (1528); both were printed by A. Weyssenhorn at Augsburg.

20 Re-printed in *ML*1551, pp 400f.

21 Published in Hermannsburg, 1860; transl. by C. J. H. Fiek.

22 Items of note may be listed as follows:
Die Historia Thome Mün/tzers,/ des anfengers der Düringischen Auffrhur/ seer nützlich zu lesen (1525);
Vnderricht Philip. Melancht. / wider die Lere der / Widerteuffer auss / dem latein verdeutschet, durch/ Just. Jonas (1528);
Das weltliche Oberkeit den/ Widerteuffern mit leibliche Straffe zu wehren/ schüldig sey (1534);
Etliche propositiones wi/der die Lere der Widerteuffer gestelt (1535);
Wider das gottslesterlich vñ/ scheudlich buch/ so zu Münster im druck newlich ist ausgangen/ Etliche Propositiones (1535);
Verlegung etlicher vnchrist/licher Artikel/ welche die Widerteuffer furgeben (1536).
The second in the list indicates no printer (President White Library); the other items may be found re-printed in the order given in *ML*1551, pp. 473f, 382f, 281f, 391f, 282f.

23 Note also the works, *Dass vn/ser Christus Jesus warer Gott sey/ Zeug/neuss der heyligen geschrifft, Wi/der die newen Juden vñ Arria/ner, vnter Christlichen namen, / welche die Gottheyt Christi ver / leugnen.* (Nürnberg, Fr. Peypus, 1526); *Von der/ Erbsund, das sye der Christen Kynder gleich als/ wol verdamb als der heyden./ Vnd von dem heyligen Tauff ob er die Erbsund hynweg nem.* (Nürnberg, Fr. Peypus, 1527).

24 *Der Widdertaufer lere vñ gcheimnis . . . ..* p. cij.

25 *Von dem Geist der Widerteuffer . . . .*, p. Bij.

26 Friedmann, Robert, ''Conception of the Anabaptists,'' IX *CH* (1940) 341-65,

344. The works of Karl Ecke, Wilhelm Neuser, C. Sachsse, Lydia Müller, Anne-marie Lohmann may be mentioned in this category.

27 According to Holl, Thomas Müntzer introduced the authentic modern note, that religious reform is impossible without social reform at the same time, when he said economic change was necessary because the hard-working peasants didn't have time to read the Bible. "Luther und die Schwärmer," in *Gesammelte Aufsätze zur Kirchengeschichte* (Tübingen, J. C. B. Mohr, 1923), I, 445. The characteristic Anabaptist attitude to the state brings Holl to the judgment: "In this, our German concept is sharply distinguished from the sect-influenced English-American. We value the union with the state, the furthering and deep-ening of the (national) community, as a good which ranks higher than the free movement of the individual." p. 466.

28 Heyer, Fritz, "Der Kirchenbegriff der Schwärmer," 56 *SVRG* (1939) 156:1-108.

29 *Infra*, p. 13.

30 *Infra*, p. 28.

31 Report of the Second Disputation at Zürich (October 26-28, 1523), *CR*, LXXXIX, 641. The Disputations afford a primary source worthy of special note in Ana-baptist history, and have been too little sought. Several reports are well-known; *infra*, p. 17.

32 *CR*, XC, 355f.

33 *CR*, XCI, 188f.

34 *CR*, XCI, 577f.

35 Printed by Christopher Froschouer, Tiguri (Zürich).

36 Both works were printed by C. Froschouer at Zürich. With Menius' two best-known works they are the most frequently used contemporary writings about the radical groups.

37 See Bohatec, Josef, *Calvins Lehre von Staat und Kirche* (Breslau, M. & M. Mar-cus, 1937); volume 147 *Untersuchungen zur Deutschen Staats- und Rechtsge-schichte*, section III.

38 *CR*, XXXV, 45-142.

39 See his *Psychopannychia* (Orleans, 1534), and especially the second edition of 1544; *CR*, XXXIII, 165-232. Also, *Contra la secte phantastique et furieuse des Libertins, que se nomment spirituels* (Geneva, 1545); *CR*, XXXII, 145-252. Müller, Karl, "Calvin und die 'Libertiner'," XL *ZKG* (1922) N. F. 3:83-129.

40 Bullinger, Heinrich, *Der Wiederteuffern ursprung / fürgang / Secten wäsen / . . . .* (Zürich, Christoffel Froschower, 1541), p. 29a.

41 On Egli's significance as editor of sources, *infra*, p. 15.

42 Article by Loserth in *ML*, I, 606-08.

43 *Ibid.*, pp. 646-48. Like Erhard's writings, Fischer's are found in this country only in the Mennonite Historical Library at Goshen College, Goshen, Indiana.

44 Article by Christian Neff, *ML*, I, 333-34.

45 See Schottenloher, Karl, "Philip Ulhart: Ein Augsburger Winkeldrucker und Helfershelfer der 'Schwärmer' und 'Wiedertäufer' (1523-1529)," 4 *Historische Forschungen und Quellen* (1921) 1-160. Christoph Froschouer was one of the courageous champions of the "ars diabolica," following Hübmaier from Zürich to Nikolsburg after the split of Evangelicals and radicals.

46 Zieglschmid, A. J. F., ed., *Die Aelteste Chronik der Hutterischen Brüder* (Cayuga Press, Inc., Ithaca, N. Y., Carl Schurz Memorial Foundation, 1943), Footnote 2, p. xxv. (Hereafter cited as *Z*).

47 Hege, Christian, "Pilgram Marpeck's *Vermahnung*," in Neff, Christian, ed., *Gedenkschrift zum 400 Jährigen Jubiläum der Mennoniten oder Taufgesinnten 1525-1925* (Ludwigshafen am RH. Konferenz der Süddeutschen Mennoniten E. V., 1925), p. 178. (Hereafter, *Gedenkschrift*).

48 *Infra*, Chapter III. See Rembert, Karl, *Die 'Wiedertäufer' im Herzogtum Jülich* (Berlin, R. Gaertners Verlagsbuchhandlung, 1899), p. 207.

49 The corner-stone of the *Ausbund* was a section of 51 hymns from Swiss Brethren of the Auspitz Colony, imprisoned in Passau, Bavaria, 1535-37. Many of the early leaders and martyrs had given songs to the movement, including Felix Manz, Georg Wagner, Leonhard Schiemer, Hans Schlaffer, Georg Blaurock and Hans Hut. Later were added hymns from the Dutch Mennonites' *Het Offer des Heeren* (1562/63) and *Ein schön Gesangbüchlein geistlicher Lieder*, with 5 songs from the Bohemian Brethren. There may have been a first edition, no longer extant,

about 1570 or 1571; one dated 1583 is known, and is probably the first edition complete. There have been more than 30 editions in Europe and America, and the book is still used by the Old Order Amish. See article by Christian Hege in I *ML* (1913) 97; also, Bender, Harold S., "The First Edition of the Ausbund," III *MQR* (April, 1929) 2:147-50; Correll, Ernst, "The Value of Hymns for Mennonite History," IV *MQR* (July, 1930) 3:215.

50 Tieleman Jansz van Braght (1625-64) edited in 1660 a record of martyrdom which has gone through many editions: *Bloedig Tooneel of Martelaarsspiegel der Doopsgezinde en weerloose Christenen*. The latest edition, in English, was published at Scottdale, Pennsylvania, in 1938. Like the Ausbund, it indicates the central significance of suffering in the eschatology of the Anabaptists, and is of basic importance for understanding the movement; see Stauffer, Ethelbert, "Märtyrertheologie und Täuferbewegung," LII *ZKG* (1933) 545-98, 554, 559. The historical dependability of the Martyrs' Mirror was discussed by Samuel Cramer in "De Geloofwaardigheid van van Braght," *DB* (1899) 63-164, (1900) 184-210. A valuable critical edition is *A Martyrology of the Churches of Christ Commonly Called Baptist* (London, Hanserd Knollys Society, 1850-53), 2 volumes, ed. by Edw. B. Underhill.

51 See Chapter V of this writing.

52 On Mennonite historiography, article by Hege in *ML*, II, 96-101.

53 Appearing during the decade, 1839-49, they comprised the five volume *Geschiedenis der Doopsgezinden;* 1839—Friesland, 1842—two volumes on Groningen, Overyssel and Ost-Friesland, 1847—two volumes on Holland, Zeeland, Utrecht and Gelderland. Also of interest is the *Geschiedkundig naar den Waldenzischen Oorsprong van de Nederlandsch Doopsgezinden* (1844). His publishers were W. Eekhoff and J. B. Wolters, Leeuwarden en Groningen.
See article by J. Loosjes in *ML*, I, 335-36.

54 His "Ketzer-Geschichte," the third part of *Chronica, Zeÿtbüch und Geschichtbibel* (Strassburg, Balthassar Beck, 1531), is of special worth.
On Franck, see article by Neff in *ML*, I, 668-74; Bischof, Herman, *Sebastian Franck und deutsche Geschichtsschreibung* (Tübingen, Ernest Riecker, 1857), Hegler, A., *Geist und Schrift bei Sebastian Franck* (Freiburg i. B., J. C. B. Mohr, 1892), Oncken, Hermann, "Sebastian Franck als Historiker," 82 *HZ* (1889) 385-435; Reimann, Arnold, *Sebastian Franck als Geschichtsphilosoph* (Berlin, Alfred Unger, 1921), volume I of *Comenius-Schriften zur Geistesgeschichte*.
Note also Teufel, Eberhard, "Die Deutsche Theologie und Sebastian Franck im Lichte der neueren Forschung," N.F. 11 *Theologische Rundschau* (1939) 304-15, N.F. 12 (1940) 99-129.

55 See his *Kirchen- und Ketzer-Historie* (Frankfurt am Mayn, Thomas Fritsch, 1700), 2 volumes; shortly before he had become famous for *Die erste Liebe, eine Darstellung des äusseren und inneren Lebens der ersten Christen* (Frankfurt, 1696); printed in usable edition by Buchh. der Evang. Gesellschaft at Stuttgart, no date, edited by A. C. Lämmert.
On Arnold, see article by Neff in *ML*, I, 85-86; Seeberg, Erich, *Gottfried Arnold: die Wissenschaft und die Mystik seiner Zeit* (Meerane i. Sa., E. R. Herzog, 1923); Schröder, William Freiherr von, *Gottfried Arnold* (Heidelberg, Carl Winters Univ.-Buchh., 1917), volume 9 of *Beiträge zur Neueren Literaturgeschichte; Studien zu den Deutschen Mystikern des Siebzehnten Jahrhunderts, No. 1*.

56 von Mosheim followed a familiar line of thinking in his published works—*De rebus Christianorum ante Constantinum magnum commentarii* (C. F. Weygand, 1739), Dissertation at Helmsstedt, and other writings; he published many rare materials on "heretics," and especially on Servetus in *Anderweitiger Versuch einer vollständigen und unpartheyischen Ketzergeschichte* (Helmsstedt, C. F. Weygand, 1748-50), 2 volumes, and was especially long remembered in England and America (!).

57 Füsslin, Johann Konrad, *Neue und unpartheyische Kirchen- und Ketzerhistorie der mittlern Zeit* (Frankfurt and Leipzig, C. G. Hilschern, 1770-74), 3 volumes. He is sometimes called "the Swiss Gottfried Arnold"; note also his *Beyträge zur Erläuterung der Kirchen-Reformations-Geschichten des Schweizerlandes* (Zürich, Conrad Orell & Co., 1741-53), 5 volumes in III.
On Füsslin, see article by Neff in *ML*, II, 22.

58 *Infra*, p. 14.

59 *Ein Apostel der Wiedertäufer* (Leipzig, S. Hirzel, 1882), pp. iv, 30.

60 Ritschl, Albrecht, *Geschichte des Pietismus* (Bonn, Adolph Marcus, 1880); I, 22-36.

61 Kautsky, Karl, *Communism in Central Europe in the Time of the Reformation* (London, T. Fisher Unwin, 1897), also Bax, E. Belfort, *Rise and Fall of the Anabaptists* (London, Swan Sonnenschein & Co., Ltd., 1903). For a more sound study of like import, see Pascal, R., *The Social Basis of the German Reformation* (London, Watts & Co., 1933).

62 *The Social Teaching of the Christian Churches* (N. Y., The Macmillan Co., 1931); II, 693f. The German edition appeared in 1912; Troeltsch depended largely upon secondary sources, but his historical sense was sound; he was not pre-committed to hostile sources, nor was he afraid to discuss objectively the logic of free religious association.

63 *Ibid.*, II, 729f. See footnote 440, p. 949, praising Alfred Hegler's original research in *Geist und Schrift bei Sebastian Franck* (*op. cit.*), pp. 1-10. See also "Die Täufer und Spiritualisten," in "Protestantisches Christentum und Kirche in der Neuzeit," in P. Hinneberg's *Die Kultur in der Gegenwart* (Leipzig and Berlin, B. G. Teubner, 1922).

64 Article by Köhler in *Die Religion in Geschichte und Gegenwart* (Tübingen, J. C. B. Mohr, 1927-31), 2nd ed. V., 1915-17, 1915.

65 Tübingen, J. C. B. Mohr, 1925.

66 Karlsruhe i. B., Heinrich Schneider, 1936. Thesis at Heidelberg. Here used as it appears as a section of *Menno Simons (1496-1561)*, same publisher, same date.

67 *Geschichte des Münsterischen Aufruhrs* (Leipzig, T. O. Weigel, 1855), 3 books, 3rd not published; *Beilagen* especially important. Note also *Die Münsterischen Humanisten und ihr Verhältniss zur Reformation* (Münster, Theissingische Buchh., 1851).
On Cornelius, see article by H. Cornelius and C. Neff in *ML*, I, 372-74.

68 *Supra*, p. 12. Also, *Die Reformation und die älteren Reformparteien* (Leipzig, S. Herzel, 1885); IV *Vorträge und Aufsätze aus der Comenius-Gesellschaft* (1897) 1 & 2, for "Die Anfänge der Reformation und die Ketzerschulen."
On Keller, article by Neff in *ML*, II, 480.

69 Zürich, J. Schabelitz, 1879. On Egli, see article by C. Bergmann in *ML*, I, 508-09. (Hereafter, sources cited as *Egli*).

70 Wien, Carl Gerold's Sohn, 1883; XLIII *Fontes Rerum Austriacarum* (Hist. Comm. Kaiserl. Akad. der Wiss. in Wien), 2te Abth. (Hereafter, cited as *Beck*). On Beck, see article by Loserth in *ML*, I, 149.

71 s 'Gravenhage, Martinus Nijhoff, 1903-14. See Dosker, Henry Elias, "Recent Sources of Information on the Anabaptists of the Netherlands," *Papers of the American Society of Church History* V, (Second Series, 1917) 49-71. Hereafter, cited as *B. R. N.* On Cramer, see article by Fleischer in *ML*, I, 377-81.

72 Wolkan, Rudolph, *ed.*, *Geschicht-Buch der Hutterischen Brüder* (Macleod, Alberta and Wien, Carl Fromme Ges. m.b.H., 1923).
Zieglschmid, A. J. F., *ed.*, *op. cit.*; unfortunately, the utility of this volume backed by the Carl Schurz Memorial Foundation is seriously limited by peculiar typography.

73 Ridemann, Peter, *Rechenschaft unserer Religion, Lehr und Glaubens, von den Brüdern, so man die Hütterischen nennt, ausgangen. . . . 1565* (Ashton Keynes, Wilts., England, Cotswald-Bruderhof, 1938).
Several pamphlets have also been published by these colonies, which joined the Hutterians after World War I under the leadership of Eberhard Arnold, and have in Hutterian fashion migrated from Germany to England, and lately to Alto Paraguay.

74 The statement of the *Verein's* plan is found on pp. v-vi of Bossert, Gustav, *ed.*, *Quellen zur Geschichte der Wiedertäufer: Herzogtum Württemberg* (Leipzig, M. Heinsius Nachf., 1930). Hereafter cited as WtQ1930. Also Schornbaum, Karl, *ed.*, *Quellen zur Geschichte der Wiedertäufer:Markgraftum Brandenburg* (Leipzig, M. Heinsius Nachf., 1934); Hereafter, *WtQ1934*. And Müller, Lydia, *ed.*, *Glaubenszeugnisse oberdeutscher Taufgesinnter* (Leipzig, M. Heinsius Nachf., 1939); hereafter, *WtQ1938*. The three volumes appear as XIII:1, XVI:2, XX:1 of *Quellen und Forschungen zur Reformationsgeschichte*. On the post-war status of the series see the report in XXIII *MQR*, (January, 1949) 1:48-52. Two more

volumes in the series have recently appeared but were not available at the time of this study: Krebs, Manfred, *ed.*, *Quellen zur Geschichte der Täufer: Baden und Pfalz* (Gütersloh, C. Bertelsmann Verlag, 1951), XXI in *QFRG:* Schornbaum, Karl, *ed.*, *Quellen zur Geschichte der Täufer: Bayern, II. Abteilung* (Gütersloh, C. Bertelsmann Verlag, 1951), XXIII in *QFRG.*
75 Article by Cornelius Bergman in *ML*, I, 451-56.

THE QUEST FOR THE ESSENCE OF ANABAPTISM

1 Rauschenbusch, Walter, "The Zürich Anabaptists and Thomas Müntzer," IX *The American Journal of Theology* (1905) 91-106, 92.
2 *Beck*, footnote 2, p. 12.
3 *Ibid.*, p. 13.
4 As they called Zwingli and Luther, and other Evangelicals.
5 Schlaffer, Hans, "Ein Kurzer Underricht zum Anfang Eines Recht Christlichen Lebens," in *WtQ*1938; p 85.
6 Müller, Nikolaus, *Die Wittenberger Bewegung, 1521 und 1522* (Leipzig, M. Heinsius Nachf., 1911). Second edition No. 43 (1521), p. 88.
7 *Ibid.*, p. 143.
8 *Ibid.*, p. 160.
9 Wiswedel, W., *Bilder und Führergestalten aus dem Täufertum* (Kassel, J. G. Oncken, 1928-30), 2 volumes. I, 30.
10 *WtQ*1934; No. 6, (testimony of February, 1525), p. 7.
11 Barge, Hermann, *Andreas Bodenstein von Karlstadt* (Leipzig, Friedrich Brandstetter, 1905). I, 352. Further, II, 188f, for other evidences of a "Puritan" lay movement. The sharp ethical concern is common ground for both Wittenberg and Zürich radicals, but the latter gave attention to internal church discipline and were little concerned with general social reform.
12 First Sermon (March 9, 1522), *WA*, X, 3:1f, 6-7.   The sermons were preached on successive days and are of mollifying effect, a moderation in contrast with his later bitterness toward those who seemed to press too far and too fast.
13 Third Sermon (March 11, 1522); *ibid.*, p. 26.
14 Fourth Sermon, (March 12, 1522); *ibid.*, pp. 36f. The rulers were to make necessary rules putting down the "outward" forms.
15 "Wider die himmlischen Propheten," *WA*, XVIII, 37f, 111.
16 Second Sermon (March 10, 1522), p. 18.
17 Discussed in Loewenich, Walter v., *Luthers Theologia Crucis* (Munich, Chr. Kaiser Verlag, 1929); II:2 in *Forschungen zur Geschichte und Lehre des Protestantismus*, pp. 16, 39.
18 *Supra*, p. 5.
19 *op. cit.*
20 *WA*, XXX, 3:510f.
21 *WA*, LIV, 116f; XXX, 2:209f; XXVIII, 336f.
22 *WA*, XVIII, 279f.
23 *WA*, XVIII, 344f.
24 Third Sermon (March 11, 1522), p. 21.
25 Köhler, Walter, "Zu Luthers Kirchenbegriff," 21 *Die Christliche Welt* (April 18, 1907) 16:371-77, 373.
26 Bainton, Roland H., "The Development and Consistency of Luther's Attitude to Religious Liberty," 22 *Harvard Theological Review* (1929) 2:107-49.
27 "Wider die himml. Propheten" (*op. cit.*), p. 103.
28 Fifth Sermon (March 13, 1522), p. 45.
29 Bainton, Roland H., *Concerning Heretics . . . An anonymous work attributed to Sebastian Castellio* (New York, Columbia University Press, 1935). pp. 43-44.
30 They based their assumption upon Luther's "Von der Freiheit eines Christen Menschen," as noted in *WtQ*1938, p. xiii.
31 Böhmer, H., "Urkunden zur Geschichte des Bauernkrieges und der Wiedertäufer," 50/51 *Kleine Texte für Theologische und Philologische Vorlesungen und Uebungen* (1910) 1-35, 11f.
32 Franz, Günther, *Der deutsche Bauernkrieg* (München and Berlin, R. Oldenburg, 1933, 2 volumes. I, 408ff. Also Unruh, B. H., "Die Revolution 1925 und das

Täufertum,'' in Neff, Christian, *ed.*, *Gedenkschrift zum 400. Jährigen Jubiläum der Mennoniten oder Taufgesinnten, 1525-1925* (Ludwigshafen am RH, Konferenz der Süddeutschen Mennoniten E. V., 1925). pp. 35f. (Hereafter, *Gedenkschrift*)

33 Brandt, Otto H., *Thomas Müntzer: Sein Leben und seine Schriften* (Jena, Eugen Diedrichs Verlag, 1933), pp. 18-21.
On Müntzer, see Lohmann, Annemarie, ''Zur geistigen Entwicklung Thomas Müntzers,'' 47 *Beiträge zur Kulturgeschichte des Mittelalters und der Renaissance* (1931) 1-71. Also, in Schottenloher, Karl, *ed.*, *Bibliographie zur Deutschen Geschichte im Zeitalter der Glaubensspaltung, 1517-1585* (Leipzig, Karl W. Hiersemann, 1933-39). 5 volumes. Items 15957, 15995, 16001a. (Hereafter, *KSch*).

34 ''Ermahnung zum Frieden auf die Zwölf Artikel der Bauernschaft in Schwaben. 1525,'' *WA*, XVIII, 279f, 297.

35 *Ibid.*, p. 315.

36 ''Wider die räuberischen und mörderischen Rotten der Bauern. 1525,'' *WA*, XVIII, 344f, 358.

37 Scheel, Otto, ''Individualismus und Gemeinschaftsleben in der Auseinandersetzung Luthers mit Karlstadt 1524/25,'' XVII *ZTK* (1907) 352-75, 358. For the study in contrasts, see Müller, Karl, *Luther und Karlstadt* (Tübingen, J. C. B. Mohr, 1907), and, by the same author. *Kirche, Gemeinde und Obrigkeit nach Luther* (Tübingen, J. C. B. Mohr, 1910).

38 His brother-in-law, Gerhard Westerburg. was with him. Cornelius, C. A., *Geschichte des Münsterischen Aufruhrs* (Leipzig, T. O. Weigel, 1855), I, 39.

39 Bainton, Roland H., *loc. cit.*, p. 119.

40 Thus Otte, Joh. Heinrich, *Annales Anabaptistici* (Basel, Jacob Werenfels, 1672), p. 8, said the Swiss movement stemmed from Müntzer and Nicolaus ''Storck'', and from the work of Martin Borrhaus (Cellarius), who went from Wittenberg to join Oecolampadius, serving as Professor of Theology at the University of Basel until his death in 1564. p. 15.

41 Arnold, Gottfried, *Kirchen- und Ketzer-Historie* (Frankfurt am Mayn, Thomas Fritsch, 1700), 2 volumes. II: XVI, XXI, 262f. Both roots are to be strongly distinguished from Münster; 264a.

42 Letter of September 5, 1524; printed in *Gedenkschrift*, pp. 89-99. The latter was made available through Cornelius, C. A., *op. cit.*, I, 240. Cf. also p. 45, ftn. 1.

43 *Supra*, p. 13.

44 Burrage, Henry S., *A History of the Anabaptists in Switzerland* (Philadelphia, American Baptist Publication Society, 1882). Burrage gave a paramount place to Erasmus in the coming of the Swiss Reformation. Harold S. Bender minimizes the importance of Erasmus in the development of Conrad Grebel; see ''Conrad Grebel, the First Leader of the Swiss Brethren (Anabaptists),'' X, *MQR*, (1936) 5-45, 91-137, 151-60; XII *MQR*, (1938) 27-54, 114-34. p. 32. The Hutterians treasured the memory of Erasmus for his insight into the ethics of the New Testament; Müller, Lydia, ''Der Kommunimus der mährischen Wiedertäufer,'' 45 *SVRG* (1927).
On Erasmus, *Infra*, p. 53.

45 *The Complaint of Peace* (Chicago & London, Open Court Publ. Co., 1917). pp. 25-26.

46 Lüdemann, H., *Reformation und Täufertum in ihrem Verhältnis zum christlichen Princip* (Bern, W. Kaiser, 1896. p. 30.

47 Burckhardt-Biedermann, Th., *Bonifacius Amerbach und die Reformation* (Basel, R. Reich, 1894). pp. 30f.

48 Newman, Albert Henry, *A History of Anti-Pedobaptism* (Philadelphia, American Baptist Publication Society, 1897). pp. 103f. One of the best books of source material in this period is Kessler's *Sabbata*, edited by Emil Egli and Rudolph Schock (St. Gall, Fehr'sche Buchhandlung, 1902).

49 Usteri, J. M., ''Darstellung der Tauflehre Zwinglis,'' and ''Zwinglis Corres pondenz mit den Berner Reformatoren ueber die Tauffrage,'' 55 *TSK* (1882) 205f, 616f. Leo Jud was one of those who repeatedly expressed doubts regarding the union of Church and State (after the Cappel War), and in regard to infant baptism; Usteri, J. M., ''Leo Judae ueber die heilige Taufe,'' 56 *TSK* (1883) 618-20.

50 It has been claimed that it was the dispute with the Anabaptists on the issue of baptism that led Zwingli to the position that all sacraments are symbols only;

XXVII *Goshen College Record, Review Supplement* (1926) 4:11-12. A better known interpretation is that which attributes the symbolic view of the Eucharist to Hoen of the Brethren of the Common Lot; Hyma, Albert, *The Christian Renaissance* (N. Y. & London, The Century Co., 1925). pp. 332f.

51 Egli, Emil, *Die Züricher Wiedertäufer zur Reformationszeit* (Zürich, Friedrich Schulthess, 1878). pp. 14-17. Also No. 692 (April E,? 1525) in *Egli; 1*, 308-14. See also Burrage, Henry S., "The Anabaptists of the Sixteenth Century," III *Papers of the American Society of Church History* (1890) 145-64, 150. Zwingli was dealing in those compromises necessary to make the whole people officially Protestant. Of all leaders in the Continental Reformation he was the least disturbed by a close linking of secular authorities with the life of the Church.

52 On Grebel, see article by Neff in *ML*, II, 163-69; also articles by Bender, Harold S., *loc. cit.*; Yoder, Edw., articles in XXVII *Goshen College Record, Review Supplement* (1926) 33-37; *MQR*, I, 41-53; II, 229-59; III, 132-46. A biography by Bender has appeared: *Conrad Grebel (c. 1498-1526), the Founder of the Swiss Brethren Sometimes Called Anabaptists* (Goshen, Indiana, The Mennonite Historical Society, 1950). xvi, 326p.

53 *Egli*, No. 646 (Feb. 18 & 25, 1525), p. 289.

54 Loserth, Johann and Beck, Josef R., "Georg Blaurock und die Anfänge des Anabaptismus in Graubündten und Tirol," VII *Vorträge und Aufsätze aus der Comenius-Gesellschaft* (1889) 1-30, 1 & 2 parts. p. 9.

55 For the positive Anabaptist teaching on Baptism, *infra*, p. 76.

56 See *Preface*.

57 *Supra*, p. 24.

58 Zili challenged Zwingli for not having a similar policy in Zürich, and also objected to the oath required of the preachers at ordination. Horsch, John, *Mennonites in Europe* (Scottdale, Penna., Mennonite Publishing House, 1942); volume I of *Mennonite History*. p. 92.

59 Egli, Emil, *Die St. Galler Täufer* (Zürich, Friedrich Schulthess, 1887). p. 42.

60 There were repeated mandates against Anabaptists in Bern through the years—September 3, 1585; July 29, 1597; etc.—indicating that the movement was not utterly crushed out, although cruelly persecuted and scattered. A Commission for Anabaptist Matters was set up in 1589, and an Anabaptist Chamber as late as 1699.

61 Celio Secundo Curione was strongly idealistic concerning the example of the Early Church, and serves as a link between Swiss "Anabaptism" and the Italian Reformers in Naples, Venice and the Grisons. Benrath, Karl, "Wiedertäufer im Venetianischen um die Mitte des 16. Jahrhunderts," 58 *TSK* (1885) 9-67, 23.

62 On the extraordinary group which gathered in the city in the course of time, see Cantimori, Delio, "Inconti Italo-Germanici Nell'eta della Riforma," Reprint. pp. 77-78.

63 Burckhardt, Paul, *Die Basler Täufer* (Basel, R. Reich, 1898). pp. 13f.

64 Oecolampadius' report on the First Disputation led to a counter-report by Hübmaier, followed by a lengthy exchange. Smithson, R. J., *The Anabaptists* (London, James Clarke & Co., Ltd., 1935). pp. 176-77. On December 29, 1529, he participated in a Third Disputation with the Anabaptist leaders in jail.

65 Note the planning in the Martyr Synod (1527); *infra*, p. 101.

66 On Hübmaier (? - 1528), see the article by Loserth in *ML*, II, 353-63; also the article by Hegler in *RE³*, VIII, 418-24. Further, Loserth, Johann, *Doctor Balthasar Hubmaier und die Anfänge der Wiedertaufe in Mähren* (Brünn, R. M. Rohrer, 1893); *ibid.*, "Die Stadt Waldshut und die vorderösterreichische Regierung," XXXVII *Archiv für österreichische Geschichte* (1891) 93-147; Mau Wilhelm, *Balthasar Hübmaier* (Berlin, Dr. Walter Rothschild, 1912). XL *Abhandlungen zur Mittleren und Neueren Geschichte;* Newman, A. H., "Balthazar Hübmaier and the Moravian Anabaptists," XXVII *Goshen College Record, Review Supplement* (1926) 10:4-22; Sachsse, Carl, *D. Balthasar Hubmaier als Theologe* (Berlin, Trowitzsch & Sohn, 1914). XX *Neue Studien zur Geschichte der Theologie und der Kirche;* Vedder, Henry C., *Balthasar Hübmaier: The Leader of the Anabaptists* (N. Y. & London, G. P. Putnam's Sons, 1905). VIII *Heroes of the Reformation*.

67 Sachsse, Carl, *op. cit.*, pp. 187, 190.

68 *Ibid.*

69 For a fuller discussion, *infra*, p. 78. Schubert, Hans von, *Revolution und Reformation im XVI. Jahrhundert* (Tübingen, J. C. B. Mohr, 1927); no. 128 in *Sammlung Gemeinverständliche Vorträge und Schriften aus dem Gebiet der Theologie und Religionsgeschichte*. p. 26.

70 Heyer, Fritz, "Der Kirchenbegriff der Schwärmer," 56 *SVRG* (1939) 156:1-108, 68. See the discussion in Chapter V.

71 Horsch, John, *op. cit.*, p. 315.

72 *Beck*, p. 9.

73 Burckhardt, Paul, *op. cit.*, pp. 123-24. Egli, Emil, *Die Züricher Wiedertäufer* (*op. cit.*), p. 31.

74 Egli, Emil, *Die St. Galler Täufer* (*op. cit.*), pp. 44-45.

75 Neuser, Wilhelm, *Hans Hut. Leben und Wirken bis zum Nikolsburger Religionsgespräch* (Berlin, Hermann Blanke, 1913). p. 19. On the radical circles at Nürnberg see article on Albrecht Dürer by Karl Rembert in I *ML* (1913) 486-93.

76 Testimony No. 14 (November 28, 1529), printed in *WtQ*1930, pp. 921-22. Other documents on this strange episode follow. See Bossert, Gustav, "Augustin Bader von Augsburg, der Prophet und König, und seine Genossen, nach den Prozessakten von 1530," X *ARG:Texte und Untersuchungen* (1912/13) 117-65, 209-41, 297-349.

77 See article on "Augsburger Täufergemeinde" by Hege in *ML*, I, 92-96. On Denck and the middle cities see Keller, Ludwig, *Ein Apostel der Wiedertäufer* (Leipzig, S. Hirzel, 1882). pp. 6-12. On the Martyr Synod, see *infra*, p. 101.

78 He wanted the inner and non-sectarian truth sought by all parties. "Falsche Propheten reden nur von Schrift und nicht auch von Gegenschrift." Keller, Ludwig, *op. cit.*, p. 71. This theme was dominant in Sebastian Franck.

79 Hulshof, Abraham, *Geschiedenis van de Doopsgezinden te Straatsburg van 1525 tot 1557* (Amsterdam, J. Clausen, 1905). pp. 5f.

80 Loserth, Johann, "Studien zur Pilgram Marpeck," in *Gedenkschrift*. p. 140.

81 On Hofmann, see article by Neff in *ML*, II, 326-35; article by Hegler in *RE*³, VIII, 222-27; Krohn, Barthold Nicolaus, *Geschichte der Fanatischen und Enthusiastischen Wiedertäufer, Melchior Hofmann und die Secte der Hofmannianer* (Leipzig, Bernhard Christoph Breitkopf, 1758); zur Linden, Friedrich Otto, *Melchior Hofmann, ein Prophet der Wiedertäufer* (Haarlem, de Erven F. Bohn, 1885). XI:2 *Verhandelingen uit gegeven door Teylers Godgeleerd Genootschap*. Further, in *KSch*: 8518, 8521.

82 Article on Nicolaus von Amsdorf by Neff in *ML*, I, 58. See also Neff's article on "Johann Bugenhagen," *ibid.*, p. 290. B. reported the Flensburg Disputation, and was led thereby into violent controversy with Hofmann.

83 *Infra*, pp. 40f.

84 *Supra*, p. 20.

85 On Denck, see article by Neff in *ML*, I, 401-14; Coutts, Alfred, *Hans Denck (1495-1527): Humanist and Heretic* (Edinburgh, Macniven and Wallace, 1927); Keller, Ludwig, *op. cit.* Further, in *KSch*: 3684, 3697, 3699, 3701, 3704.

86 On Hetzer, see article by Neff in *ML*, II, 225-31; article by Hegler in *RE*³, VII, 325-29; Keim, Theodor, "Ludwig Hetzer. Ein Beitrag zur Characteristik der Sektenbewegung in der Reformationszeit," I *Jahrbücher für Deutsche Theologie* (1856) 215-88; Weis, Frederic Lewis, *The Life and Teachings of Ludwig Hetzer* (Dorchester, Massachusetts, Underhill Press, 1930).

87 On Bünderlin, see article by Neff in *ML*, I, 298-300; Nicoladoni, Alexander, *Johannes Bünderlin von Linz und die oberösterreichischen Täufergemeinde in den Jahren 1525-1531* (Berlin, R. Gaertners Verlags, 1893).

88 *Supra*, p. 11.

89 On Schwenckfeld, note the *Corpus Schwenckfeldianorum* (Norristown, Penna., The Board of Publication of the Schwenckfelder Church, 1907ff); final Editor, Elmer E. S. Johnson. (Hereafter cited as CS). Also Ecke, Karl, *Schwenckfeld, Luther, und die Gedanken einer apostolischen Reformation* (Berlin, Martin Warneck, 1911); article by Grützmacher in *RE*³, XVIII, 72-81. Further in *KSch*: 19623, 19624, 19649, 19722.

90 Schlaffer, Hans, "Gebet und Danksagung," in *WtQ*1938, 96-98, 97.

91 Stadler, Ulrich, ''Vom lebendig wort und geschribnen,'' *WtQ*1938, 212-15, 214.
92 *Ibid.*, p. 212.
93 Arnold, Gottfried, *op. cit.*, II, XVI, XXII: 267.
94 Horsch, John, *op. cit.*, quoting one of Denck's associates: ''I have found, as it were, a middle way between popery and Lutheranism, by which I have avoided all separation, and am striving alone for a good, upright Christian life.'' p. 158. Refuting Denck's reported recantation, see Keller, Ludwig, *op. cit.*, p. 222.
95 Quoted in Keller, Ludwig, *op. cit.*, p. 55.
96 Nicoladoni, Alexander, *op. cit.*, pp. 107, 131.
97 *Ibid.*, p. 138.
98 Hegler, A., *Geist und Schrift bei Sebastian Franck* (Freiburg i. Br., J. C. B. Mohr, 1893), pp. 262-63. Troeltsch regarded Franck as the prototype of a third church-view besides the Church and sect-types: the individual Christian, modern and without formal attachment. Troeltsch, Ernst, *The Social Teaching of the Christian Churches* (New York, The Macmillan Co., 1931). 2 volumes. II, 933f. Note also Glawe, Walther, *Sebastian Francks Unkirchliches Christentum* (Leipzig, Dörffling & Franke, 1912). Paracelsus, in the first article of his ''De septem punctis idolatriae Christianae,'' discoursed upon the uselessness of going to Church. All ''forms'' are idolatry; Peuckert, Will-Erich, *Pansophie* (Stuttgart, W. Kohlhammer, 1936). p. 261. However, some of the most significant mystics also wrestled with the meaning of community, and this may suggest another dividing line in our discussion of types; Bornkamm, Heinrich, *Mystik, Spiritualismus und die Anfänge des Pietismus im Luthertum* (Giessen, Alfred Töpelmann, 1926). 44 *Vorträge der theol. Konf. zu Giessen.* p. 11.
99 Wenger, John C., ''Pilgram Marpeck, Tyrolese Engineer and Anabaptist Elder,'' IX *CH* (1940) 24-36, 24. Further on Marpeck, see articles by Wenger in XII *MQR* (1938) 136f, 167f, 205f, 269f; Loserth, Johann, ''Studien zu Pilgram Marpeck,'' and Hege, Christian, ''Pilgram Marpeck's Vermahnung,'' in *Gedenkschrift*, pp. 134f, 178f. Also *KSch*: 14832.
100 Burrage, Champlin, *The Church Covenant Idea* (Philadelphia, American Baptist Publication Society, 1904). Chapter I, and especially pp. 15f.
101 Text published in *Gedenkschrift*, pp. 185f.
102 Loserth, Johann, *loc. cit.*, pp. 152ff.
103 *Ibid.*, pp. 166f.
104 *CS*, III, 830-34. This appeared after a debate in which Capito and Schwenckfeld faced Jakob Kautz; the Brethren based their cause upon the Great Commission.
105 *Ibid.*, VIII, 161f. This was to refute the *Vermanung* of the Brethren; it called forth the *Verantwortung.*
106 *Ibid.*, VII, 161f, for a discussion of the relation of Schwenckfeld to the Anabaptists, with bibliography.
107 *Ibid.*, III, 489-90.
108 Loserth, Johann, *loc. cit.*, p. 150.
109 He also was indebted to Hoen; Hyma, Albert, *The Christian Renaissance* (*op. cit.*), p. 332.
110 Apparently Calvin learned from the Strassburg Reformers something of the church discipline and missionary intensity which marked the Anabaptists, and appropriated from them. See article on Calvin in *ML*, I, 314-17; also Hulshof, Abraham, *op. cit.*, Ch. XI. Cf. Schwarz, Rudolf, *ed.*, *Johannes Calvins Lebenswerk in seinen Briefen* (Tübingen, J. C. B. Mohr, 1909), I, No. 96 (March 24, 1543), pp. 163-64.
111 For a thorough treatment of possible links between Anabaptism and Pietism, with a generally negative conclusion as to the significance of such ties, see Friedmann, Robert, *Mennonite Piety Through the Centuries* (Goshen, Indiana, Mennonite Historical Society, 1949). Esp. first four chapters.
112 Dosker, Henry Elias, *The Dutch Anabaptists* (Philadelphia, The Judson Press, 1921). pp. 87-88.
113 Kühler, W. J., *Geschiedenis der Nederlandsche Doopsgezinden in de Zestiende Eeuw* (Haarlem, H. D. Tieck Willink & Zoon, N. V., 1932). Chapter III.
114 On Hans Hut, see article by Loserth in *ML*, II, 370-75; see also article by Hegler in *RE*[3], VIII, 489-91; Neuser, Wilhelm, *Hans Hut, Leben und Wirken bis zum Nikolsburger Religionsgespräch* (Berlin, Hermann Blanke, 1913).

115 Testimony No. 19 (March 26, 1527), at Nürnberg; in *WtQ*1934, p. 19.

116 Wappler, Paul, *Die Täuferbewegung in Thüringen von 1526-1584* (Jena, Gustav Fischer, 1913) ; II *Beiträge zur neueren Geschichte Thüringens.* pp. 26f.

117 Testimony No. 45 (Sept. 22, 1527), in *WtQ*1934, p. 37.

118 No. 51 (Hans Hut's answers to questioning), in *WtQ*1934, p. 55.

119 In his final deposition of Oct. 5, 1527, he said that he gave up revolution through Denck's influence; Keller, Ludwig, *op. cit.,* pp. 41-42.

120 Meyer, Christian, ''Zur Geschichte der Wiedertäufer in Oberschwaben: 1. Die Anfänge des Wiedertäuferthums in Augsburg,'' I *Zeitschrift des Historischen Vereins für Schwaben und Neuberg* (1874) 207-56, 231ff.

121 *WtQ*1938, p. 10 ff.

122 Rembert, Karl, *Die 'Wiedertäufer' im Herzogtum Jülich* (Berlin, R. Gaertners Verlagsbuchh., 1899), p. 207.
On Campanus, see article by Rembert in *ML*, I, 317-24; also article by Hegler in *RE*3, III, 696-98; note ''Dissertatio de Joanne Campano Anti-Trinitario'' in Schelhorn, J. G., ed., *Amoenitates Literariae* (Frankfurt & Leipzig, Daniel Bartholomew & Söhne, 1729), Volume XI, pp. 1-92.

123 Sixteen Articles (August 10, 1532) ; Detmer, Heinrich, and Krumbholtz, Robert, ed., *Zwei Schriften des Münsterischen Wiedertäufers Bernhard Rothmann* (Dortmund, Fr. Wilh. Ruhfus, 1904), p. LIII.

124 In the ''Bekentnisse van beyden Sacramenten,'' in which Rothmann also portrayed the Supper as a symbol of Christian communism. Schiedung, Hans, *Beiträge zur Bibliographie und Publizistik uber die Münsterischen Wiedertäufer* (Münster, Heinrich Buschmann, 1934), p. 11.

125 Quoted and discussed in Bergfried, Ulrich, *Verantwortung als Theologisches Problem im Täufertum des 16. Jahrhunderts* (Wuppertal-Elberfeld, A. Martini & Gruttefien, 1938), p. 45.

126 Confession of Dionisius of Diest (1534) ; Niesert, Joseph, *Münsterische Urkundensammlung* (Coesfeld, Bernhard Wittneven, 1826), I *Urkunden zur Geschichte der Münsterischen Wiedertäufer.* p. 48.

127 Cf. the discussion of eschatology in Hase, Karl, *Neue Propheten: Drei historische-politische Kirchenbilder* (Leipzig, Breitkopf and Härtel, 1851), III— ''Das Reich der Wiedertäufer,'' pp. 145f, 244.

128 Cornelius, C. A., *Die Niederländischen Wiedertäufer während der Belagerung Münsters 1534 bis 1535* (München, Akademie, 1861), Reprint. p. 5.

129 Burrage, Champlin, *op. cit.,* p. 22.

130 Bouterwek, K. W., ''Zur Wiedertäufer-Literatur,'' I *Zeitschrift des Bergischen Geschichtsvereins* (Bonn, 1864) 3:280-344; article by Keller in XXIX *ADB* (1889) 362-70.

131 Geisberg, Max, *Das Wiedertäuferreich* (München, Hugo Schmidt Verlag, 1929), The key city becomes a total pattern and symbol of impending world sovereignty; Schiedung, Hans, *op. cit.,* p. 75.

132 Dosker, Henry Elias, *op. cit.,* p. 83.

133 Liefmann, Robert, *Die Kommunistischen Gemeinden in Nord-Amerika* (Jena, Gustav Fischer, 1922), p. 7. Liefmann depended upon Kautsky at this point.

134 Schubert, Hans von, ''Der Kommunismus der Wiedertäufer in Münster und seine Quellen,'' X:11 *Sitzungsberichte der Heidelberger Akademie der Wissenschaften. Phil.-Hist. Klasse* (1919). pp. 3-7.

135 Detmer, Heinrich, *Bilder aus den religiösen and sozialen Unruhen in Münster während des 16. Jahrhunderts* (Münster, Coppenrathsche Buchh., 1903-04), 3 volumes. II—''Bernhard Rothmann,'' p. 156.

136 The parallelism with early Mormon experience and teaching will not escape the reader. Ochino was banished from Zürich at the age of 76 for saying this, although probably only using a traditional formula to cover the patriarchs; Bainton, Roland H., ''The Immoralities of the Patriarchs According to the Exegesis of the Late Middle Ages and of the Reformation,'' *Harvard Theological Review* (1930), p. 39-49, 45. See discussion with an immense amount of material in Rockwell, William Walker, *Die Doppelehe des Landgrafen Philipp von Hessen* (Marburg, N. G. Elwertsche Verlagsbuchh., 1904).

137 Detmer, Heinrich, *op. cit.,* I (''Johann von Leiden''), 46. There is no Anabaptist source for Polygamy; witness Hofmann's excommunication of Klaus

Frey. *Ibid.*, III (''Ueber die Auffassung von der Ehe und die Durchführung der Vielweiberei in Münster während der Täuferherrschaft''), 230f.

138 *Z*, p. 87. See article by Loserth on the Diener der Notdurft *ML* I, 440-42.

139 On Huter, see article by Loserth in *ML*, II, 375-78. Also, in Horsch, John, *The Hutterian Brethren, 1528-1931.* (Goshen, Indiana, Mennonite Historical Society, 1931); number II of *Studies in Anabaptist and Mennonite History.*

140 *Z*, p. 65.

141 Müller, Lydia, *loc cit.*, pp. 53f.

142 Several letters and reports are printed in *WtQ*1930, pp. 1086f.

143 *Infra*, p. 104.

144 *Infra*, Chapter V.

145 Krohn, Barthold Nicolaus, *op. cit.*, p. 248.

146 Braght, T. J, van, *A Martyrology of the Churches of Christ Commonly called Baptist* (London, Hanserd Knollys Society, 1850-53), 2 volumes. II, 195f.

147 Kühler, W. J., *op. cit.*, p. 4.

148 On Menno (1496?-1561) see the article by Cramer in *RE*³, XII, 586-94; biography by Horsch, John, *Menno Simons* (Scottdale, Penna., Mennonite Publishing House, 1916); Krahn, Cornelius, *Menno Simons* (Karlsruhe i. B., Heinrich Schneider, 1936). Further in *KSch*: 15576.

149 Brons, A., *Ursprung, Entwicklung und Schicksale der Taufgesinnten oder Mennoniten* (Norden, Diedr. Soltau, 1884), p. 64.

150 Mrs. Brons attributes the glorification of the Early Church primarily to the Brethren of the Common Lot; *ibid.*, pp. 56f.

151 Bergfried, Ulrich, *op. cit.*, pp. 49-50.

152 Krahn, Cornelius, *op. cit.*, pp. 124f.

153 *Ibid.*, pp. 104-05.

154 Horsch, John, *Menno Simons* (*op. cit.*,), p. 50.

155 Quoted in Horsch, John, ''Menno Simons' Attitude toward the Anabaptists of Münster,'' X *MQR* (1936) 55-72, 57. The Hutterians called the Münster event a Lutheran error; *Z*, p. 144.

156 Krahn, Cornelius, *op. cit.*, pp. 143ff.

157 Friedmann, Robert, ''Conception of the Anabaptists,'' IX *CH* (1940) 4:341-65. For a stimulating classification of the Anabaptists in terms of radically Christian discipleship, see Bender, Harold S., ''The Anabaptist Vision,'' XIII *CH* (March, 1944) 1:3-24. For a conservative statement of inter-relationships in the early period, see Friedmann's ''The Encounter of Anabaptists and Mennonites with Anti-Trinitarianism,'' XXII *MQR* (1948) 3:139-162.

158 According to a suggestive discussion in an article of that title by Roland H. Bainton, in XXI *The Journal of Religion* (1941) 2:24-34.

CHRISTIAN PRIMITIVISM: THE FALL OF THE CHURCH

1 See *Preface.*

2 Lovejoy, Arthur O., *et al.*, *A Documentary History of Primitivism and Related Ideas* (Baltimore, Johns Hopkins Press, 1935), (Volume I — ''. . . . in Antiquity'') p. ix. Lovejoy also made representative studies of primitivism in the Church Fathers; cf. his ''The Communism of St. Ambrose,'' III *The Journal of the History of Ideas* (1942) 4:458-68, and '''Nature' as Norm in Tertullian,'' reprinted in *Essays in the History of Ideas* (Baltimore, Johns Hopkins Press, 1948), pp. 308-38. For the use of primitivist motifs in the Middle Ages, see Boas, George, *Essays on Primitivism and Related Ideas in the Middle Ages* (Baltimore, Johns Hopkins Press, 1948).

3 According to Hans von Schubert, Sebastian Franck drew upon a source which defended theft on the ground that all things are common ''as the Greek philosophers say.'' Von Schubert suspected Seneca's Epistle 90 was the source, and also showed the influence of Seneca's primitivism upon Erasmus, Colet and More. Von Schubert, Hans, ''Der Kommunismus der Wiedertäufer in Münster und seine Quellen,'' X *Sitzungsberichte der Heidelberger Akad. der Wiss.—Phil.-Hist. Klasse* (1919) 11:46-47.

4 Burdach, Konrad, *Reformation, Renaissance, Humanismus* (Berlin and Leipzig, Paetel Brothers, 1926), 2d. edition. p. 174f.

5 Pastor, Antonio, *The Idea of Robinson Crusoe* (Watford, Herts., England, Góngora Press, 1930), p. 302.

6 Bissell, Benj., *The American Indian in English Literature of the Eighteenth Century* (New Haven, Yale University Press, 1925), pp. 17-19. Chinard, Gilbert, *L'Exoticisme Amèricain dans la Litterature Francaise au XVIᵉ Siècle* (Paris, Libraire Hachette et Cⁱᵉ, 1911), p. xvi.

7 Egli, No. 691, p. 307. When a group escaped from Zürich prison, March, 1526, some suggested going to "den roten Juden" over the sea. Correll corrected the date (given by Egli as April, 1525) and the phrase by reference to the material in the Zürich State Archives. It should read "Inden" instead of "Juden", and Correll considers the report a serious suggestion. Correspondence of 5/4/44.

8 Stadelmann, Rudolph, *Vom Geist des ausgehenden Mittelalters* (Halle, Max Niemeyer, 1929), XV *Deutsche Vierteljahrschrift für Literaturwissenschaft und Geistesgeschichte.* p. 223.

9 Ferguson, Wallace K., "Humanist Views of the Renaissance," XLV *The American Historical Review* (October, 1939) I: reprint, p. 3f.

10 Hyma, Albert, *The Christian Renaissance* (N. Y. & London, The Century Co., 1925). See also Ullmann, C., *Reformers before the Reformation* (Edinburgh, T. & T. Clark, 1855), 2 volumes, translated.

11 Hyma, Albert J., *The Youth of Erasmus* (Ann Arbor, University of Michigan Press, 1930), Mestwerdt, Paul, *Die Anfänge des Erasmus* (Leipzig, Rudolph Haupt, 1917); volume II *Studien zur Kultur und Geschichte der Reformation.* On his relation to Anabaptism see Rembert, Karl, *Die 'Wiedertäufer' im Herzogtum Jülich* (Berlin, R. Gaertners Verlagbuchh., 1899), p. 194.

12 Burckhardt-Biedermann, Th., *Bonifacius Amerbach und die Reformation* (Basel, R. Reich, 1894), "Good God! What unchristian strife has sprung from books when simple Love alone is 'Christian'!" p. 37.

13 *Supra,* p. 7.

14 Benz, Ernst, *Ecclesia Spiritualis* (Stuttgart, W. Kohlhammer, 1934). Cf. also Grundmann, Herbert, *Studien über Joachim von Floris* (Leipzig and Berlin, B. G. Teubner, 1927).

14b *Ibid.,* p. 22.

14c *Ibid.,* p. 27.

14d *Ibid.,* p. 36.

14e *Ibid.,* p. 37.

14f *Ibid.,* p. 310.

14g *Ibid.,* pp. 313, 362f.

14h *Ibid.,* p. 357.

14i *Ibid.,* p. 66.

15 Hobhouse, Walter, *The Church and the World in Idea and in History* (London, Macmillan & Co., Ltd., 1910), pp. ix-x.

16 Heering, G. J., *The Fall of Christianity* (N. Y., Fellowship Publications, 1943), First published in 1928—*De Zondeval van het Christendom.*

17 *Ibid.,* p. 33.

18 Hyma, Albert, The *Christian Renaissance (op. cit.)*, p. 61.

19 Lovejoy, A. O., *et al., op. cit.,* pp. 32f, 61f.

20 Z., p. 298.

21 Lovejoy, A. O., *et al., op. cit.,* p. 53. Cf. also Boas George, *op. cit.,* pp. 103, 119.

22 "Ein Epistl an die gmain zu Rottenburg geschrieben, darinnen hübsche erklärungen der 12 haupt stück unsers christlichen glaubens begriffen sein," *WtQ*1938, p. 56.

23 Spitalmeier's court testimony, Nürnberg; No. 70 (Dec. 1527), in *WtQ*1934, p. 64.

24 *Beck,* pp. 169-73.

25 Rideman, Peter, *Rechenschaft unserer Religion, Lehr und Glaubens, von den Brüdern, so man die Hutterischen nennt, ausgangen . . . . 1565* (Ashton Keynes, Wilts., England, Cotswold-Bruderhof. 1938), p. 92f.

26 "Eine liebe unterrichtung Ulrichen Stadlers, diener des Worts, der sünd halben und des ausschluss, wie er darinen stehe, auch gemainschaft der zeitlichen güeter halben. Wider die, so des Herrnwerk pand und strick schelten, mit warhaftiger zeugnus heiliger geschrift, wie hernach volget," in *WtQ*1938, pp. 215-27, 225.

27 Lovejoy, A. O. *et al., op. cit.*, pp. 96, 119f, 140f. Boas, George, *op. cit.*, pp. 43, 111, 122, 212-13. Cf. Boas, on the monks' use of New Testament texts: "Such texts give us a verbal picture of the Christian who is ascetic, poor in worldly goods, free even when enslaved by a terrestrial master, careless of the future, wise without learning. It is not to be wondered that such a person was confused with the pagan Sage of the 'ethical period' nor that the monastic life was described as 'the life of philosophy'." p. 107.
On the other hand, medieval Christian primitivism also had its anti-intellectual expressions; Gregory the Great spoke contemptuously of those "who receive more the talents of the learned than the simple life of the innocent." p 122.

28 Given May 12, 1531; printed in *WtQ*1934, No. 267, pp. 243-47, 244.

29 Lovejoy, A. O. *et al., op. cit.* p. 112 Boas, George, *op. cit.*, pp. 30. 127-28, 187.

30 Hut, Hans, "Vom geheimnus der tauf, baide des zaichens und des wesens, ein anfang eines rechten warhaftigen Christlichen lebens; Joan:5," printed in *WtQ*1938, pp. 14-27, 17.
Schlaffer, Hans, "Ein kurzer bericht und leer eines recht christlichen lebens;" *ibid.*, pp. 94-96, 95.
In Sebastian Franck's writing Nature was extolled as Life and Being, and Art was condemned as appearance and sham; he favored the peasants and liked the fable of the town and country mouse. Reimann, Arnold, *Sebastian Franck als Geschichtsphilosoph* (Berlin, Alfred Unger, 1921); I *Comenius-Schriften zur Geistesgeschichte*, p. 97.

31 *Supra*, p. 51.

32 Mestwerdt, Paul, *op. cit.*, pp. 32, 43. The normative use of the Early church probably came to the Anabaptists largely from Zwingli; Köhler, Walter, "Ulrich Zwingli und die Reformation in der Schweiz," in Pflugk-Harttung, Julius von, *Im Morgenrot der Reformation* (Hersfeld, Vertriebsanstalt christl. Kunstwerk, 1912), pp. 669-715, 675.

33 Lovejoy, A. O., *et al., op. cit.*, p. 19. Boas George, *op. cit.*, p. 21.

34 "Eine liebe unterrichtung Ulrichen Stadlers," printed in *WtQ*1938, pp. 215-27, 226.

35 *WtQ*1938, p. xxi.

36 Stauffer, Ethelbert, "Märtyrertheologie und Täuferbewegung," LII *ZKG* (1933) 545-98, 549. Recently translated in large part by Robert Friedman, XIX *MQR* (1945) 3:179-214.

37 Schlaffer, Hans, "Ein Kurzer Underricht zum Anfang Eines Recht Christlichen Lebens," printed in *WtQ*1938, pp. 84-93, 84.

38 Wilbur, Earl Morse, *ed., A History of the Polish Reformation by Stanislaus Lubieniecki*. MSS, p. 33. Book III, Chapter 32, in Eusebius' *Historia Ecclesiae.*

39 Wilbur, E. Morse, *A History of Unitarianism* (Cambridge, Harvard University Press, 1945), pp. 142-43. Also, Trechsel, Fr., *Die protestantischen Antitrinitarier vor Faustus Socin.* (Heidelberg, Karl Winter, 1844), 2 volumes. I, 123.

40 Krahn, Cornelius, *Menno Simons*, p. 136.

41 Bainton, Roland H., "The Left Wing of the Reformation," XXI *The Journal of Religion* (1941) 2:124-34, 125, 128. In Sebastian Franck's scheme of history there is a Fall at those times when the "Church" and the "World" are co-extensive, amalgamated: with Constantine, when the Saxons were "converted" by the sword of Charlemagne, or in the territorial principle of the Reformers. Endriss, Julius, *Sebastian Francks Ulmer Kämpfe* (Ulm a. D., Dr. Karl Hohn, 1935), p. 5.

42 Z, p. 34.

43 *Supra*, p. 47.

44 Seeberg, Erich, *Gottfried Arnold: die Wissenschaft und die Mystik seiner Zeit* (Meerane i.Sa., E. R. Herzog, 1923), p. 435.

45 It is interesting to note that the periodization of Christian history remains the same whether the triumph of the Eusebian martyr-history under Constantine is regarded with delight or dismay. Luther took the triumph at face value, the radicals looked behind it to perceive the inward meaning of corruption and compromise in the apparent glory. William Cave (1637-1713) took the reign of the Great Emperor for the heyday of Christianity; Gottfried Arnold used Cave's periodization of history, but deplored the consequent institutionalization and confessionalism. Schröder, William Freiherr von, *Gottfried Arnold* (Heidelberg,

Carl Winters Univ.-Buchh., 1917); IX *Beiträge zur Neueren Literaturgeschichte; Studien zu den Deutschen Mystikern des Siebzehnten Jahrhunderts*, Heft 1. p. 20.

46 Baur, August, *Zwinglis Theologie* (Halle, Max Niemeyer, 1885-89). 2 volumes. II, footnote p. 68.

47 Seeberg, Erich, *op. cit.*, p. 455.

48 Here was the inevitability of the Anabaptist attack upon the Reformers, who also belonged to the fallen condition of the Church; Heyer, Fritz, "Der Kirchenbegriff der Schwärmer," 56 *SVRG* (1939) 156:1-108, 13-15.

49 *Z*, p. 183.

50 True religion can never be popular, peddled on the market-place. Hegler, A., *Geist und Schrift bei Sebastian Franck* (Freiburg i. B., J. C. B. Mohr, 1892), p. 254.

51 "Artikel und handlung, so Michael Sattler zu Rotenburg am Neckar mit seinem blut bezeuget hat," in *WtQ*1938, p. 39. "No, . . . we shall arm and equip ourselves with the prayer that God strive for us. Also I say the Turk remains a Turk and is a Turk; but the so-called Christians remain Christians according to the flesh but persecute the true Christians, drive them from house and home; they are Turks in spirit." Quoted from the Testimony of Hans Schmidt in Württemberg (1950); in *WtQ*1930, p. 656.

52 "Wir zwingen niemands zum glauben . . . ."! — a proud boast! *Z*, p. 75. For further discussion, *infra*, p. 91.
"Christus thut niemand zwingen
Zu seiner Herrlichkeit,
Allein wird's dem gelingen,
Der willig ist bereit,
Durch rechten Glaub und wahre Tauff
Würkt Buss mit reinem Herzen,
Dem ist der Himmel kauft."
Ausbund (Lancaster, Joh. Bär & Bohn, 1856), 7th Penna. edit. p. 43.

53 Evans, Austin P., *An Episode in the Struggle for Religious Freedom: The Sectaries of Nuremberg, 1524-1528* (N. Y., Columbia University Press, 1924), pp. 53f. See Harder, Ernst, "Die Frühesten Vorkämpfer der Toleranzgedankens," XXIII *Monatsschriften der Comenius-Gesellschaft* (1914) 9:173-79. Denck at this time went beyond the appeal to private interpretation and spoke for the independent meeting.

54 Egli, Emil, *Analecta Reformatoria* (Zürich, Zürcher & Furrer, 1899). 2 volumes; I, 103. Lord Acton once stated that Anabaptists and Catholics shared a common conviction at this point, that the State is not responsible for religion. "The Protestant Theory of Persecution," in *Essays on Freedom and Power* (Boston, Beacon Press, 1948), Ed. Gertrude Himmelfarb. Ch. IV, p. 95.

55 *Beck*, pp. 14-15.

56 No. 247 (1564), Reported in *WtQ*1930, p. 242. "Christ alone is King!"— Heyer, Fritz, *loc. cit.*, p. 89.

57 Bainton, Roland H., *David Joris: Wiedertäufer und Kämpfer für Toleranz im 16. Jahrhundert* (Leipzig, M. Heinsius Nachf., 1937), Erg. Bd. VI *ARG*, p. 87.

58 "The Seven Articles" (February 24, 1527); *Beck*, pp. 41-44.

59 This was the watershed between *Spiritualisten* and *Täufer*. On the Anabaptist attitude to congregational discipline, see Horsch, John, *Mennonites in Europe* (Scottsdale, Penna., Mennonite Publishing House, 1942); volume I of *Mennonite History*, pp. 323f.

60 *Infra*, p. 88.

61 Heyer, Fritz, *loc. cit.*, p. 15. According to Heyer the Reformers allowed for more freedom in "forms" than did the Anabaptists. Heyer fails to distinguish between the radicals' initial protest against all formalism and the Anabaptists' final insistence upon certain disciplines to maintain the integrity of the congregation. *Infra*, p. 78.

62 Although the assertion of inner experience was so pronounced, the Anabaptists proper did not go as far as the Spiritualists in eliminating "forms." A great exchange between Marpeck and Schwenckfeld on Baptism clarified

the two positions in this respect. Marpeck said his opponents were so hyper-critical that they would not have followed even Jesus in a group when He was on earth; the command to gather a people could not, Marpeck said, he avoided. The sense of the meaning of history and its fulfillment lay strongly upon the Anabaptists, while the Spiritualists tended to hang issues upon the philosophical speculation in which historical choices were little seen. Loserth, Johann, "Studien zur Pilgram Marpeck," in Neff, Christian, ed., Gedenk-schrift, pp. 134f, 150.

63 For discussion of their positive teaching, infra, p. 85.

64 On Karlstadt, see article by G. Hein in ML, II, 463-65; also, Barge, Her-mann, Andreas Bodenstein von Karlstadt (Leipzig, Friedrich Brandstetter, 1905), 2 volumes. Further, in KSch: 9627, 9636, 9638.

65 No. 73 (Dec. 25, 1521); Müller, Nikolaus, Die Wittenberger Bewegung, 1521 und 1522 (Leipzig, M. Heinsius Nachf. 1911), 2nd edition; p. 170.

66 Barge, Hermann, op. cit., II, 259.

67 WtQ1938, p. xiv. Also, Müller, Lydia, "Der Kommunismus der mährischen Wiedertäufer," 45 SVRG (1927) 1:123, 38. There is, however, a Mennonite finding in which Zwingli's interpretation is attributed to the influence of the radicals. Supra, p. 28.

68 WtQ1930, pp. 200, 204.

69 Confession of the Ansbach Anabaptists, No. 176 (May 10, 1529); WtQ1934, p. 166. Also, "Urlaub brüeff Anthoni Erdtfordters an die zu Clagen fort beschrieben in Kärnten und überantwort," printed in WtQ1938, pp. 258-62, 262.

70 Many old monks attributed the "Fall" to the growth of the hierarchy; we have here a link of monachism and radical Protestantism. Seeberg, Erich, op. cit., p. 279.

71 Matthew 18:20 was always a favorite text of the Anabaptists!

72 Z, p. 36.

73 One testified they met by the oak in Esslingen wood; No. 99 (July 10, 1539); testimony printed in WtQ1930, p. 71. For constitutive discussion, infra, p. 108.

74 Harder, Ernst, loc. cit., p. 177.

75 WtQ1930, No. 174, p. 148f.

76 Testimony of Ambrose Spitalmeier, No. 31 (c. Sept. 9, 1527); WtQ1934, p. 27.

77 Krahn, Cornelius, op. cit., p. 130.

78 Hanss Schlaffer, quoted in WtQ1938, p. 93.

79 Egli, Emil, Die Züricher Wiedertäufer zur Reformationszeit (Zürich, Friedrich Schulthess, 1878), p. 23.

80 Infra, p. 76

81 There were various attempts, all unsuccessful; article, "Bann," by Neff in ML, I, 115-19.

82 "The Five Articles," in WtQ1938, pp. 236-57, 245.

83 No. 623 (Jan. c.20, 1525); Egli, p. 276f.

84 WtQ1938, pp 236-57, 256. The positive form of this discussion will be found below, p. 109.

85 Müller, Lydia, op. cit., p. 59.

86 Haupt, Hermann, "Ein oberrheinischer Revolutionär aus dem Zeitalter Kaiser Maximilians I.," Erg. Bd. VIII Westdeutsche Zeitschrift für Geschichte und Kunst (1893) 77-228; quoted, p. 115.

87 Ibid., quoted p. 201.

88 Supra, p. 60. We may note parallel thinking in later radicals: Francis Hotman dated the "Fall" of France with the end of the grand old Frankish kingdom, the going over to Rome. Gerard Winstanley dated the "Fall" of England with the Norman conquest, the beginning of the system of rents and tithes. Even Karl Marx had a primitivist myth in the explanation he gave for the shift from collective to private land ownership.

89 Infra, p. 110.

90 According to John Horsch, the late American Mennonite scholar, their attitude has always been soundly Biblical and pessimistic toward the world to this day. "The Hutterians . . . believe that modern progress has changed neither the individual human heart nor the character of the world . . . The modern idea of Christ as the saviour of the world, in the sense that he is the leader in move-

ments for world regeneration through reform, falls short by far of representing his true saviourhood. He is the Redeemer of those only who have been personally saved, and in consequence own and follow him as their Lord. The world is to be overcome—not assimilated.'' Horsch, John, *The Hutterian Brethren* (*op. cit.*), footnote 128, p. 134.

91 Seeberg, Erich, *op. cit.*, pp. 262f.

92 Bainton, Roland H., *David Joris* (*op. cit.*), p. 30.

93 Bouterwek, K. W., *loc. cit.*, p. 299. This dualism of churchly and social restitution is familiar in St. Augustine.

94 *Z*, pp. 35f. Also, *Beck*, p. 11.
On the relation of the Anabaptists to the Waldenses, see Dosker, Henry Elias, *op. cit.*, pp. 16f. Also, for an argument that the South Germans were uniquely influenced, see Nicoladoni, Alexander, *Johannes Bünderlin von Linz* (Berlin, R. Gaertners Verlag, 1893), pp. 45f. On classification, *supra*, p. 12.

95 Bouterwek, K. W., *loc. cit.*, p. 304.

96 For general discussion, see Heyer, Fritz, *loc. cit.*, pp. 24f. Complete pessimism is expressed in the Nineteen Articles of Galenus Abrahams and Spruyt (c. 1650), wherein all hope of erecting an apostolic church is abandoned. John Smyth represented a similar despair of reclaiming the lost thread of authority. Troeltsch, Ernst, *The Social Teaching of the Christian Churches* (N. Y., The Macmillan Co., 1931), II, 766.

97 *Infra*, Chapter V.

98 Heyer, Fritz, *loc. cit.*, p. 22.

99 *Supra*, p. 53.

100 Quoted in Rembert, Karl, *op. cit.*, p. 197.

101 Ritschl, Albrecht, ''G. Witzels Abkehr vom Luthertum,'' II *ZKG* (1877-78) 386-417, 396f. Ritschl, whose use of the theme in theology is so well known in America, traces the normative use of the apostolic community back to Joachim of Fiore.
On Witzel, see article by Tschackert in *ADB*, XLIII, 657-62; article by Kawerau in *RE*³, XXI, 339-409; Schmidt, G. L., *Georg Witzel: Ein Altkatholik des XVI. Jahrhunderts* (Wien, Wm. Braumüller, 1876). Further in *KSch*: 22711a, 22712, 22736.

102 Detmer, Heinrich, and Krumbholtz, Robert, *ed.*, *op. cit.*

103 Schiedung, Hans, *Beiträge zur Bibliographie und Publizistik ueber die Münsterischen Wiedertäufer* (Münster, Heinrich Buschmann, 1934), p. 11.

104 Rembert, Karl, *op. cit.*, footnote 2 on p. 244. Franck's writings were widely read among the Anabaptists.
On the popularity of the theme ''Restitution'' see Bainton, Roland H., ''Changing Ideas and Ideals in the Sixteenth Century,'' VIII *Journal of Modern History* (1936)4: footnote, p. 428.

105 Whitney, Lois, *Primitivism and the Idea of Progress* (Baltimore, Johns Hopkins Press, 1934), p. 1.

THE RESTITUTION

1 Heyer, Fritz, ''Der Kirchenbegriff der Schwärmer,'' 56 *SVRG* (1939) 2:1-108, 18.

2 *WtQ*1934, p. 61.

3 Heyer, Fritz, *loc. cit.*, pp. 99-102.

4 Schlaffer, Hans, ''Ein Kurzer Unterricht zum Anfang Eines Recht Christlichen Lebens,'' in *WtQ*1938, p. 92.

5 Hut, Hans, ''Vom geheimnus der tauf . . . . .,'' in *WtQ*1938, p. 14.

6 *Beck*, pp. 41-44. The Seven Articles were defined at a noted conference called under the leadership of Michael Sattler, a great leader of the new movement, to serve the Anabaptist congregations as a guide against false teaching. Cf. Blanke, Fritz, ''Beobachtungen zum ältesten Täuferbekenntnis,'' XXXVIII *ARG* (1940) 240-49. Cf. McGlothlin, M. J., *Baptist Confessions of Faith* (Philadelphia, American Baptist Publication Society, 1911). pp. 2-9.

7 Hut, Hans, "Vom geheimnus der tauf," in *WtQ*1938, p. 27.

8 This was a favorite Anabaptist argument; Schlaffer, Hans, "Kurtze und ainfältige vermanung vom kindertauf, wie derselbig nit mag beibracht werden auss heiliger schrift" (1528), in *WtQ*1938, p. 100. Stadler, Ulrich, "Etlich schöne tröstliche sendbrief, underrichtungen und leeren. . . . Vom der erbsünd, tauf, urtl der sünd zum tod, gemainschaft und andern nutzlichen sachen," *ibid.*, p. 233. Reported in the Disputation at Lütisberg (1533), in Egli, Emil, *Die St. Galler Täufer* (Zürich, Friedrich Schulthess, 1887), footnote 5, p. 54. Testimony of the Grüninger *Täufer* (June 4f, 1527), No. 1201 in *Egli*, II, 547.

9 Testimony in *WtQ*1930, p. 240.

10 Dosker, Henry Elias, *The Dutch Anabaptists* (Philadelphia, The Judson Press, 1921), pp. 106f.

11 *Z*, p. 27.

12 Testimony of Sept. 22, 1527; No. 25, in *WtQ*1934, p. 38.

13 The oldest was by Hübmaier and the second came thirteen years later from the hand of Peter Ridemann; Heyer, Fritz, *loc. cit.*, p. 9.

14 Müller, Lydia, "Der Kommunismus der mährischen Wiedertäufer," 45 *SVRG* (1927) 1:1-123, 37.

15 Hut, Hans, "Vom geheimnus der tauf . . .," in *WtQ* 1938, p. 21.

16 Testimony (February 7, 1525), No. 636 in *Egli*, I, 284.

17 Krahn, Cornelius, *Menno Simons (1496-1561)*, p. 124f.

18 Hut, Hans, *loc. cit.*, p. 25.

19 Loserth, Johann, *Doctor Balthasar Hubmaier und die Anfänge der Wiedertäufer in Mähren* (Brünn, R. M. Rohrer, 1893), p. 2.

20 Only an adult might qualify under the Great Commission; *infra*, Chapter V.

21 Bergfried, Ulrich, *Verantwortung als Theologisches Problem im Täufertum des 16. Jahrhunderts* (Wuppertal-Elberfeld, A. Martini & Grüttefien, 1938), p. 98. It has been wrongly asserted that the Anabaptists were "Confessionless" groups. This is only true in the sense that ethical rather than doctrinal issues generally concerned them, and they used the ban for moral government but rarely to enforce intellectual conformity. Schwenckfeld and Franck are the true points of departure for Confessionless Christianity. Heyer, Fritz, *loc. cit.*, p. 47.

22 "Ein Ausschnitt aus Peter Walpots 'Kinderlehre'," printed in *WtQ*1938, p. 257; also Rideman, Peter, *Rechenschaft unserer Religion, Lehr und Glaubens, von den Brüdern, so man die Hütterischen nennt, ausgangen . . . 1565.* pp. 79f.

23 A Hutterian observer condemned the Nikolsburg congregational life because Hübmaier baptized large numbers into the church every Sunday who certainly did not know the full meaning of their commitment; nor were the members subject to any system of congregational government. Testimony at Erlangen (Jan. 17, 1529), No. 145; printed in *WtQ*1934, p. 132.

24 Müller, Lydia, *loc. cit.*, pp. 42-43.

25 "Rechenschaft und bekanntnus des glaubens . . ." (Trieste, 1539), in *WtQ*1938, p. 204; "Ein Rechenschaft von unsern lieben brüedern Jeronime, Michel und Hänssl," (1536), p. 209.

26 Quoted in Nicoladoni, Alexander, *Johannes Bünderlin von Linz und die oberösterreichischen Täufergemeinde in den Jahren 1525-1531* (Berlin, R. Gaertners Verlag, 1893), p. 155.

27 *Z*, pp. 110-12.

28 *Z*, pp. 83f.

29 *WtQ*1938, p. xvii.

30 No. 174 (August 1557?), *WtQ*1930, p. 148.

31 Rideman, Peter, *op. cit.*, p. 141; "Rechenschaft und bekanntnus. . . ." (Trieste, 1539), *WtQ*1938, p. 197.

32 Article by Neff, "Bann," in *ML*, I, 115-19.

33 Letter of Sept. 5, 1524, Grebel and associates to Müntzer; Rauschenbusch, Walter, "The Zürich Anabaptists and Thomas Müntzer," IX *American Journal of Theology* (1905) 91-106, 94, 95.

34 *Beck*, pp. 41-44.

35 "Von der Eeschaidung zwischen glaubigen und unglaubigen," in *WtQ*1938, pp. 253f. Separation was permissible, but not a commandment; p. 255.

36 Quotation from Hübmaier in Newman, A. H., "Balthazar Hübmaier and the

Moravian Anabaptists,'' 27 *Goshen College Record, Review Supplement* (1926) 10:4-22, 12.

37 Quotation from Hübmaier in Vedder, Henry C., *Balthasar Hübmaier*, pp. 212-14. Hübmaier intrigued Baptist scholars of an earlier generation, perhaps in part because he took a more orthodox view of the use of the sword than most Anabaptists. Today, his significance as an Anabaptist leader is generally depreciated by students of the movement.

38 Bergfried, Ulrich, *op cit.*, p. 20.

39 Testimony at Kirchheim (March 24, 1566), No. 120 in *WtQ*1930, p. 1084.

40 Testimony of Wolfgang Wüst at Beiersdorf (Jan. 3, 1528), Nos. 78 & 79 in *WtQ*1934, p. 71.

41 Fourth in the Seven Articles (Feb. 24, 1527), in *Beck*, pp. 41-44; also, article by Hege, ''Absonderung,'' in *ML*, I, 11-12.

42 Huter, Jakob, ''Anschleg und fürwenden der blinden und verkerten welt, und aller gottlosen gegen den fromen,'' *WtQ*1938, p. 170.

43 *Ibid.*, p. 153.

44 *Z*, p. 357.

45 A late criticism, quoted in Wotschke, Theodor, *Geschichte der Reformation in Polen* (Leipizg, R. Haupt, 1911), volume I of *Studien zur Kultur und Geschichte der Reformation.* p. 225.

46 Hege, Christian, ''The Early Anabaptists in Hesse,'' V *MQR* (1931) 157-78, 159.

47 *Z*, pp. 250, 307. *Infra*, p. 230.

48 See article by Ernst Correll, ''Ehe,'' in *ML*, I, 509-26.

49 Heyer, Fritz, *loc. cit.*, p. 58.

50 On this particular aspect of the Brethren's radicalism, see Egli, Emil, *Die Züricher Wiedertäufer zur Reformationszeit* (Zürich, Friedrich Schulthess, 1878), p. 12. Also, Unruh, B. H., in *Gedenkschrift*, p. 42. This was perhaps not a social attack so much as part of their broad-gauged warfare with the establishment.

51 Testimony of Ambrosius Spitelmeier (c. Sept. 9, 1527), No. 31 in *WtQ*1934, pp. 27, 28.

52 *Supra*, p. 45.

53 *Z*, pp. 107f; also Heyer, Fritz, *loc. cit.*, pp. 81f.

54 *Z*, pp. 212f.

55 Article by Neff, ''Aelteste,'' in *ML*, I, 39-40; also Correll, Ernst, *Das Schweizerische Täufermennonitentum* (Tübingen, J. C. B. Mohr, 1925), p. 37.

56 *Ibid.*, p. 45.

57 Wolkan, Rudolph, *ed.*, *Geschicht-Buch der Hutterischen Brüder*, p. 220.

58 *WtQ*, 1938, p. 246.

59 The Articles of Kyburg (May 2, 1525), No. 703 in *Egli*, p. 320. The Regensperg Articles (May E., 1525), No. 729, *ibid.*, pp. 340-43.

60 Rideman, Peter, *op. cit.*, pp. 40, 94-5.

61 ''Eine liebe unterrichtung Ulrichen Stadlers . . . .,'' in *WtQ*1938, p. 222.

62 Conclusion to the 3d of Five Articles (1547), *ibid.*, p. 247.

63 Horsch, John, *The Hutterian Brethren, 1528-1931*, pp. xvi, 4.

64 In the Five Articles (1547), printed in *WtQ*1938, p. 244.

65 Testimony of Hans Hut (1527), No. 51 in *WtQ*1934, pp. 41-44.

66 Letter to the authorities at Zürich (March, 1526), No. 940 in *Egli*, II, 449.

67 Certain groups frowned upon the rigor which developed in Hutterian discipline; Confession of the Windesheim Anabaptists (April 16, 1531), No. 242 in *WtQ*1934, pp. 219, 238.

68 *WtQ*1938, p. 109.

69 Brandhuber, Wolfgang, ''Ein sendbrief an die gmain Gottes zu Rottenburg am In'' (1529), in *WtQ*1938, p. 138.

70 In *WtQ*1934, p. 36.

71 Smith, C. Henry, *The Story of the Mennonites* (Berne, Indiana, Mennonite Book Concern, 1941), p. 65.

72 *Beck*, pp. 41-44.

73 The second of the Five Articles (1547), in *WtQ*1938, p. 242.

74 Confessions of several newly baptized at Beiersdorf (1528), No. 82 in *WtQ*1934, p. 84.

75 Confession of Ansbach Anabaptists (May 10, 1529), No. 176, *ibid.*, p. 165.
Also in Langenmantel, Hans, "Ein anders gespräch vom abentmahl Christi und seiner gemeinschaft aufs kurzeste," in *WtQ*1938, p. 135; Zaunring, Georg, "Ain kurtze annzaigung des abentmals Christy," *ibid.*, p. 145.

76 *Z*, p. 186.

77 Schiemer, Leonhard, "Ein Epistl an die gmain zu Rottenburg geschrieben . . . ," in *WtQ*1938, p. 54.

78 No. 369 (June 23, 1523), in *Egli*, I, 133.

79 Article by Neff, "Abendmahl," in *ML*, I, 6-9.

80 "The Donatist peasant rising believed only in the sacramental power of 'pure' priests, and not in its character *indelibilis*: this was the beginning of the great series of sect-movements, with their hostility to the Church. . . . ."; Troeltsch, Ernst, *The Social Teaching of the Christian Churches* (N. Y., The Macmillan Co., 1931), I, 209f. Also footnote, p. 338.

81 Repeatedly the Anabaptist before the court would testify that he avoided the communion because he was unworthy; see instances in *WtQ*1930, pp. 199, 240. 252f.

82 Confession of Simon Krausshaars von Neckar-Gröningen (May, 1559), No. 190, *ibid.*, pp. 178f.

83 Zaunring, Georg, in *WtQ*1938, p. 147.

84 *WtQ*1938, p. xiv. Menno used the same simile: "Gelijck als dan een natuurlijck brood van veel korens in de meulen gebroocken met water gekneet/van des vyers hittighydt tot een broodt gebacken wordt/alsoo wordt oock de gemeynte Christi uyt veel geloovigen/ met de meulen des Godlijcken woordts in have herten gebroken/ met dat water des Heyligen Geests/ en met dat vyer der reynder ongeverweder liefden i en een lichaem gedoopt." Cited in Krahn, Cornelius, *Menno Simons*, p. 142.

85 No. 247 (1564) in *WtQ*1930, p. 241.

86 "Rechenschaft und bekenntnus des glaubens. . . ." (Trieste, 1539), in *WtQ*1938, p. 201.

87 "Contra Anabaptistarum opinionem." (August, 1557?), No. 174 in *WtQ*1930, pp. 148f.

88 *WtQ*1938, p. 210.

89 Newman, A. H., *A History of Anti-Pedobaptism* (Philadelphia, American Baptist Publication Society, 1897), p. 88.

90 Correll, Ernst, *op. cit.*, footnote on p. 28.

91 Burckhardt-Biedermann, Th., *Bonifacius Amerbach und die Reformation* (Basel, R. Reich, 1894), p. 91.

92 For the definitive Mennonite treatment of this point, see Hershberger, Guy Franklin, *War, Peace and Nonresistance* (Scottdale, Penna., The Herald Press, 1944), pp. 219f. For further exposition of the distinction here made between "defencelessness" (or nonresistance) and "pacifism," see Littell, Franklin H., "The Inadequacy of Modern Pacifism," *Christianity and Society* (Spring, 1946) 1:18-23.

93 Heyer, Fritz, *loc. cit.*, p. 85.

94 *Ibid.*, p. 89.

95 Rideman, Peter, *op. cit.*, p. 118.

96 "Anschleg und fürwenden der blinden und verkerten Welt . . . ," in *WtQ*1938, p. 186.

97 *Ibid.*, p. 186.

98 *Ibid.*, p. 199.

99 *WtQ*1938, p. 186.

100 Fourth of Five Articles (1547)), *ibid.*, p. 252.

101 No. 623 (Jan. c. 20, 1525), in *Egli*, I. 276f.

102 See article by Neff, "Eid," in *ML*, I, 535-46.

103 *WtQ*1938, p. 249.

104 No. 205 (May 18, 1560), in *WtQ*1930, p. 198.

105 *WtQ*1938, p. 97.

106 From the testimony of some who came from the Swiss to join the Hutterians (1543)); *ibid.*, p. 265.

107 Smithson, R. J., *The Anabaptists* (London, James Clarke & Co., Ltd., 1935), p. 125, with a reference to *BRN*.

108 *Z*, p. 205.
109 *Supra*, p. 64.
110 Supra, p. 45. The Report of the Colloquy of Emden (1578), in Arnold, Gottfried, *Kirchen- und Ketzer-Historie* (Frankfurt am Main, Thomas Fritsch, 1700), II: XVI, XXI, 272a.
111 *Z*, p. 307.
112 Fourth in the Five Articles (1547), in *WtQ* 1938, p. 249.
113 Stauffer, Ethelbert, "Märtyrertheologie und Täuferbewegung," LII *ZKG* (1933) 545-98, 588. The baptismal formulae were martyr-confessionals.
114 Mannhardt, W., *Die Wehrfreiheit der Altpreussischen Mennoniten* (Marienburg & Danzig, B. Hermann Hemmpels Wwe., 1863); van der Smissen, H. "Der Grundsatz der Wehrlosigkeit in seiner historischen Entwicklung dargestellt," 35 *Mennonitische Blätter* (1888) 21:121-24, 22:129-30; Vos, K., *De Weerlosheid der Doopsgezinden* (Amsterdam, J. H. DeBussy, 1924). In general, these writers assert that the Anabaptist nonresistance was not a dogmatic question but a matter of historical   development and decline.
115 Cf. Horsch, John, "An Historical Survey of the Position of the Mennonite Church on Nonresistance," I *MQR* (1927) 3:5-22, 4:3-20.

THE GREAT COMMISSION

1 *Supra*, p. 41. Since the preparation of this MSS, a stimulating study of the same area has come to the writer's hand: Wiswedel, Wilhelm, "Die alten Täufergemeinden und ihr missionarisches Wirken," 40 *ARG* (1943) 183-200, 45 *ARG* (1948) 115-32.
2 This name has been given them by certain authors who rightly find the terms "*Wiedertäufer*" and "*Täufer*" inaccurate and restrictive. See *Preface*. "Evangelical Anabaptists" seems best to indicate their overwhelming sense of mission. Friedmann, Robert, "Conception of the Anabaptists," IX *CH* (1940) 341-65, 362.
3 *Egli*, No. 674 (March 16-25, 1525), I, 299: One testified that he slept home during the services; and besides he read in his testament "who believes and is baptized. . . ." See also No. 1631 (Dec. 26, 1529); here the Great Commission (Mk 16) and the Ban (Mt 18) are linked together as the basic Anabaptist ordinances; I, 692. "Rechenschaft und bekanntnus des glaubens. . . ." (Trieste, 1539) stressed Mk 16; *WtQ*1938, p. 193. When Hanss Schlaffer was called up before the authorities at Schwatz, 1528, he answered on Mt 28, Mk 16; van Braght, T. J., *A Martyrology of the Churches of Christ Commonly Called Baptist* (London, Hanserd Knollys Society, 1850-53), I, 50. The central authority in Hübmaier's "Von dem christl. Tauff der Gläubigen" is Mt 28:29; Sachsse, Carl, *D. Balthasar Hubmaier als Theologe*, pp. 19-20. With Menno Simons the demand for righteousness was primary, and the second order was Mt. 28:29, Mk. 16:15; quoted in Horsch, John, *Menno Simons*, p. 50. See *WtQ*1934, p. 186. Questions prepared for the Windesheim *Wiedertäufer* indicated an expectation of testimony based on the Great Commission and the *Acts;* No. 260 (May, 1531), pp. 236-37. The testimony of Julius Lober, who had a brother in Moravia, was built on the promise of salvation to him who believes and is baptized. His proof texts were Mt 5, Mt 28 and Mk 16, Lk 3, Acts 3.8.19; No. 267 (April 18, 1548), pp. 353-55. See *Z*, p. 31.
4 *Beck*, p. 64.
5 *WtQ*1938, p. 15 (Hans Hut), p. 92 (Hanss Schlaffer), p. 112. B. Hübmaier wrote to the authorities that he knew no other order but preach, believe, baptize; *Egli*, I, 449. When at St. Gall Uolimann was summoned before the Council, April 25, 1525, for going on his own authority with Baptism and the Supper, he said the original order was teaching, believing, baptizing; and this lasted to the time of Tertullian and Cyprian when they began to baptize sick children. Heath, Richard, *Anabaptism from its Rise at Zwickau to its Fall at Münster* (London, Alexander & Shepheard, 1895), p. 39. (Heath's book contains interesting material in spite of an erroneous central thesis.)
6 *WtQ*1934, No. 44 (Sept. 20, 1527), p. 34 (Hans Spitelmair).

7 *Z*, pp. 269f. See also p. 60; Baptism stands on Mk 16, Mt 28 (Hanss Schlaffer, 1528). And on pp. 250f, a statement by Gabrielites who joined the Hutterians in 1545 begins on Baptism, based on Mt 28 and Mk 16. See *WtQ*1938, pp. 236f. At an examination of various people at Erlangen, 1527, Hans Ritter the Nodler said: 1) the Lord commanded ''go ye . . . .''; 2) man must submit under God as animals under man; 3) they went to flowing water, filled a hat and poured; *WtQ*1934, No. 16, p. 16. ''Question. 'What do you hold concerning infant baptism?' Answer. 'I consider it nothing else than a human institution.' Qu. 'By what then will you prove, or establish your baptism?' Ans. 'By Mark xvi.' '' Confession of an Anabaptist at Antwerp, 1551; vanBraght, T. J., *op. cit.*, I, 436-37.

8 *WtQ*1934, No. 353 (April 27, 1534), p. 338.

9 Ludwig Hetzer marked them with a cross on the forehead, reading the Great Commission; *ibid.*, Nos. 137, 138, 139 (July 6, 1528), pp. 124-29, 125.

10 So one writer concluded, referring to the excellent example of the Master, baptized by John in his thirtieth year; *WtQ*1938, p. 93.

11 Note Calvin's treatment of the matter in ''Brieve Instruction pour armer tous bons fidèles contre les Erreurs de la Secte Commune des Anabaptistes,'' XXXV *CR* (1868) cols. 45-142, 58. Calvin did not restrict the command in time, but held Jesus was speaking primarily of preaching and not baptizing.

12 They emphasized Mt 10:1-15 rather than Mt 28:19, but had the whole world in prospect. On the Franciscan movement as a World Mission see Benz, Ernst, *Ecclesia Spiritualis* (Stuttgart, W. Kohlhammer, 1934), p. 66.

13 Horsch, John, *Mennonites in Europe* (Scottdale, Penna., Mennonite Publishing House, 1942), p. 315. Horsch, John, *The Hutterian Brethren, 1528-1931* (Goshen, Ind., Mennonite Historical Society, 1931). Applicants for baptism and church membership were instructed in their duty to be willing to go to the provinces as missionaries; footnote 36, p. 29. The oldest missionary hymn, 23 verses of 8 lines each, was composed by the Hutterians; pp. 27f. Hans Hut testified that he was baptized by Hans Denck in terms of Mk 16 and the last of Matthew; how seriously he took the instruction is recorded in his great evangelistic trips; *WtQ*1934, No. 57 (1527), pp. 41-44. See also the statement of Georg Nespitzer at Ansbach; No. 206 (July 12, 1530), pp. 186-88. Hut baptized him while Jörg read the Great Commission, ''go to all creatures. . . .''

14 Latourette, Kenneth S., ''New Perspectives in Church History,'' XXI *The Journal of Religion* (1941) 4:432-43, 438f.

15 *WtQ*1938, p. 95 (Hanss Schlaffer).

16 *WtQ*1930, No. 947 (Dec. 4, 1590), p. 658.

17 *Beck*, footnote 2, p. 39 (instructions to Jörg Zaunring).

18 The Anabaptists said the *Schriftgelernten* have no *creütz;* they were as though the goldsmith only talked to the metal and didn't take it into his shop; *WtQ*1938, p. 74 (Leonhard Schiemer).

19 ''Ein Brieff D. Mart. Luthers Von den Schleichern und Winckelpredigern'' (1532), *WA*, XXX, 3, 510f. p. 519.

20 *Ibid.*, p. 521.

21 Cited by Menius, Justus, *Von dem Geist der Wiederteuffer* (Wittemberg, 1544). Microfilm from Columbia Library (UTS). p. fiij.

22 *Ibid.*, p. fij.

23 ''Bekandtnuss and verantwortung Hansen Schlaffers. . . .,'' *WtQ*1938, p. 111.

24 *WtQ*1930, No. 113 (April 14, 1563), p. 1057 (Glock).

25 Ecke, Karl, *Schwenckfeld, Luther, und der Gedanke einer apostolischen Reformation* (Berlin, Martin Warneck, 1911), pp. 90f. Capito wrote that C. S. stood for ''kirchendienst, das ist predig und reichung der sacrament, gar niderlegung und also warten mit zweien oder dreien. . . . bis der h. geist wider keme wie am pfingstag zu Hierusalem.'' *WtQ*1930, No. 65 (May 21, 1534), p. 990f.

26 *Ibid.*, pp. 108f.

27 The church was where ''two or three are gathered together,'' ''unpartheyisch''; Report on the Tübingen Colloquy (May 28, 1535), *CS*, V, 336. It was founded in the freely preached evangel, Christ with us to the end of the world (Mt 28: 20); ''Was die warhafftig Christlich Kirch sei'' (c. 1530), *CS*, V, 57.

28 ''*Freiwilligkeitskirche*'' was a term used by their enemies, in part justified by their championing of Erasmus against Luther in the controversy over the Free

Will. It also conveys their sociological significance as voluntary religious association in lands controlled by Catholic and Protestant state churches.

29 *WtQ*1938, pp. 178-79 (Jacob Huter). See also p. 238: "Da steet abermals, am ersten soll man predigen, darnach glauben, zum driten, die da glauben, taufen. Die kindlen können nit glauben, sie wissen nichts von Gott, von Christo, darumb ist inen der tauf nit angeben in der kindheit." (The Five Articles) Infant Baptism is refuted on "preach and baptize," for they must first have the faith; *WtQ*1930, No. 169 (April 9, 1557), p. 143. Permitting Infant Baptism indicates that the full values of mature decision are not known (Mk 16:16!); *Egli*, No. 1201 (June 4, 1527), p. 547. The answer of Christ *De baptismo parvulorum* is Mt 28, then Mk 16; *WtQ*1934, No. 228 (Hans Hechtlein, 1530), pp. 200-01. The two main influences launching Hans Hut on his great evangel seem to have been studying Mk 16, Mt 28, and Acts 19:1-7 on Infant Baptism, and Müntzer's "Hoch verursachte schutzrede. . . .''; Neuser, Wilhelm, *Hans Hut. Leben und Wirken bis zum Nikolsburger Religionsgespräch* (Berlin, Hermann Blanke, 1913). Footnote 40, pp. 12-13, and footnote 63, p. 15. Thomas van Imbroek, who was of large influence on Campanus, is recorded (May 5, 1558): "They asked him why he did not have his children baptized? He answered: 'The Scripture teaches nothing of infant baptism; and they who will be baptized according to God's word must first be believers!'" van Braght, T. J., *op. cit.*, II, 139.

30 *Beck*, p. 67.
31 *Ibid*, No. 795 (August, 1525), p. 377.
32 Article by Neff, "Beck," in *ML*, I, 148-49.
33 From a letter of Peter Glock, April 14, 1563; *WtQ*1930, No. 114, p. 1068.
34 *Ibid.*, No. 113 (April 14, 1563), p. 1061. Hanss Schmidt said he was commissioned "to be a light to the world" (Mt 5:14); No. 947 (Dec. 4, 1590), pp. 652f.
35 This proof text was roundly stated by Jakob Huter in his "Brief an den Landeshauptmann in Mähren''; "Und wir sagen und wolten, das alle welt wer wie wir und möchten iederman zu disem glauben bringen und bekeeren, so wurde alles krüegen und ungerechtigkait ein end haben." *WtQ*1938, p. 163.
36 For this office the Brethren went back to the earliest times of the Church. The highest responsibility in the community was to be sent out to lead the heathen to Christ; article by Loserth in *ML*, I, 438-40.
37 For an example of missioners calling out large numbers in Moravia; cf. *Z*, p. 171. Peter Rideman reported to Hans Amon on what he found in the groups of Württemberg and Hesse; pp. 193f. For example of the way areas were affected by the missioners: arts. "Aargauer Täufer," "Baden, Grossherzogtum," in *ML*, I 4-6, 103-07. For reports to Peter Walpot on missionary travels; *WtQ*1930, No. 122 (Sept. 30, 1566), pp. 1086f.
38 On the loss of discipline due to the advent of economic refugees, see Horsch, John, *The Hutterian Brethren, 1528-1931*, p. xvi.
39 *Infra*, footnote 53, p. 103.
40 The word to all creatures seemed to imply a new creation thereby, a new community not built with stones but by the Word; Hege, Chr., "Pilgram Marpecks Vermahnung," in *Gedenkschrift*, p. 245. Jörg von Passau wrote in a letter (1529): "Nachdem der almechtig got uns erofnet hat sein geheimnus nach seinem veterlichen willn, wie ir ermanet seit durch das evangelium, das euch gepredigt ist, in allen creaturen, die uns weisen den weg der gerechtigkeit, dardurch wir komen zum ewigen reich durch Jesum Cristum." *WtQ*1934, Nos. 186-87, pp. 169f.
41 After Zwingli's "Vom Tauf, Widertauf und Kindertauf. . .," an Edict of the Zürich Council forbade the corner meetings and suggested that the foreign enemies of Infant Baptism might earn their penny elsewhere; Loserth, Johann and Beck, Josef R., "Georg Blaurock und die Anfänge des Anabaptismus in Graubündten und Tirol," VII *Vorträge und Aufsätze* (1889) 1-30, 3. On return Blaurock was whipped into exile; *Egli*, No. 1110 (June 5, 1527), II, 530.
42 *Egli*, No. 646 (Feb. 18 and 25, 1525), p. 289.
43 *Ibid.*, No. 837 (Oct. 8, 1525), p. 395.
44 On his capacity as a powerful missioner see *Beck*, pp. 79f. *Z*, p. 49.
45 *Z*, p. 56.

46 *Egli*, No. 824 (Sept. 20, 1525), I, 391; report of a convert of Teck's, No. 953
    (April 11, 25, May 2, 1526), I, 457-58. See No. 1357 (Jan. 21, 1528), II.
47 See article by Hege, "Augsburger Täufergemeinde," in *ML*, I, 92-96.
48 *Beck*, pp. 310-312.
49 Stauffer, Ethelbert, *loc. cit.*, p. 578. When Andreas Neff, leading Schwenck-
    felder, made submissions, C. S. heard of it and wrote (Sept. 29, 1545), praying
    God might give him grace to be strong and carry through "ritterlich";
    *WtQ*1930, No. 136, p. 103f; No. 139, p. 109. There are four weapons of the
    true *Ritter* of Christ: faith, hope, love and *Gelassenheit*; Friedmann, Robert,
    "Concerning the True Soldier of Christ: A Hitherto Unknown Tract of the
    Phillipite Brethren in Moravia," V *MQR* (1931) 87-99, 91.
50 *WtQ*1938, p. 88 (Hanss Schlaffer).
51 Ludwig Hetzer, quoted in Weis, Frederick Lewis, *The Life and Teachings of
    Ludwig Hetzer* (Dorchester, Mass., Underhill Press, 1930), p. 110.
52 "Die viert epistel vom Jacob Huetter, an die gmain Gottes in Mähren," in
    *WtQ*1938, pp. 150-59, 154.
53 The effectiveness of the Hutterian missioners among the depressed classes is
    portrayed in Nos. 634, 667, 716, 721 in *WtQ*1930. It is Bossert's final conclu-
    sion that the Schwenckfelders won more preachers and women from the
    nobility, while the Anabaptists drew mostly from the peasants; p. xii. Ac-
    counts of those fleeing to Moravia, debts and small goods, indicate their station
    as tradespeople and craftsmen; No. 261 (Nov. 9, 1569), p. 249. No. 262 (Oct. 27,
    1569). Properties inventoried sometimes indicate a fair degree of prosperity;
    *WtQ*1934, No. 27 (1527), pp. 23-24. On the general problem of the relation
    of Anabaptism ("Handwerker Christentum"?) to social forces, see Loesche,
    Georg, "Archivalische Beiträge zur Geschichte des Täufertums und des Protes-
    tantismus in Tirol und Voralberg," 47 *Jahrbuch der Gesellschaft für die Ge-
    schichte des Protestantismus im ehemaligen und im neuen Osterreich* (1926) 1-161.
    p. 3. The flooding in of economic refugees accentuated the problem of organi-
    zation within the Moravian communities, and many new colonists returned to
    their former stations when conditions were better or when persecution threatened
    the Moravian life. There may be here a kind of reaction against city life and
    commercial complexities, and idealization of *"die Bedürfnislosigkeit"*; Correll,
    Ernst, *op. cit.*, pp. 61-62. *WtQ*1930, No. 198 (June 27, 1559), p. 185: A definite
    form of confession and submission was provided for those who returned, would
    submit, and re-establish themselves in the fabric of a stable society. See also
    the case of Hans Volmar of Geradstatten, who after rebaptism went to Moravia
    and then returned and made submission; No. 64, p. 44. Also Christmann
    Schmidt of Diegenbach, who was banished on return; No. 70, p. 47. Konrad
    Wirtemberger of Zaisersweiher, who returned but refused to conform, was
    expelled and exiled; No. 68, p. 46. Appollonia of Horrheim and husband came back
    from Moravia and submitted; Nos. 73-4, p. 49. Very apparently the migration
    to Moravia was only an economic movement to many.
54 *WtQ*1934, No. 12 (1527), p. 15; one of the men was Hans Ritter the Nodler,
    who accompanied Hans Hut.
55 *WtQ*1930, No. 231 (Feb. 5, 1563), p. 227. Poor relief records, pp. 231f. A
    General Rescript (July 13, 1538), p. 68, early mentioned journeymen going up
    and down in the land and wandering off to Moravia.
56 *Ibid.*, No. 241, pp. 234f. Here is a typical process of confiscation against those
    who have been in Moravia for some years: 1) Are there children, how old, and
    are they also Anabaptist? 2) If no other kin are eligible, who has a just claim
    to the goods and property? See No. 251 (Dec. 24, 1565): questions over goods
    and money of *Wiedertäufer* who had gone 28 years before to Moravia. And
    No. 263 (Oct. 7, 1570): judgment on an estate; the daughter had married an
    Anabaptist and lived in Moravia, and her part was laid by.
57 *WtQ*1934, p. 18. Proof by authorities that a man should not wander, but stay
    with his wife and children; No. 150 (Feb. 1, 1529), pp. 143-46. Note Calvin's
    opposition to the "barefooted evangel" of the Libertines, which was no more
    ecclesiastical than social; Müller, Karl, "Calvin und die 'Libertiner'," XL
    ZKG (1922) N.F.III:83-129. Luther, himself a good Hausvater, stated the fam-
    ily as one of the orders of "natural" responsibility (*Schöpfungsordnungen*),
    against the wandering *Schwärmer* as well as against Catholic celibacy.

58 A wanderer examined by Joh. Brenz; *WtQ*1930, No. 169 (April 9, 1557), p. 146. A familiar phrase in the hearings was "wife and children not of his faith," which may have been to protect them from the authorities but was probably due to the fact that the father had travelled widely in guild circles and broken loose from the state church.

59 *WtQ*1938, p. 214 (Ulrich Stadler).

60 *WtQ*1934, No. 254 (April 30, 1531), p. 231: "di armen fruma leut auf apostolisch ire guter gemein halten" in terms of the Great Commission.

61 Correll, Ernst, *op. cit.*, p. 18.

62 *Supra*, p. 43.

63 *Z*, p. 105

64 *Ibid.*, p. 112.

65 *Ibid.*, p. 134. *WtQ*1934, pp. 144f.

66 *Z*, p. 157.

67 *Beck*, p. 99. *Supra*, p. 81.

68 *Ibid.*, p. 226; in 1556, during the dispute among the Swiss Brethren on the Incarnation, many came over to the Hutterians who stood on Reformation ground. Melchoir Waal served as missioner among the Swiss to 1559, and from 1561 for the Hutterians; Wolkan, Rudolph, *ed.*, *Geschicht-Buch der Hütterischen Brüder*, pp. 304, 311, 391. Testimony of the group coming over, stating their complaint against the Swiss; *WtQ*1938, pp. 265f. Many were won by Hanss Schmidt, Hutterian "Diener des Worts" in Württemberg who wrote, among other tracts, "Warumb man in das Märherland ziehen soll"; pp. 267, 269-70.

69 On the occasion of the splits, *Beck*, pp. 113f. *Z*, p. 134. Gabriel Ascherham wrote that he had never opposed Infant Baptism and during a long series of acrimonious polemics permanently alienated both enemies and friends; p. 250.

70 A notable effort was made in 1538; *Z*, p. 181.

71 On Stadler and his group, *Beck*, p. 133; *WtQ*1938, 212f.

72 *WtQ*1938, p. 226.

73 *Z*, p. 102.

74 Rideman, Peter, *Rechenschaft unserer Religion, Lehr und Glaubens von den Brüdern, so man die Hütterischen nennt, ausgangen. . . . 1565.* The Great Commission was stated as the first argument against Infant Baptism, p. 70.

75 *Z*, pp. 176f. While imprisoned in Hesse, 1540, and not knowing what his end might be, he wrote a beautiful "unpartheyisch" admonition to the Brethren; see pp. 212f.

76 *Beck*, footnote on p. 41.

77 "Die viert epistel vom Jacob Huetter . . . ,"*WtQ*1938, pp. 150-59, 152.

78 *WtQ*1934, No. 66 (Dec. 23, 1527), p. 61. Storch sent out 12 apostles through Germany, p. 9.

79 See chapter on Hut in Brush, John, *Radical Eschatology of the Continental Reformation;* MSS in Sterling Library, Yale PhD Thesis, 1942. Further, *supra*, p. 39.

80 *WtQ*1934, Nos. 206, 227, 242.

81 "Die Chronik von Clemens Sender," XXIII *Die Chroniken der Deutschen Städte* (Leipzig, S. Hirzel, 1894), p. 192.

82 "Urgicht. . . . .16. September 1527," in Meyer, Christian, "Zur Geschichte der Wiedertäufer in Oberschwaben: 1. Die Anfänge des Wiedertäuferthums in Augsburg," I *Zeitschrift des Historischen Vereins für Schwaben und Neuberg* (1874) 207-56, 223.

83 Article by Hegler, *RE*³, VIII, 489-91.

84 Neuser, Wilhelm, *op. cit.*, pp. 26f. He travelled so widely that his trips cannot be traced, and also sent out apostles who were especially effective among the handworkers.

85 Article by Loserth, *loc. cit.*, p. 371; Mt 24, Mk 13, Lk 17—the last things.

86 "7 Urteile der Wiedertäufer," No. 234 (1530); *WtQ*1934, p. 212.

87 See article by Neff, "Jakob von Campen," in *ML*, I, 324-25. Deventer, Zwolle, Amsterdam and Leyden were among the most important centers; Cornelius, C. A., *Die Niederländischen Widertäufer während der Belagerung Münsters 1535* (München, Akademie, 1869), p. 4.

88 Bouterwek, K. W., "Zur Wiedertäufer-Literatur," I *Zeitschrift des Bergischen Geschichtsvereins* (1869) 280-344, 294. In the day of wrath the devil will be

overthrown from his present reign: "In Summa, Gottes volk, welches übrig bleibt, das unbeflecht und rein in allem Gehorsem sein soll, über die ganze Erde, zu Dienste stehen." p. 311.

89 *Ibid.*, p. 310.

90 Quoting Rothmann, with discussion; Heyer, Fritz, *loc. cit.*, p. 68.

91 Bouterwek, K. W., *loc. cit.*, p. 347.

92 Bainton, Roland H., "The Immoralities of the Patriarchs According to the Exegesis of the Late Middle Ages and of the Reformation," 23 *Harvard Theological Review* (1930) 39-49, footnote 28, p. 45.

93 *WtQ*1934, p. 131.

94 *WtQ*1934, p. 65; this is from the Nikolsburger Articles (1527) which here express Anabaptist sentiments. *WtQ*1938, p. 225 (Stadler).

95 Heyer, Fritz, *loc. cit.*, p.54. One rose to challenge the preacher in church and defend the corner-preacher; *Egli*, II, 581. Sattler held his meetings in field and woods; II, 589-91. The court at Marbach, July 10, 1539, heard one say they met "by the oak in Esslingen wood," on Sunday morning while others were in church; *WtQ*1930, No. 99, p. 71. Part of any pledge of submission was to avoid the small corner meetings; if those who submitted fell back, their property was forfeit.

96 Heyer, Fritz, *loc. cit.*, p. 16.

97 *WtQ*1938, p. 225 (Stadler).

98 *Ibid.*, p. 165 (Huter).

99 Jacob Huter, in writing the lords against persecution, reported in moving language the sick and helpless and orphans among them; *WtQ*1938, p. 162.

100 On the general place of hymnology in the movement, cf. Correll, Ernst, "The Value of Hymns for Mennonite History," IV *MQR* (July, 1930) 3:215f. Also Ramaker, A. J., "Hymns and Hymn Writers Among Anabaptists of the Sixteenth Century," III *MQR* (April, 1929) 2:93f.

101 Written by Swiss Brethren in prison at Passau, 1535-37. *Supra*, p. 10.

102 This is the stock phrase describing the martyrs in the Greater Chronicle; *Beck*, p. 1. On the origins of the material in vanBraght's *Martelaarspiegel* see article in *ML*, I, 252-53. Also van Braght, T. J., *op. cit.*, pp. viii.

103 The three-fold baptism; *WtQ*1938, pp. 77f (Leonhard Schiemer).

104 The cup Jesus drank; *WtQ*1934, p. 51 (Huter).

105 *WtQ*1938, p. 203; (*Rechenschaft* at Trieste, 1539).

106 Müller, Lydia, *op. cit.*, p. 59.

107 *WtQ*1938, p. 155 (Huter).

108 *WtQ*1930, No. 947 (Dec. 4, 1590), pp. 658-59, 662.

109 *WtQ*1938, p. 67 (Schiemer).

110 *WtQ*1938, p. 154.

111 Holl, Karl, "Luther und die Schwärmer," sec. 7 of *Gesammelte Aufsätze zur Kirchengeschichte* (Tübingen, J. C. B. Mohr, 1923), p. 429. "Dan warhaftig inerlich wort ist ewige und almechtige kraft Gottes gleichfermig in menschen wie in Got, und vermag alle ding."—in *WtQ*1938, p. 214 (Stadler).

112 See quotations of observers; *Beck*, p. xx.

113 Clemen, Otto, "Das Prager Manifesto Thomas Müntzers," XXX *ARG* (1933) 73-81, 75. It was with Joachim of Fiore that *Leiden* first became eschatological, signifying in mysterious fashion an effective opposition to the Great Church in the Age of the Spirit; Benz, Ernst, *op. cit.*, p. 298.

114 It must be admitted that Menno and his associates represented a reaction against all eschatology; nevertheless, they looked for the Thousand Years of Peace which should be ushered in with Christ's coming. *Beck*, p. xviii.

115 Johnson, John W., "Balthazar Hubmaier and Baptist Historic Commitments," IX *The Journal of Religion* (1929) 50-65, 54f.

116 Article by Loserth in *ML*, II, 353-63, 360.

117 On their expectancy, *WtQ*1938, p. xvi.

118 Article, "Apokatastase," in *ML*, I, 77.

119 Stauffer, Ethelbert, *loc. cit.*, quoting and discussing Menno, p. 566. On the martyr church as the type of Stephen, see Benz, Ernst, *op. cit.*, pp. 335f.

120 *Supra*, p. 74.

121 Pannabecker, Samuel Floyd, *The Development of the General Conference of the*

Mennonite Church of North America in the American Environment; MSS at Sterling Library, PhD Thesis 1944, p. 36; exclusiveness and growth of agrarian life mark the loss of missionary enterprise; p. 618: the foreign missionary enterprise was the first outside program to commend itself to the church of America, suggesting an earlier affinity.

122 Cf. Payne, Ernest A., *The Anabaptists of the Sixteenth Century and their Influence in the Modern World* (London, Carey Kingsgate Press, 1949).

SELECT BIBLIOGRAPHY

Source Books and Bibliographies

Bainton, Roland H., *Bibliography of the Continental Reformation*: *Materials available in English* (Chicago: American Society of Church History, 1935), No. 1 of *Monographs in Church History*.

Beck, Josef, *ed., Die Geschichts-Bücher der Wiedertäufer in Osterreich-Ungarn* (Wien: Carl Gerold's Sohn, 1883); XLIII *Fontes Rerum Austriacarum* (Hist. Comm. Kaiserl. Akad. der Wiss. in Wien), 2te Abth.

Bossert, Gustav, *ed., Quellen zur Geschichte der Wiedertäufer*: *Herzogtum Württemberg* (Leipzig: M. Heinsius Nachf., 1930); XIII:1 *Quellen und Forschungen zur Reformationsgeschichte.*

Braght, T. J. van, *A Martyrology of the Churches of Christ Commonly called Baptist* (London: Hanserd Knollys Society, 1850-53). 2 volumes, edited by Edward B. Underhill.

Cramer, Samuel, and Pijper, F., *ed., Bibliotheca Reformatoria Neerlandica* (s' Gravenhage: Martinus Nijhoff, 1903-14). 10 volumes.

Egli, Emil, *ed., Actensammlung zur Geschichte der Zürcher Reformation in den Jahren 1519-1533* (Zürich: J. Schabelitz, 1879), 2 volumes.

Friedmann, Robert, "Die Briefe der österreichischen Täufer," XVI *ARG* (1929) 30-80, 161-87.

Geisberg, Max, *ed., Das Wiedertäuferreich* (München: Hugo Schmidt Verlag, 1929). 16 facsimiles.

Hege, Christian, and Neff, Christian, *ed., Mennonitisches Lexikon* (Frankfurt am Main and Weierhof (Pfalz): H. & N., 1913, 1937, ...). 2 volumes; 3d forthcoming.

Horsch, John, *ed., Catalogue of the Mennonite Historical Library* (Scottdale, Penna.: Mennonite Publishing House, 1929).

Krebs, Manfred, *ed., Quellen zur Geschichte der Täufer: Baden und Pfalz* (Gütersloh: C. Bertelsmann Verlag, 1951). XXI *Quellen und Forschungen zur Reformationsgeschichte.*

Müller, Lydia, *ed., Glaubenszeugnisse oberdeutscher Taufgesinnter* (Leipzig: M. Heinsius Nachf., 1934); XX:1 *Quellen und Forschungen zur Reformationsgeschichte.*

Schornbaum, Karl, *ed., Quellen zur Geschichte der Wiedertäufer: Markgraftum Brandenburg* (Leipzig: M. Heinsius Nachf., 1934); XVI *Quellen und Forschungen zur Reformationsgeschichte.*

Schornbaum, Karl, *ed.*, *Quellen zur Geschichte der Täufer: Bayern, II. Abteilung* (Gütersloh: C. Bertelsmann Verlag, 1951). XXIII *Quellen und Forschungen zur Reformationsgeschichte.*

Schottenloher, Karl, *Bibliographie zur Deutschen Geschichte im Zeitalter der Glaubensspaltung, 1517-1585* (Leipzig: Karl W. Hiersemann, 1933-39). 5 volumes.

Wolkan, Rudolph, *Geschichts-Buch der Hutterischen Brüder* (Macleod, Alta., and Vienna: Carl Fromme Ges. m.b.H., 1923).

Zieglschmid, A. J. F., *Die älteste Chronik der Hutterischen Brüder* (Philadelphia, Penna.: Carl Schurz Memorial Foundation, 1943).

Works of General Significance

Bainton, Roland H., "The Left Wing of the Reformation," XXI *The Journal of Religion* (1941) 2: 124-34.

Bender, Harold S., "The Anabaptist Vision." XIII *Church History* (1944) 3-24.

Bergfried, Ulrich, *Verantwortung als Theologisches Problem im Täufertum des 16. Jahrhunderts* (Wuppertal-Elberfeld: A. Martini & Grüttefien, 1938). Inaugural Dissertation at Tübingen.

Bergmann, Cornelius, *Die Täuferbewegung im Kanton Zürich bis 1660* (Leipzig: M. Heinsius Nachf., 1916); volume V of *Quellen und Forschungen zur Schweizerischen Reformationsgeschichte.*

Bouterwek, K. W., "Zur Wiedertäufer-Literatur," I *Zeitschrift des Bergischen Geschichtsvereins* (Bonn, 1864) 3:280-344.

Brons, A., *Ursprung, Entwickelung und Schicksale der Taufgesinnten oder Mennoniten* (Norden, Diedr. Soltau, 1844).

Burckhardt, Paul, *Die Basler Täufer* (Basel, R. Reich, 1898).

Burrage, Champlin, *The Church Covenant Idea* (Philadelphia: American Baptist Publication Society, 1904).

Burrage, Henry S., *The History of the Anabaptists in Switzerland* (Philadelphia: American Baptist Publication Society, 1882).

Correll, Ernst, *Das Schweizerische Täufermennonitentum* (Tübingen: J. C. B. Mohr, 1925).

Dosker, Henry Elias, *The Dutch Anabaptists* (Philadelphia: The Judson Press, 1921).

Ecke, Karl, *Schwenckfeld, Luther und die Gedanke einer Apostolischen Reformation* (Berlin: Martin Warneck, 1911).

Egli, Emil, *Die St. Galler Täufer* (Zürich: Friedrich Schulthess, 1887).

Egli, Emil, *Die Züricher Wiedertäufer zur Reformationszeit* (Zürich: Friedrich Schulthess, 1878).

Evans, Austin Patterson, *An Episode in the Struggle for Religious Freedom: the Sectaries of Nuremberg, 1524-1528* (N. Y.: Columbia University Press, 1924).

Friedmann, Robert, "Conception of the Anabaptists," IX *CH* (1940) 341-65.

Hege, Christian, *Die Täufer in der Kurpfalz* (Frankfurt am Main: Hermann Minjon, 1908).

Hegler, Alfred, *Beiträge zur Geschichte der Mystik in der Reformationszeit* (Berlin: C. A. Schwetschke & Sohn, 1906); Erg. Bd. I *ARG*.

Heyer, Fritz, "Der Kirchenbegriff der Schwärmer," 56 *SVRG* (1939) 156:1-108, Heft 2.

Horsch, John, "The Faith of the Swiss Brethren," IV *MQR* (1930) 241-66; V (1931) 7-27, 128-47, 245-54.

Horsch, John, *The Hutterian Brethren, 1528-1931* (Goshen, Ind.: Mennonite Historical Society, 1931); volume 2 of *Studies in Anabaptist and Mennonite History*.

Horsch, John, *Mennonites in Europe* (Scottdale, Penna.: Mennonite Publishing House, 1942); volume 1 of *Mennonite History*.

Hulshof, Abraham, *Geschiedenis van de Doopsgezinden te Straatsburg van 1525 tot 1557* (Amsterdam: J. Clausen, 1905).

Kühler, W. J., *Geschiedenis der Nederlandsche Doopsgezinden in de Zestiende Eeuw* (Haarlem: H. D. Tjeck Willink & Zoon N. V., 1932).

Loserth, J., "Der Communismus der Mährischen Wiedertäufer in 16. und 17. Jahrhundert," 81 *Archiv für österreichische Geschichte* (1895) 135-322.

Lüdeman, H., *Reformation und Täufertum in ihrem Verhältnis zum christlichen Princip* (Bern: W. Kaiser, 1896).

Müller, Lydia, "Der Kommunismus der mährischen Wiedertäufer," 45 *SVRG* (1927) 142:1-123, Heft 1.

Neff, Christian L., *ed., Gedenkschrift zum 400. Jährigen Jubiläum der Mennoniten oder Taufgesinnten 1525-1925* (Ludwigshafen: Konferenz der Süddeutschen Mennoniten E. V., 1925).

Newman, Albert Henry, *A History of Anti-Pedobaptism* (Philadelphia: American Baptist Publication Society, 1897).

Rembert, Karl, *Die 'Wiedertäufer' im Herzogtum Jülich* (Berlin: R. Gaertners Verlagsbuchh., 1899).

Smith, C. Henry, *The Story of the Mennonites* (Berne, Ind.: Mennonite Book Concern, 1941.

Smithson, R. J., *The Anabaptists* (London: James Clarke & Co., Ltd., 1935).

Smucker, Donovan E., "Anabaptist Historiography in the Scholarship of Today," XXII *MQR* (1948) 116-27.

Stauffer, Ethelbert, "Märtyrertheologie und Täuferbewegung," LII *ZKG* (1933) 545-98.

Trechsel, Fr., *Die Protestantischen Antitrinitarier vor Faustus Socin.* (Heidelberg: Karl Winter, 1844). 2 volumes.

Troeltsch, Ernst, "Die Täufer und Spiritualisten," in "Protestantisches Christentum und Kirche in der Neuzeit," in P. Hinneberg's *Geschichte der christlichen Religion: Die Kultur der Gegenwart* (Leipzig and Berlin: B. G. Teubner, 1922).

Wappler, Paul, *Die Stellung Kursachsens und der Landgrafen Philipp von Hessen zur Täuferbewegung* (Münster i. W.; Aschendorffsche Buchh., 1910), 13/14 *Reformationsgeschichtliche Studien und Texte.*

Wappler, Paul, *Die Täuferbewegung in Thüringen von 1526-1584* (Jena: Gustav Fischer, 1913); volume II *Beiträge zur neueren Geschichte Thüringens.*

Wessel, J. H., *De Leerstellige Strijd tusschen Nederlandsche Gereformeerden en Doopsgezinden in de Zestiende Eeuw* (Assen: Van Gorcum & Co., 1945). XXXI *Hist. Bibliothek.*

Wilbur, Earl Morse, *A History of Unitarianism* (Cambridge, Mass.: Harvard University Press, 1945), volume I.

Wiswedel, W., *Bilder und Führergestalten aus dem Täufertum* (Kassel: J. G. Oncken, 1928-30), 2 volumes; 3rd to be published.

Special Studies of Note

Bainton, Roland H., *Concerning Heretics. . . . An anonymous work attributed to Sebastian Castellio* (N. Y.: Columbia University Press, 1935); volume XXII of the *Records of Civilization: Sources and Studies.*

Bainton, Roland H., *David Joris: Wiedertäufer und Kämpfer für Toleranz im 16. Jahrhundert* (Leipzig: M. Heinsius Nachf., 1937); Erg. Bd. VI *ARG.*

Barge, Hermann, *Andreas Bodenstein von Karlstadt* (Leipzig: Friedrich Brandstetter, 1905), 2 vols.

Bender, Harold S., "Conrad Grebel, the First Leader of the Swiss Brethren (Anabaptists)," X *MQR* (1936) 5-45, 91-137, 151-60.

Bender, Harold S., *Conrad Grebel (c. 1498-1526), The Founder of the Swiss Brethren* (Goshen, Ind.: The Mennonite Historical Society, 1950), No. 6 of *Studies in Anabaptist and Mennonite History.*

Benrath, Karl, "Wiedertäufer im Venetianischen um die Mitte des 16. Jahrhunderts," 58 *TSK* (1885) 9-67.

Benz, Ernst, *Ecclesia Spiritualis* (Stuttgart: W. Kohlhammer, 1934).

Brandt, Otto H., *Thomas Müntzer: Sein Leben und seine Schriften* (Jena: Eugen Diedrichs Verlag, 1933).

Cornelius, C. A., *Geschichte des Münsterischen Aufruhrs* (Leipzig: T. O. Wiegel, 1855). 3 books, 3rd not published.

Coutts, Alfred, *Hans Denck (1495-1527):Humanist and Heretic* (Edinburgh: Macniven & Wallace, 1927).

Detmer, Heinrich, *Bilder aus der religiösen und sozialen Unruh in Münster während des 16. Jahrhunderts* (Münster: Coppenrathsche Buchh., 1903-04), 3 vols.

Friedmann, Robert, *Mennonite Piety Through the Centuries* (Goshen, Ind.: The Mennonite Historical Society, 1949), No. 7 of *Studies in Anabaptist and Mennonite History.*

Hegler, A., *Geist und Schrift bei Sebastian Franck* (Freiburg i. B.: J. C. B. Mohr, 1892).

Holl, Karl, "Luther und die Schwärmer," in volume I of *Gesammelte Aufsätze zur Kirchengeschichte* (Tübingen: J. C. B. Mohr, 1923).

Horsch, John, *Menno Simons* (Scottdale, Penna.: Mennonite Publishing House, 1916).

Keller, Ludwig, *Ein Apostel der Wiedertäufer* (Leipzig: S. Hirzel, 1882).

Krahn, Cornelius, *Menno Simons (1496-1561)* (Karlsruhe i. B.: Heinrich Schneider, 1936).

Linden, Friedrich Otto zur, *Melchior Hofmann, ein Prophet der Wiedertäufer* (Haarlem: de Ervon F. Bohn, 1885); XI *Verhandelingen uit gegeven door Teylers Godgeleerd Genootschap* (1885) 2.

Loesche, Georg, "Archivalische Beiträge zur Geschichte des Täufertums und des Protestantismus in Tirol und Voralberg," 47 *Jahrbuch der Gesellschaft für die Geschichte des Protestantismus in ehemaligen und in neuen Osterreich* (1926).

Loserth, Johann, *Doctor Balthasar Hubmaier und die Anfänge der Wiedertaufe in Mähren* (Brünn: R. M. Rohrer, 1893).

Mau, Wilhelm, *Balthasar Hubmaier* (Berlin: Dr. Walter Rothschild, 1912); XL *Abhandlungen zur Mittleren und Neueren Geschichte.*

Nestler, Hermann, *Die Wiedertäuferbewegung in Regensburg* (Regensburg: Josef Hobbel, 1926).

Neuser, Wilhelm, *Hans Hut. Leben und Wirken bis zum Nikolsburger Religionsgespräch* (Berlin: Hermann Blanke, 1913). Dissertation at Bonn.

Nicoladoni, Alexander, *Johannes Bünderlin von Linz und die oberösterreichischen Täufergemeinde in den Jahren 1525-1531* (Berlin: R. Gaertners Verlag, 1893).

Sachsse, Carl, *D. Balthasar Hubmaier als Theologe* (Berlin: Trowitsch & Sohn, 1914); XX *Neue Studien zur Geschichte der Theologie und der Kirche.*

Schiedung, Hans, *Beiträge zur Bibliographie und Publizistik über die Münsterischen Wiedertäufer* (Münster i. Westf: Heinrich Bornkamm, 1934).

Schubert, Hans von, "Der Kommunismus der Wiedertäufer in Münster und seine Quellen," X *Sitzungsberichte der Heidelberger Akademia der Wissenschaft. Phil. Hist. Klasse* (1919) 11.

Weis, Frederick Lewis, *The Life and Teachings of Ludwig Hetzer* (Dorchester, Mass.: Underhill Press, 1930). Dissertation at Strassburg.

Wenger, John C., "Pilgram Marpeck. . . .," XII *MQR* (1938) 137-66, 167f, 205-56.

Wenger, John C., "Pilgram Marpeck, Tyrolese Engineer and Anabaptist Elder," IX *CH* (1940) 24-36.

INDEX